THE POWER OF eLEARNING

Piedmont College Library

RELATED TITLES OF INTEREST

Using Technology in Learner-Centered Education:
Proven Strategies for Teaching and Learning
David G. Brown, Gordon McCray, Craig Runde,
and Heidi Schweizer
ISBN: 0-205-35580-3

Instructing and Mentoring the African American
College Student: Strategies for Success
in Higher Education
Louis B. Gallien Jr. and Marshalita S. Peterson
ISBN: 0-205-38917-1

Emblems of Quality in Higher Education:
Developing and Sustaining High-Quality Programs
Jennifer Grant Haworth and Clifton F. Conrad
ISBN: 0-205-19546-6

Grant Writing in Higher Education:
A Step-by-Step Guide
Kenneth T. Henson
ISBN: 0-205-38919-8

Writing for Publication: Road
to Academic Advancement
Kenneth T. Henson
ISBN: 0-205-43319-7

Learner-Centered Assessment
on College Campuses: Shifting the
Focus from Teaching to Learning
Mary E. Huba and Jann E. Freed
ISBN: 0-205-28738-7

The Adjunct Professor's Guide to Success:
Surviving and Thriving in the College Classroom
Richard E. Lyons, Marcella L. Kysilka,
and George E. Pawlas
ISBN: 0-205-28774-3

Success Strategies for Adjunct Faculty
Richard E. Lyons
ISBN: 0-205-36017-3

Teaching College in an Age of Accountability
Richard E. Lyons, Meggin McIntosh,
and Marcella L. Kysilka
ISBN: 0-205-35315-0

An Introduction to Interactive Multimedia
Stephen J. Misovich, Jerome Katrichis,
David Demers, and William B. Sanders
ISBN: 0-205-34373-2

Teaching Tips for College and University
Instructors: A Practical Guide
David Royse
ISBN: 0-205-29839-7

Creating Learning-Centered Courses
for the World Wide Web
William B. Sanders
ISBN: 0-205-31513-5

Faculty of Color in Academe: Bittersweet Success
Caroline Sotello Viernes Turner
and Samuel L. Myers Jr.
ISBN: 0-205-27849-3

The Effective, Efficient Professor:
Teaching, Scholarship and Service
Phillip C. Wankat
ISBN: 0-205-33711-2

The Student Guide to Successful Online Learning:
A Handbook of Tips, Strategies, and Techniques
Ken W. White and Jason D. Baker
ISBN: 0-205-34104-7

The Online Teaching Guide: A Handbook
of Attitudes, Strategies, and Techniques
for the Virtual Classroom
Ken W. White and Bob H. Weight
ISBN: 0-205-29531-2

For further information on these and other related titles, contact:

College Division
ALLYN AND BACON, INC.
75 Arlington Street, Suite 300
Boston, MA 02116
www.ablongman.com

THE POWER OF eLEARNING

The Essential Guide
for Teaching in the Digital Age

SHIRLEY WATERHOUSE
Embry-Riddle Aeronautical University

Boston ■ New York ■ San Francisco
Mexico City ■ Montreal ■ Toronto ■ London ■ Madrid ■ Munich ■ Paris
Hong Kong ■ Singapore ■ Tokyo ■ Cape Town ■ Sydney

Executive Editor and Publisher: *Stephen D. Dragin*
Senior Editorial Assistant: *Barbara Strickland*
Marketing Manager: *Jennifer Armstrong*
Editorial-Production Service: *Omegatype Typography, Inc.*
Composition and Prepress Buyer: *Linda Cox*
Manufacturing Buyer: *Andrew Turso*
Cover Administrator: *Joel Gendron*
Electronic Composition: *Omegatype Typography, Inc.*

For related titles and support materials, visit our online catalog at www.ablongman.com.

Between the time Website information is gathered and then published, it is not unusual for some sites to have closed. Also, the transcription of URLs can result in typographical errors. The publisher would appreciate notification where these errors occur so that they may be corrected in subsequent editions.

Library of Congress Cataloging-in-Publication Data

Waterhouse, Shirley A.
    The power of elearning : the essential guide for teaching in the digital age / Shirley Waterhouse.
        p. cm.
    Includes bibliographical references and index.
    ISBN 0-205-37564-2 (alk. paper)
        1. Computer-assisted instruction—Handbooks, manuals, etc.   2. Educational technology—Handbooks, manuals, etc.   3. Teachers—Effect of technological innovations on.
    I. Title.

LB1028.5.W375 2005
371.33'4—dc22

                                                                                    2004050565

Printed in the United States of America

10   9   8   7   6   5   4   3   2   1   09   08   07   06   05   04

*To the many friends who provided me so much moral support
for this project and many similar ones through the years and especially
to Barbara Benson-Braunstein, Barbara Cravotta Buchner,
Margaret DiGaetano, M.D., Pat Nelson, and Toni Stoughton.*

CONTENTS

CHAPTER SEVEN

External Resources   142

CHAPTER EIGHT

Coursesite Design and Maintenance   166

PART III   COURSE MANAGEMENT   185

CHAPTER NINE

Intellectual Property Rights and Course Policies   187

CHAPTER TEN

Course Delivery   207

CHAPTER ELEVEN

eLearning Assessment   237

PREFACE

PURPOSE

Educators and trainers today are facing a new and perhaps unique challenge—keeping up with their students, who are often more technically savvy than their instructors. Students also have high expectations about the use of computer technology in their educations. An institution's use of technology is often a major consideration when today's students and their parents select a college or school. For these reasons, among many others, instructors and trainers at all levels must develop an awareness of elearning and an understanding of how to use it. If you are an instructor and have no plans to retire very soon, the old question of whether you are going to use elearning has already been answered. The new question is not *if* you are going to start, but *when.*

The workplace is changing also. Preparation for today's world requires that students know how to find and use information rapidly. They must also learn how to learn, because lifelong learning will be essential in their careers. They must be prepared to work in a global environment where team collaborations through the use of technology will be commonplace. We have a responsibility to prepare students for this changing workplace, and elearning can help us do this. Traditional methods of instruction, although still relevant, must be reinforced by new elearning practices. The Internet and computers, the foundations of elearning, create a means to dramatically improve traditional education and training. Elearning makes it easy for students to engage in student-centered learning activities relevant to the real world. The web provides a host of new learning opportunities such as virtual experiments, online field trips, online tutoring, worldwide collaborations, and digital library resources, among many, many others. There is now—through technology—an unprecedented opportunity to reinvent education.

Nevertheless, the power of elearning does not come from the technology alone. Rather it is unleashed when teachers know how to use technology to create better instruction. This explains why the focus of this book is on elearning pedagogy and not on technology alone. The book is intended to help you along the path of elearning discovery. It is straightforward and practical, as opposed to being abstract and theoretical. Many of its concepts are based on the commonsense strategies that many experienced teachers have discovered through trial and error. The book presents information on how to combine basic teaching principles with elearning strategies to bring about positive changes in the instructional environment. It is intended to help you avoid the mistakes made by some of your elearning predecessors who failed to focus on elearning pedagogy when they introduced technology into their teaching. Some of those pioneers in elearning used computers simply because they were available or because they were led to believe that computers would somehow magically bring improvements in their instruction. Too often, they were disappointed in the results. Technology to the end of better instruction—not technology for its own sake—should be your goal as an elearning instructor. Your elearning journey may require a commitment to changing the way you teach, and it will certainly demand that you make a significant investment of your time. But the journey is well worth it. The payoff of elearning is commensurate with the informed effort you will expend in using it. The goal of this book is to help you make your efforts in elearning informed efforts.

ABOUT THE PRIMARY AUTHOR

My teaching and consulting career spans over 30 years. I started teaching in 1972 at Mainland High School in Daytona Beach, Florida. A year later, I became an instructor at Daytona Beach Community College (DBCC), where I taught for six years. During this period I published my first book, on word processing, not long after word processing software first appeared in the commercial market. In 1976, I was awarded a substantial federal grant to design and implement an innovative, individualized computer-based learning environment at DBCC. At this point, computer-based learning was a new concept in the community college system. Shortly after completing this project, I published my second book. Like the book you have in your hand, it was about the use of computer technology, and like my first book it addressed another concept that was new at the time—office automation.

In 1979, I left teaching to become a corporate consultant. In this capacity, I designed and implemented technology-training programs for large corporations and governmental agencies in the United States. After traveling back and forth across the states for 10 years, in 1989 I returned to full-time teaching as a faculty member in the Department of Computer Science at Embry-Riddle Aeronautical University (ERAU). For the past 16 years, I have taught—either full-time or part-time—in ERAU's graduate and undergraduate programs. From 1989 to 1996 I worked full-time in the Department of Computer Science at ERAU, where I taught applications software. During this period I published my third and fourth books, books respectively about how to use the Enable and the Lotus Smart Suite productivity software packages. During this seven-year period, I also received one of the highest honors to which a teacher can aspire. Eleven semesters during this time period, ERAU graduating seniors voted me the outstanding teacher in the Computer Science Department. No achievement before or since has meant more to me. As we all know, most of us enter teaching not for fame or fortune, but in the hope we will have a positive impact on the lives of the students we teach. I have always considered my outstanding teacher awards to be evidence that my hope was to some small degree realized.

In 1996, after completing a doctorate in Educational Technology, I was asked to create and become the director of a new Department of Educational Technology at ERAU. Embry-Riddle is almost unique among institutions of higher learning. Considered by many to be the leading aviation- and aerospace-focused university in the world, it has two residential campuses and over 130 teaching centers located around the globe. Using technology effectively in the delivery of education became an ERAU priority, and a very rewarding and challenging mission for me. As ERAU's Director of Educational Technology, I lead the university's elearning initiatives and faculty technology development program. About three years ago, I published a fifth book with coauthor Ramon Harris, *A Ten Step Guide to Establishing Instructional Technology Systems*.

Over the past few years, I have also returned to part-time consulting with educational institutions desiring to implement elearning and establish technology training programs for faculty. One of the most rewarding consulting responsibilities for me has been to create and conduct two series of workshops about using technology in education. One is a faculty series on elearning pedagogy. The other is for administrators and addresses elearning strategic planning. These consulting endeavors have taken me throughout the United States as well as the Middle East, where I have not only conducted workshops but also delivered keynote addresses at elearning conferences. For more information on my workshops and keynote speaking engagements, visit http://shirleywaterhouse.com.

I have a passion for teaching and elearning, a passion I want to share with you through my book. My goal is to help teachers, professors, and trainers at all levels learn to use elearning by providing a starting place, a frame of reference, guidelines, examples, tools, and resources that have worked for me and for others. I have witnessed the struggle some instructors go through in getting started with elearning, in committing to change the way they teach, and in understanding how to apply elearning's power. I hope this book will make your own personal striving in elearning a little easier than it would be otherwise. As the title of my book indicates, elearning can empower one to improve the world of instruction significantly. However, elearning's power is merely a potential until it is actualized through the efforts of instructors. The true power of elearning is in your hands, and in the hands of the teachers of the future.

ABOUT CONTRIBUTING AUTHORS

You will notice that the collective "we" is often used to refer to the "authors" of this book. This is appropriate in part because I did not work on this project alone. While my name is on the cover of the book, and I can take the credit for initiating the book and doing the research, there were others who made very significant contributions to this work. The individual beyond myself who contributed most to the book is Dr. Rodney Rogers. Dr. Rogers provided invaluable insight from the perspective of a professor in higher education and spent hundreds of hours making major editorial contributions to every chapter in this book. There were also sixteen other reviewers of the book, including an instructional designer, faculty and administrators in higher education, and teachers and administrators in K–12. Four of the reviewers reside in countries outside of the United States, including Australia, the United Kingdom, the United Arab Emirates, and Saudi Arabia. Dr. Rogers's affiliation, and those of the book's reviewers, are listed in the acknowledgments section.

I also consider the hundreds of authors whose articles and books are referenced throughout the book to be contributors. In addition, the sponsors of the numerous websites illustrated or referenced in the book made significant contributions. The instructors and administrators throughout the world who have attended one of my workshops and provided me with insight on how to help instructors and institutions implement elearning have likewise influenced this book. Finally, the thousands of students who have provided me with inspiration throughout my career and have taught me so much about teaching and learning are in a real sense participants in the book's creation.

CONTENT AND ORGANIZATION

This book is composed of three parts. Part One is an overview in three chapters of the subject of elearning. Chapter 1 discusses elearning fundamentals. It defines elearning terms, explores the major advantages of elearning as well as its major challenges, and advances guidelines on how to get started using elearning. Chapter 2 describes elearning pedagogy. It explains how the educational principles put forward in three well-known pedagogical works can be adapted to an elearning environment. These three works are Chickering and Gamson's *Seven Principles,* Bloom's *Taxonomy of Intellectual Behaviors,* and Gagne's *Nine Events of Instruction.* Chapter 2 also explores how elearning can create a student-centered learning environment. Chapter 3 explains the importance of instructional planning and provides an elearning planning model called VPODD, which is an acronym for Vision, Profile, Objectives, Design, and Development.

Part Two—in five chapters—identifies elearning tools and resources, and investigates how to use them effectively. Chapter 4 provides an overview of the software tools commonly used in elearning. Chapter 5 describes tools for creating information to disseminate to students and provides guidelines for designing word processor documents and presentation graphics slide shows for web viewing. Chapter 6 explains how to use electronic forums and chats. Chapter 7's subject is web resources. It provides numerous examples of the growing number of web-based instructional materials—including digital libraries—readily available for use in elearning. Chapter 8 describes how to organize, design, and maintain an elearning coursesite.

The three chapters of Part Three of the book address the specifics of course delivery and elearning assessment. Chapter 9's subject is intellectual property rights and course policies. It discusses copyright and fair use guidelines and touches the controversial subject of how instructors can establish an understanding with their institutions about the ownership of elearning materials they create. Chapter 9 also explains the importance of various kinds of policies and procedures in an elearning environment. Chapter 10 addresses course delivery, with an emphasis on how to help students succeed in elearning. The chapter explains "getting-started" activities and provides many examples of such activities. It also offers suggestions about how to deal with the behavior of different kinds of "problem" students, including shy students, students with special needs, disgruntled students, and others. Chapter 10 explains how to facilitate team projects in an elearning environment. Finally, Chapter 11 offers suggestions about assessing student performance, coursesite effectiveness, and the overall effectiveness of an elearning course.

PRACTICAL RESOURCES INCLUDED IN THE BOOK

This book is a practical guide to elearning that explores the wide breadth of topics one must consider when creating and delivering elearning courses. It is written in plain English with a minimum of technical and educational jargon. The elearning terms used are—I hope—clearly defined when they are introduced. The book makes every effort to illustrate generalizations and abstractions with concrete suggestions and examples. For instance, it does not simply inform you that you should implement a cogent and detailed policy about the use of email in an elearning course. It also provides a specific example of such a policy. You will discover that the book abounds in such "practical" resources. You will find, for example:

- Checklists and tips
- Specific guidelines
- Example discussion and team project topics
- Example elearning policies and procedures
- Example assessment instruments
- Numerous bibliographic references, most of which can be accessed online
- Numerous URL references, accessible at http://shirleywaterhouse.com

THE BOOK'S AUDIENCE

This book was written in the hope that it will appeal to a wide audience. Simply put, it is intended for anyone who wants to learn about the basics of elearning. Although thoroughly researched, it is distinctly informal and unscholastic in tone, though perhaps not entirely unscholarly. It will be most helpful to instructors who are elearning novices. However, the book is also appropriate for instructors who have some limited experience in elearning, such as instructors who were the first to adopt learning management systems. This group is comfortable with the technology but wants to learn more about elearning pedagogy. Its members are ready to change their methods and implement effective elearning strategies that go beyond the basic use of learning management systems. This book is also intended for those who supervise teachers, professors, or trainers, and those who teach individuals in these groups.

This book should likewise prove helpful for students studying to be educators or trainers. No formal program of study in education or instructional design is complete unless its students graduate with a thorough knowledge of elearning theory and practice. The book is also intended for those indirectly involved in elearning, such as individuals who sell or maintain elearning services, software, and hardware. A good understanding of elearning theory and practice will enable them to serve their potential customers better. In summary, the book is intended for individuals in the following groups:

- Faculty in higher education, including teachers of teachers
- Teachers in K–12
- Instructional designers
- Elearning developers
- Corporate trainers
- Students studying to be teachers
- Supervisors and administrators of teachers, faculty, or trainers
- Students studying to be supervisors and administrators in an educational environment
- Individuals who sell or maintain elearning services, software, and hardware

Before reading this book, you—the audience—should be aware of several premises, ideas, and assumptions that underlie its design and construction:

- Instructors will use learning management software—for example, Blackboard, Desire-2Learn, WebCT, or a similar LMS—to construct elearning coursesites and resources.

- Instructors will find it necessary to create elearning resources individually when instructional design teams or elearning development teams are not available.
- The concepts in the book are applicable in both a face-to-face hybrid elearning delivery mode and a totally online distance-learning delivery mode.
- Most of the research referenced in the book represents work done in the United States. However, elearning principles respect no geographical boundaries. Thus the information in the book should be of interest to English-speaking readers throughout the world.
- While the book's figures and examples emphasize elearning in higher education, the concepts presented in the book are equally applicable in the K–12 and corporate training environments.
- The ▪ symbol appearing before a referenced website denotes that the URL for the website can be found at the end of that chapter.

ACKNOWLEDGMENTS

My sincerest appreciation goes to the following individuals who reviewed this book and provided me with invaluable input and guidance.

Sheryl R. Abshire, Administrative Coordinator of Technology, Calcasieu Parish Public Schools, USA

David G. Brown, Ph. D., Vice President and Dean of the International Center for Computer Enhanced Learning at Wake Forest University, USA

Michael Crock, Ph. D., Director, Information Services, Flexible Learning & Access Services, Griffith University, Australia

Charlene Douglas, Director, dot.edu®, University of Wisconsin System, USA

Colette Perry Hutton, Instructional Designer, University of Central Florida, USA

Haifa Reda Jamal Al-Lail, Ph. D., Dean of Effat College, Saudi Arabia

Tayeb A. Kamali, Ph. D., Managing Director, Higher Colleges of Technology, United Arab Emirates

Demetra Katsifli, Ph. D., Head of Academic ICT Services, Kingston University, United Kingdom

Daryl LaBello, Educational Technologist, Embry-Riddle Aeronautical University, USA

Dave Pedersen, Ph. D., Associate Director, Educational Technology Department, Embry-Riddle Aeronautical University, USA

Emilio Ramos, Ph. D., Dean of Academic and Administrative Technology, Dallas Community Colleges, USA

Rodney Rogers, Ph.D., Professor, Aeronautical Science Department, Embry-Riddle Aeronautical University, USA

Phyllis C. Self, Ph. D., Vice Provost for Academic Technology, Virginia Commonwealth University, USA

Thanks also to the Allyn and Bacon reviewers including Linda Leeper, New Mexico State University, Brenda Robinson, University of New England, Mark E. Ryan, National University, and Heidi Schweizer, Marquette University.

A special thank you to two Embry-Riddle Aeronautical University graduate students, Michelle Rea and Kris Murray Tilman, for expert assistance with bibliographic references and URLs.

THE POWER OF ELEARNING

PART I

PEDAGOGY
AND PLANNING

CHAPTER ONE

ELEARNING FUNDAMENTALS

Elearning involves improving teaching and learning using instructional strategies *enhanced* by technology, especially computer technology. Because computers can so significantly enhance an educational environment, elearning is a subject most worthy of a book explaining what it is and how to use it. This introductory chapter, which assumes the reader has little prior knowledge of the subject, provides an overview of ideas and concepts relevant to elearning. It presents in summary form many if not most of the ideas developed in more detail throughout the remainder of the book. The chapter is organized into five major sections. The first section defines and discusses basic elearning concepts. The second describes and explains learning management systems, software packages that facilitate organizing, creating, and delivering an elearning course, whereas the third section addresses the potential of elearning to improve teaching and learning. To help you see how elearning can enhance an instructional environment, this third section also identifies exemplary elearning applications currently accessible on the web. The fourth section of the chapter addresses major challenges to the use of elearning. The fifth and final section identifies steps you may take to begin using elearning effectively.

BASIC ELEARNING CONCEPTS

One premise of this book is that elearning improves learning when instructors focus first on the fundamentals of teaching and learning—that is, on pedagogical principles—rather than on elearning technology. In other words, technology is a means to an end, not an end in itself. Consequently, if you want to create an effective elearning environment, you must first understand the principles leading to effective elearning. Ultimately, of course, you must also understand how to apply technology to achieve your instructional goals. Nevertheless, pedagogy must drive technology, not the other way around (Chizmar & Williams, 2001). A second premise of the book is that elearning can enhance both courses taught in a classroom and courses taught in a distance-learning environment, where instructors and students do not routinely have face-to-face contact with each other. Distance learning will be described more thoroughly in Chapter 2. Depending on which of these two instructional environments you will teach in—traditional or distance learning—it will be up to you to determine how best to apply the elearning concepts discussed in this book.

Pedagogy, Andragogy, and eLearning Pedagogy

Three terms—*pedagogy, andragogy,* and *elearning pedagogy*—are often used in discussions about elearning. One simple definition of *pedagogy* is that it is the art or profession of teaching. Pedagogy also denotes the principles and instructional strategies related to good teaching. Because the classical Greek root of the word *(paidagōgos)* denotes a leader or teacher of boys, some purists insist that pedagogy refers to teaching children. By contrast, *andragogy*—whose root *anere* means adult—is the art or science of helping adults learn, together with related principles and instructional strategies (Knowles, 1984). In addition to denoting adult learning, androgogy sometimes references teaching conducted in a self-directed learning environment. Despite these distinctions, the term *pedagogy* is commonly used today to denote teaching individuals of any age. In this book, we prefer the broader definition and use the term *pedagogy* to include *andragogy*. By *elearning pedagogy,* we mean the pedagogical principles and related instructional strategies applicable to an elearning environment.

If you are an experienced instructor, pedagogy is not a new concept to you. You apply pedagogical principles each time you make decisions about your instructional environment or the strategies you will use to help your students learn. For example, if you teach in a traditional classroom face-to-face with students, you frequently make pedagogical decisions such as when to deliver a lecture and what to include in the lecture; when to use a classroom demonstration; what kinds of written assignments will best promote learning; when to have students deliver in-class presentations; whether, when, and how to test student learning; and how to assess the effectiveness of your instruction; among many others.

Teaching in an elearning environment, as opposed to a traditional environment, does not diminish the need to base your teaching on sound pedagogical principles. To do this, however, you will need to understand how to apply pedagogical principles in an elearning environment. To a very significant extent, elearning facilitates the application of teaching strategies difficult to implement in a traditional instructional environment. As you begin the process of adopting elearning, start by understanding elearning pedagogy. Then proceed with an understanding of the technology tools to help you apply elearning pedagogy to your teaching. You will probably conclude that elearning gives you tremendous power to enhance your teaching and your students' learning. Elearning pedagogy and the effective use of elearning, then, is the subject of this book.

Some Terms Relevant to eLearning Pedagogy

Elearning, we have seen, involves the application of computer technology to enhance teaching and learning. In this book an *elearning* course—or *course* for short—is any course of instruction that to some extent uses elearning to deliver its content. In this book, an *elearning resource*—often called a *resource*—is a component of an elearning course. Typically—but not always—an instructor creates resources using a computer, and students *access* them via a computer. When a student accesses an elearning resource for the purpose of learning, an *elearning activity*—or an *activity*—takes place. Examples of elearning activities are using the web to access course information, listening to an audio resource such as a folk song or a symphony, viewing a video resource, and communicating and/or collaborating online.

Technology facilitates creating and using elearning resources. The tools available for creating resources are described in Chapter 4. These tools range from basic computer programs such as word processor and presentation graphics software to complex computer programs for creating animations, movies, or sophisticated 3-D graphical simulations. Learning management systems, described in the next section of this chapter, are perhaps the major tools available to elearning instructors. When an instructor creates an elearning resource, he or she—implicitly or explicitly—applies an *elearning strategy*. There are several important factors to consider when devising elearning strategies and creating the related elearning resources. These factors include but are not limited to course subject matter and objectives; whether students and instructors meet face-to-face or online; student characteristics such as maturity level and technology skills; and the computer technology available in classrooms, laboratories, and a student's personal environment. Seen from this perspective, elearning pedagogy involves using sound pedagogical principles and learning strategies to create course resources that support effective teaching and learning. Chapters 2 and 3 provide further information on pedagogy and elearning planning and instructional design.

Two additional terms relevant to elearning pedagogy are *instructional technology* and *educational technology*. While these terms may have different meanings in different organizations, they typically refer to activities, departments, or personnel that focus on the application of technology in the instructional environment. In institutions using elearning, there is commonly found a department called either the *Instructional Technology Department* or the *Educational Technology Department*. Personnel working in such a department are called *instructional technologists* or *educational technologists*. We view the terms *instructional technology* and *educational technology* as synonymous, because individuals working in either area share the common goal of improving learning through the use of computer technology.

LEARNING MANAGEMENT SYSTEMS AND COURSESITES

Three factors help explain elearning's rapid rise: the proliferation of inexpensive personal computers, the widespread availability of Internet connections, and dramatic improvements in software tools for creating elearning resources. Perhaps one of the most important tool sets for an elearning instructor is a *learning management system—or LMS* for short. An LMS is simply software that enables instructors to create and organize resources—for example, course documents—on the web. The LMS also facilitates creating and using elearning resources such as electronic discussions and online tests. The testing component supports automatic grading and posting of test scores. Finally, the LMS allows an instructor to construct a *coursesite* to organize resources associated with a particular course of instruction. Students in the course view the coursesite with a web browser and access its resources using the functionality of the LMS. Some LMSs used in corporate and government training environments have more sophisticated functions including features that track employees' development of competencies, among others.

Another term to describe software used to organize, manage, and administer learning is *course management system (CMS)*. Some individuals use the terms CMS and LMS interchangeably. Others use the term *LMS* to reference software that has more sophisticated administrative functionality than CMSs. In this book, our preferred term is LMS.

Figures 1.1 and 1.2 show the opening screens for coursesites created using two popular LMSs, ▪Blackboard and ▪WebCT, respectively. Other LMSs are ▪Angel, ▪Desire2Learn,

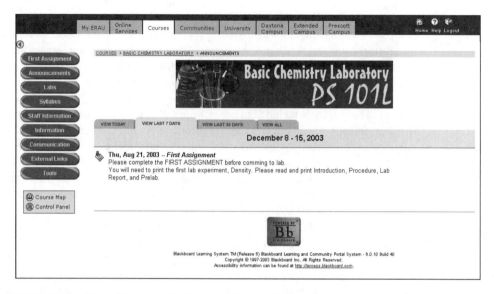

FIGURE 1.1   Basic Chemistry Laboratory Coursesite Homepage

Professor Marlene Coslow, Embry-Riddle Aeronautical University. Created in Blackboard, used with permission.

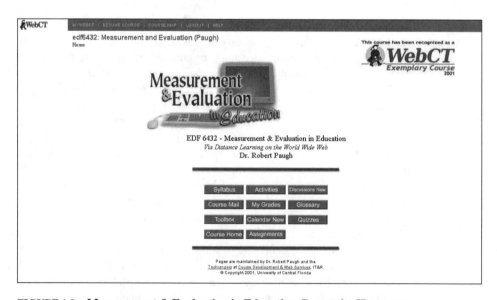

FIGURE 1.2   Measurement & Evaluation in Education Coursesite Homepage

Dr. Robert Paugh, University of Central Florida. Created in WebCT, used with permission.

■Educator, ■FirstClass, and ■LearningSpace. The coursesite in Figure 1.1 was created using Blackboard. In this example, note that a course announcement is visible when a student initially accesses the coursesite. The vertically arranged buttons at the left allow a student to access additional course resources such as assignments, lab resources, course information, and online communications. All of the resources posted in this coursesite were created by entering text in text boxes, which is the equivalent of filling in forms; by using mouse gestures; or by attaching files created with a word processor or with presentation graphics software. Figure 1.2 provides a similar example of a coursesite created with WebCT. Chapters 4 and 8 address the details of LMS functionality and coursesite design.

RISING POPULARITY OF LMS SOFTWARE

An LMS makes it easy for an instructor to create a coursesite where students can access course resources. Before LMSs appeared, instructors who wanted to make course information available on the web had to learn web authoring to make a coursesite. This involved using a computer language called HTML (hypertext markup language), a standard for web authoring. Using electronic discussions or online testing required purchasing or writing additional, more sophisticated software to implement these capabilities. Such undertakings were too intimidating for most instructors, and only a small minority used websites for teaching and learning. Gradually, LMSs emerged to fill the needs of instructors who wanted to use the web for teaching but lacked the necessary programming skills. Three of the first proprietary learning management systems—Web Course in a Box, Lotus LearningSpace, and WebCT—appeared in the early and mid-1990s. A subsequent early LMS, Blackboard, entered the market a little later but quickly became popular with instructors because of its ease of use.

There are at least two alternatives to proprietary LMS software such as Blackboard and WebCT. One is for an organization to outsource the creation of elearning coursesites to companies in business to create elearning materials. ■eCollege is one example of such a company. Another option is open-source learning management software such as the ■OKI (Open Knowledge Initiative). The OKI is an initiative being led by MIT and Stanford University with a goal of developing modular, easy-to-use learning management tools that will be freely available to any institution with a desire to use them. Other noted institutions working on the OKI initiative are the University of Michigan, Dartmouth College, North Carolina State University, the University of Pennsylvania, the University of Wisconsin–Madison, Indiana University, and Cambridge University (Gallagher, 2003). A related open-source LMS effort is the Sakai Project started by four universities—Indiana, Michigan, MIT, and Stanford (Green, 2004).

There is also an open-source effort underway in countries outside of the United States. One example is ■KEWL (Knowledge Environment for Web-Based Learning), an open-source learning management system suited for the developing world. KEWL was developed at the University of the Western Cape (UWC) and is available at no cost under an open-source license. It is a comprehensive tool that can be modified for schools in Africa and the rest of the developing world (Keats, 2003). Another example of open-source software is ■Bazaar, an online learning management and conferencing system produced by Athabasca University in Canada (Hesemeier, Kuivi, & Sosteric, 2003).

The growing popularity of LMSs throughout the instructional world is vividly illustrated by the rate at which they are being adopted in colleges and universities. When we consider the unprecedented growth in the use of the web, it is easy to imagine that LMSs and elearning are likely to experience similar growth in the next few years. For example, it took only 3 years for the web to reach its first 50 million users, once user-friendly browsers were available, compared to 15 years for television and close to 37 years for radio to reach the same number of users (Naughton, 2001). Now that easy-to-use learning management tools are available, we are likely to see a tremendous growth in their use. Kenneth Green, a noted authority on the use of computing in education, produces a yearly study—called the ▪Campus Computing Project—on the use of information technology (IT) in higher education. Green's statistics indicate that a growing number of institutions consider LMSs to be very important in their institutional IT planning. In 2003, more than four-fifths (82.3 percent) of the institutions participating in Green's survey reported the adoption of an LMS standard, up from 73.2 percent in the 2001 survey and 57.8 percent in the 2000 survey (Green, 2003b). In a study conducted by the EDUCAUSE Center for Applied Research, entitled Supporting E-Learning in Higher Education, findings revealed that 80 percent of the institutions participating in the research offer courses that utilize online sessions to complement classroom sessions, and 71 percent offer fully online courses (Arabasz, Pirani, & Fawcett, 2003).

LMS Functionality

Clearly, LMSs play a major role in the elearning environment. However, creating a coursesite and its elearning resources should not be the main focus of your instructional efforts. First, you must identify the appropriate goals for your course. Next, you must devise learning strategies to support these goals. Finally, you must understand how LMS functionality can be used to implement your instructional goals and strategies. This approach ensures that technology is used to support sound pedagogy. The four major LMS functional categories support:

1. Distribution of course information
2. Student–instructor and student–student communications
3. Student interaction with course resources
4. Online testing and grading

To use these LMS functionalities, you need to know only how to type and how to invoke the desired feature using "point and click" gestures with a mouse. No programming skills are required. Thus potential elearning instructors require very little training to be able to create coursesites. Moreover, LMSs will undoubtedly become significantly more powerful and sophisticated in the next decade, just as word processors did in the 1990s. Such changes will bring increased functionality that is even easier to use. Thus it seems likely that instructors will use LMSs in the near future as commonly as they use email and word processing programs today. This outcome is certainly desirable, in view of the fact that many elearning proponents believe all courses, labs, and seminars would be greatly enhanced by a companion coursesite (Strauss, 2002).

Example Uses of LMS Functionality

An LMS can provide convenient access to elearning for both students and instructors, but it alone cannot bring about pedagogical change. We reiterate a crucial point: If you want to improve teaching and learning using computer technology, you must use LMS tools and other available software to create course resources based on effective elearning strategies. Figure 1.3 provides examples of uses of an LMS in each of the four functional categories. As you read through this list, try to imagine how each LMS function could be used to expand and/or improve your own instructional environment. Some of the uses allow instructors to complete administrative tasks more efficiently. Others support improved communications and assessment. Still others increase opportunities for students to interact with course content.

ELEARNING'S POTENTIAL TO IMPROVE TEACHING AND LEARNING

Your elearning goal should be to improve teaching and learning. When pedagogy drives instruction, elearning can bring about powerful changes in the way you interact with students. Listed here are a few of the many advantages of using elearning, followed by a discussion

FIGURE 1.3   Examples of Practical Ways to Use an LMS

I. DISTRIBUTION OF COURSE INFORMATION AND WEB ACCESS

- Up-to-the-minute course announcements
- Course syllabus
- Course notes
- Slide show presentations for previewing or reviewing course topics
- Course documents, assignments, and materials
- Student portfolios

II. ELECTRONIC COMMUNICATIONS

- Discussion to facilitate students getting to know each other
- Discussion to preview a topic
- Discussion to summarize a topic
- Discussion to clarify confusion on a course topic or course issue
- Virtual office hours instead of face-to-face office hours
- Online tutoring
- Online chats for instructor and small groups
- Online chats to facilitate group work and team projects
- Discussion with a guest speaker or mentor

III. INTERACTION WITH CONTENT AND WEB ACCESS

- Web-based research and website URLs
- Online field trips
- Online experiments
- Online simulations
- Publishers' web-based supplemental materials
- Miscellaneous web-based resources

IV. ONLINE TESTING AND GRADING

- Self-assessments
- Review tests
- Online tests
- Automatic test grading and grade postings
- Online surveys and evaluations

of each. This section then concludes with brief descriptions of several exemplary instances of the use of elearning.

- Elearning facilitates student-centered learning.
- Elearning facilitates anytime-anyplace learning.
- Elearning facilitates student interaction with course content.
- Elearning facilitates and promotes communication and collaboration.
- Elearning makes course administration easier.
- Elearning helps track students' time on task.
- Elearning can reduce the cost of delivering instruction.
- Elearning adds a worldwide dimension to courses.

eLearning Facilitates Student-Centered Learning

The literature about teaching frequently argues that students need to be more actively involved in the learning process; that is, that students learn better in a *student-centered,* active learning environment than in an *instructor-centered* environment. The goal of *student-centered learning*—also called *active learning*—is for students to take on more of the responsibility of learning and become more *actively* involved in the learning process. In a student-centered learning environment, the spotlight is on the student, and the instructor assumes the role of facilitator. Elearning promotes student-centered learning through activities such as online self-assessment, web-based research, and electronic discussions that foster student interactions with each other and with the instructor, among other learning activities.

Although lectures occur less frequently in a student-centered environment than in an instructor-centered environment, when instructors do lecture, elearning can make lectures more interactive. For example, to reinforce the main points of a lecture, students can be assigned a web-based research activity—to be completed either in class or outside of class—in which they visit websites relevant to the lecture topic and report their findings. Students can also be tasked with sharing their responses to a class lecture in an electronic discussion in the hours following the lecture and before the next class meeting. If there appears to be some confusion about a topic addressed in the lecture, the instructor can enter the discussion to clear up the confusion. In addition, when lecture notes are posted to the coursesite, students can preview them before class or review them after class. This minimizes the need for detailed note taking, which both shortens the time required to deliver a lecture and eliminates a distraction that diverts students' attention from the lecturer.

eLearning Facilitates Anytime-Anyplace Learning

An *anytime-anyplace learning environment*—in contrast to a *traditional* or *conventional learning environment*—is one where students learn at their own convenience as opposed to having to attend regularly scheduled instructional sessions. Elearning makes it easier to create an anytime-anyplace learning environment. Students can access learning resources posted on a coursesite from any place they can access the Internet and at any time that is convenient for them. They benefit greatly from the convenience of such an environment. In addition, anytime-anyplace learning is convenient for instructors, who can create, modify, and post course resources, review grades in an online gradebook, view students' comments in an electronic discussion, or work on any other aspect of the coursesite in the office, from home, or while traveling.

Anytime-anyplace learning is of special benefit to individuals who are adult learners, learners over the age of 25, and nontraditional students. Some typical characteristics of nontraditional students are that they attend part-time; they work full-time; they have dependents, other than a spouse; they do not depend on parents for financial support, and they are single parents, among other traits (Oblinger, 2003). According to the ▪National Center for Education Statistics (NCES), three-quarters of all undergraduates are nontraditional students (2002). Adult learners and nontraditional students find it difficult to attend regularly scheduled classes. As lifelong learning becomes more important in an increasingly complex world where technology vastly influences both one's work and one's play, the number of individuals in these two learning categories is sure to continue to increase. One can easily see the appeal to students and faculty of the successful and accredited online universities and programs that provide virtual classrooms and degree programs twenty-four hours a day anywhere in the world with courses starting weekly (Greenberg, 2004).

Like nontraditional learners and adult learners, students with special needs also benefit from an anytime-anyplace learning environment. When discussions are conducted online, some but not all shy students benefit by being able to take time to compose thoughtful answers before responding. Shy students are also discussed in Chapters 6 and 10. For students with speech difficulties, being able to write responses to class discussions removes major obstacles to communication and typically results in greater achievement. For students who are wheelchair bound, online learning eliminates their having to navigate from their domiciles to a classroom. For those with sight disabilities, screen readers can parse information on the coursesite and read it aloud to students.

Anytime-anyplace learning is not only for students in higher education. There is also a growing interest in online learning in the kindergarten through high school environment (K–12). One example is the ▪Florida Virtual School (FLVS) founded in 1996. FLVS is a pioneer in online learning for the K–12 environment and is currently the largest virtual school in the United States. There are no FVS buildings, and its students and teachers can be located anywhere in the state of Florida or indeed anywhere in the world (Young, 2003). Elearning can provide many of the same benefits to students in the K–12 environment that it provides to students in higher education. Moreover, these benefits may be even more meaningful to the younger students. For example, consider what it would mean to a student in a remote mountain town to be given the opportunity to take the same high school Latin course that is available to a student in an urban or suburban setting (Kalmon, 2003).

eLearning Facilitates Student Interaction with Course Content

Technology allows an instructor to create course resources whereby students interact with course content via the web, including online experiments and online field trips, among others. For example, the ▪Froguts website, illustrated in Figure 1.4, allows students to dissect frogs virtually. Multimedia technology allows an instructor to supplement course content

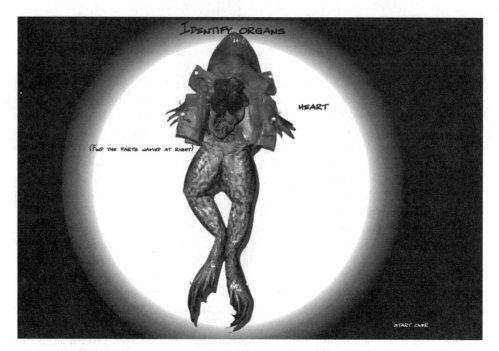

FIGURE 1.4   Illustration of Virtual Frog Dissection, Froguts, Inc.
Used with permission.

with video or audio clips. At Ohio University's ▪Wired for Books website famous authors can be heard talking about their books and reading passages from them. Chapter 7 provides a more extensive discussion of web-based resources that facilitate students' interaction with course content.

eLearning Facilitates and Promotes Communication and Collaboration

More than any elearning capability, online discussion enables students to communicate and collaborate with each other. We have already noted that some shy students feel more comfortable expressing their views and contributing to course discussion when the discussion takes place online. Often students report getting to know each other—as well as the instructor—better when there are opportunities to engage in discussions in an anytime-anyplace environment. Online discussion is a particularly important communication tool for distance-learning students whose opportunities to engage their instructor and classmates face-to-face are few or none. Also, online discussions can be conducted anonymously, providing an excellent strategy for examining sensitive topics. Problems associated with biases about gender, race, age, or appearance sometimes hinder communication; they are minimized in online discussions in which individuals are physically anonymous. Finally, elearning discussion tools not only facilitate student collaboration and team projects but also provide students with an opportunity to learn how to use technology they will very likely use in the workplace one day.

eLearning Makes Course Administration Easier

Instructors new to elearning must of course master the relevant technology and learn new instructional skills. Moreover, all instructors who use elearning to deliver a course must develop a coursesite and its related learning resources. These activities increase an instructor's workload in the short run just as developing a new course requires considerable time in any learning environment. However, in the long run, elearning can save an instructor time. For example, elearning helps instructors create and manipulate course materials more efficiently. Online electronic documents can be revised and reposted to the coursesite quickly, whereas when paper documents are revised, they also must be reprinted and redistributed by hand. By contrast, students access revised electronic documents from the coursesite at their convenience without assistance from the instructor, who simply posts an announcement to indicate that a document has been updated.

Another administrative advantage of elearning is that instructors who use an LMS can provide more timely feedback through email, virtual office hours, and online tutoring. However, care must be exercised to ensure that total weekly student contact hours do not increase when interacting online with students. A computer can subtly lure instructors as well as students to overutilize its capabilities. A related advantage is that electronic gradebooks are far easier to maintain than paper gradebooks, once you master the skills of using them.

Instructors using an LMS also report a decrease in the overall time required to create, administer, and grade a test, record the grades, and provide feedback for students on answers missed. Of course, many instructors have reservations about online testing for grades due to the increased possibilities of students' cheating on unproctored exams. As a consequence, some instructors implement alternative assessment methods. Many of these same instructors, however, continue to use the LMS online testing capability for self-testing, an activity that has the potential to improve learning dramatically. Online testing, student cheating, and alternative assessment methods are discussed in Chapter 11.

eLearning Helps Track Students' Time on Task

A common complaint of instructors is that students do not spend enough time studying. The 2003 National Survey of Student Engagement (NSSE) survey revealed that only 13 percent of full-time students spent 25 hours a week preparing for classes, the approximate number faculty members say is needed to do well in college, and more than 41 percent spent 10 or fewer hours a week (NSSE, 2003). Learning management systems provide a means of tracking how much time a student spends on any particular learning activity accessed via the LMS. These data—because they indicate which coursesite areas are most frequently accessed—also lead to an understanding of which course resources students find most useful. Such information can be of value in revising course resources to improve student learning and in counseling underachieving students, because lack of effort—that is, time on task—is quite often the root cause of academic difficulty.

eLearning Can Reduce the Cost of Delivering Instruction

Elearning has the potential to decrease the total costs of delivering instruction at the same time that it improves student learning. In the K–12 environment, not only is elearning used in instructional improvements, but it also is being used to meet instructional challenges unique to the contemporary primary and secondary educational environment. These challenges include the need to provide in-service workshops to large numbers of teachers and to establish parent–teacher communications, tasks that can be facilitated online using elearning tools. In the corporate and government environments, elearning is often used to reduce the cost of travel to training sites and to provide just-in-time training. In higher education, elearning has been applied to large enrollment courses with great success. When large enrollment courses—as opposed to courses with smaller class sizes or fewer sections—use elearning to deliver content more efficiently and to enhance teaching and learning, a greater return on a university's information technology investment is typically realized (Twigg, 2000).

Perhaps the most impressive work on the potential of elearning to reduce the cost of course delivery is the ▪Program in Course Redesign. This Pew Charitable Trusts Foundation program spanned a three-year period. Thirty participating institutions were awarded grants to redesign traditional large enrollment introductory courses for delivery in an elearning environment. The goal of course redesign was to improve student learning while at the same time making course delivery more efficient, hence decreasing associated costs. The participating institutions applied various approaches in pursuit of this goal. Some reduced the number of face-to-face lectures, others implemented online self-assessment resources, and others established online tutoring, as well as a number of additional approaches. All 30 institutions reduced course delivery costs by about 40 percent on average (from 20 percent to 84 percent) (Heterick & Twigg, 2003). Figure 1.5 lists the actual savings reported by the first 10 participating institutions, as obtained from the Program in Course Redesign website. More detailed information on the outcomes at all 30 institutions can be found on this website.

One example outcome of the Pew Program in Course Redesign is the Virginia Tech ▪Math Emporium, an innovative approach to teaching freshman math courses. Students studying calculus, linear algebra, and other mathematics subjects in the Virginia Tech Math Emporium are engaged in an exciting new way to learn where the instructional environment is a 500-workstation computer laboratory setting, instead of classrooms. Students are guided through the course material by easy-to-use computer programs. They can work individually or in groups of up to eight students, giving everyone the opportunity to learn using his or her preferred learning style. To supplement such computer-assisted learning, students can choose to work one-on-one with professors or with graduate and undergraduate student coaches as often—or as infrequently—as they perceive the need to do so. Figure 1.6 depicts the opening screen of the Math Emporium visitor's website.

Although improved course delivery was one important goal of the Pew Program in Course Redesign, a goal of equal importance was to improve learning as a result of the course redesign. When measured against the same courses delivered in a traditional learning environment, 19 of the 30 projects showed improved learning, and the remaining 11 showed no significant difference. Other significant learning outcomes were realized including increased course completion rates, improved retention, better student attitudes toward the subject matter, and increased student satisfaction with the mode of instruction compared to traditional formats (Heterick & Twigg, 2003).

FIGURE 1.5   Actual Savings of the Program in Course Redesign Round I Recipient Institutions

INSTITUTION	COURSE REDESIGNED	SAVINGS
University of Illinois at Urbana–Champaign	Statistics	$229,600
Penn State University	Elementary Statistics	190,320
University of Wisconsin–Madison	Chemistry	172,200
Virginia Tech	Mathematics	140,000
University at Buffalo	Computer Literacy	105,000
University of Colorado–Boulder	Astronomy	70,720
University of Central Florida	American Government	68,466
Indiana University–Purdue University of Indianapolis	Sociology	34,000
University of Southern Maine	Psychology	21,250
Rio Salado College	Mathematics	17,190

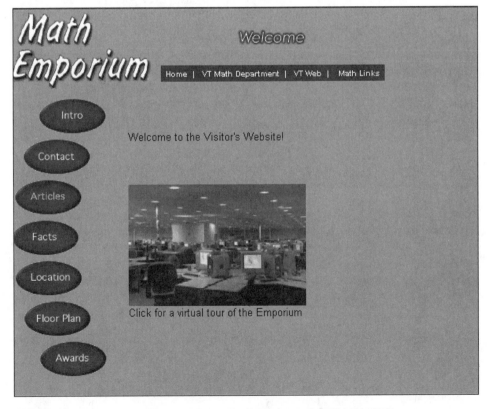

FIGURE 1.6   Math Emporium, Department of Mathematics, Virginia Tech
Used with permission.

eLearning Adds a Worldwide Dimension to Courses

One of the major reasons elearning is so powerful is that it allows you to use the vast resources of the web when you teach, thus adding a global dimension to your courses. Otherwise inaccessible resources can be integrated into course materials, and your class can become a meeting place for individuals with common interests throughout the world. Experts, no matter where their geographic location, can be invited as guest speakers or can become mentors for your class via LMS communication capabilities. One example of online mentoring is ▪MentorNet, whereby women engineering and science students who desire mentoring can be connected with experts in their particular engineering or scientific field. The opening screen of the MentorNet website is depicted in Figure 1.7.

Another site fostering worldwide collaboration is ▪THRO—Teaching Human Rights Online—offering interactive exercises freely available for individuals as well as groups. Transnational THRO Internet conferences expose participants to different cultural perspectives on issues such as terrorism, genocide, war crimes, and women's rights. These types of collaborations are critical in fostering cultural understanding in our global society. Figure 1.8 shows the opening screen of the THRO website.

The Massachusetts Institute of Technology's ▪TEK (Time Equals Knowledge) site is another example of worldwide collaborations. TEK's goal is to increase access for individuals in third world countries to the wealth of information on the Internet (Hermida, 2003). Users can submit a request for an Internet search by sending an email message to TEK in

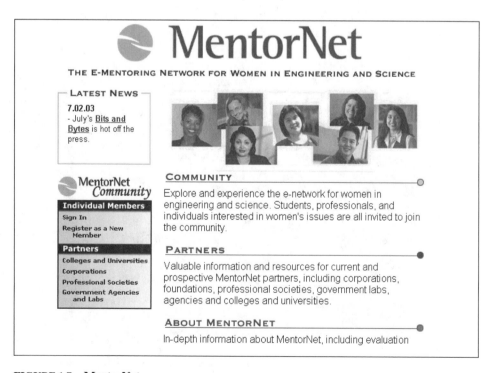

FIGURE 1.7   MentorNet

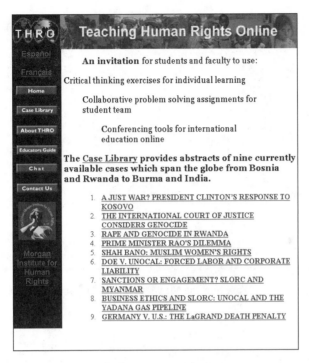

**FIGURE 1.8   Teaching Human Rights Online,
University of Cincinnati**

Used with permission.

Boston. TEK searches the web, locates appropriate pages, selects the pages to send back, compresses them, and returns them to the user via email.

Online Learning Exemplars

Many exemplary websites exist that provide specific evidence of how instructors and institutions are using the web to improve teaching and learning. Among these are the websites just described and those created by institutions participating in the Pew Program in Course Redesign. The rapid proliferation of such sites reflects an expanding worldwide interest in the power of elearning. This section identifies and briefly describes a few additional websites worthy of consideration by individuals seeking information about online learning. One such site is the ■MIT (Massachusetts Institute of Technology) OpenCourseWare site illustrated in Figure 1.9. This website reflects a growing desire among academicians to expand access to educational materials. MIT—a longtime leader in the open source movement—has now begun the admirable process of making materials for more than 2,000 MIT undergraduate subjects available to the public (Margulies, 2003).

Another example is the ■MERLOT Project—Multimedia Educational Resource for Learning and Online Teaching—which is a collection of peer-reviewed elearning coursesites. This project evaluates online learning sites by rating content quality, the potential effectiveness of course materials as teaching-and-learning tools, and the ease of use of the coursesite (Hanley, 2003). MERLOT is illustrated in Figure 1.10. Figure 1.11 illustrates

FIGURE 1.9   MIT OpenCourseWare and the MIT Department of Earth, Atmospheric, and Planetary Sciences

Used with permission.

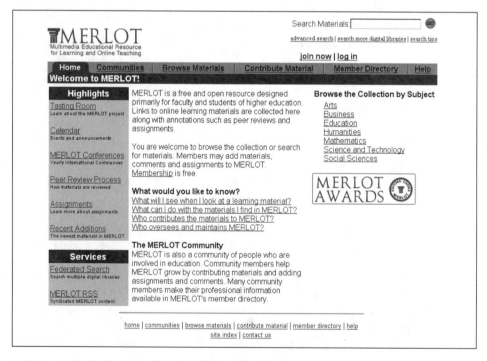

FIGURE 1.10   Multimedia Educational Resource for Learning and Online Teaching (MERLOT)

Used with permission.

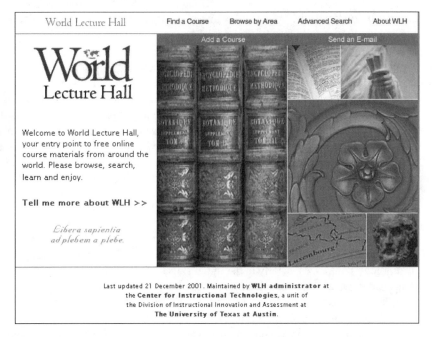

FIGURE 1.11   World Lecture Hall, The University of Texas at Austin
Used with permission.

the ▪World Lecture Hall website maintained by The University of Texas at Austin. The World Lecture Hall is a catalog of coursesites organized by discipline. It enables a user to search by discipline for websites relevant to his or her instructional interests.

MAJOR ELEARNING CHALLENGES

Challenges to elearning are simply issues that must be dealt with in order to maximize the use of elearning in the instructional world. There exist at least three categories of challenges to the use of elearning:

- Technology challenges
- Instructor challenges
- Effectiveness challenges

What follows is a discussion of challenges in each category.

Technology Challenges

Technology challenges fall into three subcategories. They are the need for a robust infrastructure, the likelihood of technology failures, and the need for more sophisticated LMS tools.

Robust Infrastructure.   A complex infrastructure is required to support elearning including personal computers for classrooms, laboratories, and offices; LMS software; and high-speed Internet access, to name only a few of the needed technologies. Also, personnel with the expertise to design and implement this infrastructure are required, as are personnel and procedures to maintain and support the system once it is implemented. All of these resource requirements are costly. Thus one of elearning's major challenges is obtaining adequate funding when so many other technology requirements, especially in administrative areas, compete for institutional funds. What is needed is a shared institutional vision whereby leadership at all levels fully endorses elearning and commits to providing the necessary resources. Including elearning goals in institutional and departmental strategic planning is required to ensure that elearning is adequately funded, implemented, and assessed (Waterhouse & Harris, 2001).

Technology Failures.   Another major challenge to elearning is technology failures. Regardless of how much time and effort you have spent to create an effective elearning environment, if the computer system supporting your course fails, your efforts may be in vain. Technology failures, especially in the initial stages of elearning adoption, can prejudice students and instructors against elearning. When this happens, it can be difficult to regain their confidence. Consequently, every conceivable effort must be made to provide a stable technology environment. Because it is inevitable that you and your students will experience some type of technology failure at some point in your shared elearning experiences, procedures for dealing with technology failures must be established. Chapter 9 discusses elearning policies and procedures in detail and includes example procedures relevant to technology failures.

Need for LMS Improvements.   Although users of current LMSs have a strong appreciation for currently supported capabilities, they also have a list of expectations as LMSs move into the next stage of maturity (Carmean & Haefner, 2003). With elearning becoming an integral component in the delivery of instruction, the scope and functionality of LMSs must continue to advance to meet the growing reliance on technology-assisted learning. Improvements are needed in the ability to share elearning resources across courses, as well as in the ability to import course content from one course management system to another. Currently, tools that enable an instructor to edit and grade students' essays and similar text-based assignments are rudimentary and must be improved. More sophisticated capabilities are needed as well in assessment tools, gradebooks, e-portfolios, communications tools, and the integration of library resources with LMSs.

Instructor Challenges

Challenges to persuading instructors to commit to elearning fall into two subcategories: the existence of disincentives and the need for supportive leadership and appropriate incentives. Addressing disincentives amounts to dispelling those that are imaginary and convincing leadership to find appropriate remedies for those that are real. Nevertheless, dealing with disincentives and incentives separately seems appropriate. Explaining why a problem exists is but a prelude to solving it.

Disincentives.   One disincentive to the adoption of elearning is a very natural and very human resistance to change. An old adage holds that fear of the known is preferable to fear of the unknown. Perhaps this idea helps explain why many of us find it difficult to adjust to a world of rapidly changing and increasingly sophisticated technology. Most instructors are accustomed to being in control of their subject matter and the way it is presented. Those who perceive that they deliver good lectures question why they should adopt elearning, especially when there is no assurance that they will be successful under the new instructional paradigm. Others who excel in face-to-face teaching may be quite disinclined to accept the challenges presented by elearning. It is difficult to see how to deal with resistance to change in the adoption of elearning, but to pretend that this resistance does not exist is naive. Adoption of elearning will occur only when instructors are convinced that change in this direction is apt to be change for the better. We believe that informing instructors about the power of elearning will help overcome this challenge. In fact, this belief explains the existence of this book.

A second disincentive to instructors' embracing elearning is the fear that elearning may eliminate their jobs. This fear may be more imaginary than real. Sophisticated online courses do have the potential to educate many people at an ultimately low cost. However, developing such courses is extremely time-consuming and expensive, given the current state of elearning technology. There seems to be little likelihood that these kinds of courses will appear in large numbers in the near future. Even when elearning does result in an increased number of online offerings, inevitably an increased number of course facilitators will also be needed.

Another disincentive is the challenging learning curve embracing elearning presents. Before they can use elearning, instructors must devise new teaching strategies, strategies yet unknown to them. Developing the required teaching and technology skills requires a significant time commitment, as does creating and refining elearning resources and coursesites to contain them. Related to this disincentive is the fear some instructors have that they will not own the learning materials they create or that they will not be credited appropriately for having created them. Stories abound about the time and effort individuals have invested in elearning only to find that their efforts do not enhance job security or that they do not own the intellectual property rights to their work. Higher education instructors not infrequently express disappointment in a general lack of recognition for their elearning efforts, including a lack of support from academic leaders and a failure on the part of their colleagues to express interest in their work (Wilson, 2001). They also report they have been reminded during the evaluation process that it is research and publications that carry the most weight in tenure and promotion decisions, with elearning efforts receiving little if any recognition. These real disincentives will not be countered until institutional leadership embraces elearning fully and appropriately credits instructors who engage in it.

A final disincentive has to do with the actual delivery of an elearning course, once the course is developed and refined. Some instructors believe that teaching in an elearning environment results in increased workloads and large amounts of undocumented work. Others perceive that they are expected to teach more students in a distance-learning mode than in a classroom. Still others report that their workloads increased due to the number of emails from distance-learning students. This disincentive is not entirely imaginary, but it often stems from an inappropriate use of elearning's tools. Chapters 9 and 10 address this issue in more detail.

Need for Supportive Leadership and Appropriate Incentives.   Before they will make the considerable effort required to adopt elearning, instructors have to be convinced in terms of their own needs and values that elearning is important (Garofoli & Woodell, 2003). Thus establishing appropriate faculty incentives is of paramount importance if an institution wishes to substantially increase its use of elearning. Such incentives are lacking at institutions in which top leadership is unsupportive of elearning. As indicated previously, before elearning can become an important factor at any institution, leaders from the top on down must strongly endorse its use and provide resources, encouragement, support, and related incentives for instructors. Most important of all, leaders must recognize and reward instructors who successfully adopt elearning.

Instructor incentives fall into two subcategories: short-term or "start-up" incentives, and long-term incentives. Short-term incentives are necessary to ensure that instructors have time to learn new teaching skills and to experiment with elearning through the development of elearning resource prototypes. Examples of such incentives are course releases and/or reduced expectations in other departmental and institutional workload requirements. In addition, leaders must supply appropriate elearning tools and provide adequate training and technical assistance for novice elearning instructors. The payoff for an institution's financial investment is that a coursesite, once developed, can be used by many different instructors who teach the course supported by the site. Reusable elearning resources and courses mean that new instructors need not spend vast amounts of time—as they now do under the conventional instructional paradigm—developing a course of instruction that has already been prepared many times before by those who preceded them.

Long-term incentives include appropriate compensation, instructor ownership rights for elearning resources they create, and recognition in the evaluation process. Institutions should consider providing additional financial compensation for faculty who devote many hours of work to develop elearning resources, and without a doubt favorable intellectual property rights agreements should be established. Chapter 9 addresses intellectual property rights in more detail.

Providing recognition for instructors using technology is critical. One example of a successful method to recognize faculty's technology efforts is the ▪Webstars website at Florida State University. This website displays photos of Florida State elearning instructors, along with a brief description of how they are using technology in their courses and links to more information on individual instructors.

Ensuring that instructors' elearning efforts count in the job evaluation process is clearly the most important long-term incentive leadership can provide. This issue seems easily addressable at institutions using elearning for consulting or internal training or in the K–12 instructional environment. In higher education, by contrast, it is more perplexing, and the rise of elearning will certainly not resolve the continuing debate in academe, especially at the undergraduate level, about the relative importance of teaching and publication. Currently, it is probably safer for senior university instructors to champion elearning than for younger yet untenured instructors to do so. The irony of this situation is that the younger instructors, having grown up with computers, are more likely to be interested in elearning than are their more senior colleagues.

Effectiveness Challenges

Elearning proponents are challenged when defending claims about its effectiveness for two reasons. First, there exists little research to support such claims. Second, the research that does exist might be better focused. Elearning effectiveness research to date typically compares test grades or final course grades of students taught the same subject in elearning and traditional instructional environments. Such an approach is at best misguided. Elearning typically changes the instructional environment from instructor centered to student centered, and it introduces many new technology tools and skills. As a consequence, assessment methodology that goes beyond grade comparisons is needed to grasp the overall effectiveness of elearning (Lockee, Moore, & Burton, 2001). Chapter 11, Elearning Assessment, discusses how to evaluate the effectiveness of elearning.

SIX STEPS FOR GETTING STARTED

For most instructors who are successfully utilizing elearning, the thought of returning to traditional instructional methods seems inconceivable. If you were to ask them to give up posting course resources for web access, to forego online testing and grading, to stop using electronic discussions, or to cease learning activities whereby students access course resources online, most would think you had lost your mind! So, what did it take to get these instructors started with elearning? Some were naturals, early adopters who eagerly wanted to try out new technologies and new teaching strategies. Others wanted to improve their instructional environment and felt elearning could help. Still others were required by their academic departments to begin using elearning. Something common to all of these instructors, however, is that they all had to start somewhere. Understanding what is involved in getting started is a major step toward your elearning success. There are several stages of the "getting-started" process. What follows briefly discusses six steps that might help you begin using elearning:

- Ask yourself why.
- Make a commitment.
- Develop a new vision for your course and how you teach.
- Determine the resources available to you.
- Acquire new technology skills and develop new instructional methods.
- Plan.

Step One—Ask Yourself Why

It is interesting to consider why instructors adopt elearning, especially early adopters. In an attempt to better understand faculty's adoption of elearning in institutions of higher learning, David Brown of Wake Forest University surveyed elearning early adopters at 42 of America's most wired college campuses (2000). His findings revealed that most instructors were motivated to engage in elearning in order to improve learning, and specifically to provide a more interactive learning experience for students. In a follow-up study involving 30 of the institutions that had participated in Brown's survey, Paul Hagner reported that 70 percent of the faculty revealed that there were no outside incentives provided them by their institutions (Hagner, 2000). The results of both surveys provide evidence that the strongest motivator for faculty's adoption of elearning is a desire to improve teaching and learning. Note, however, that these findings address attitudes of faculty who were voluntary early adopters of elearning.

Enhanced teaching and learning is and certainly should be the major motivation for adopting elearning. However, you may find that other incentives—as previously discussed—will influence your decision to begin using elearning. In any event, you probably should not "rush" all at once into the use of elearning. Determine the degree of elearning commitment that is best suited for you initially. Then ease into the field gradually. The level of implementation you choose may involve goals such as to:

- Send email to all students simultaneously.
- Provide students the convenience of web access to course materials.
- Administer online quizzes and course surveys and obtain instant results.
- Change the instructional environment to a student-centered one.
- Use the web to afford students more interaction with course content.
- Facilitate electronic communications beyond email with students.

If you are investigating the use of elearning on behalf of your academic department rather than simply for yourself, you must also determine how elearning can be applied as solutions to departmental challenges. For example, is student retention a challenge? Is there a need to improve the efficiency of course delivery in large enrollment courses, as illustrated in the Pew Program in Course Redesign?

Step Two—Make a Commitment

When you make the decision to begin using elearning, you must be ready for change, and you must be willing and able to devote the time needed to learn new technical skills and new teaching methods. Bear in mind that changing your instructional environment will likely not happen overnight. You should be realistic about the time needed to design and implement elearning. Also, be aware that elearning may increase your workload in the short run, though it may well reduce your workload in the long run, after you have developed your courses and gained experience delivering them.

Step Three—Develop a New Vision for Your Course and How You Teach

If you are an experienced instructor, you already have preferred teaching methods. If you are a novice, the way you were taught in your education will probably determine what teaching methods you use when you first become an instructor. Instructors in either circumstance— when they begin to use elearning—typically must rethink and revise the ways they approach teaching in an elearning environment. This requires understanding how student learning can be improved through the use of elearning and its associated technology tools.

One of the most frequent mistakes made by instructors new to elearning is to post course materials on the web without thinking enough about how students will use these materials. Simply posting information on a coursesite does little to improve learning. What is important is what students are asked to do with the information you put on your coursesite. You must ensure that students understand the value of the elearning assignments you give them. For example, a focused web-based research assignment will provide specific instructions about what students should look for and how they should report their findings. A related example involves the use of electronic discussions. Students must be provided thought-provoking questions that promote critical thinking.

In short, you must avoid using technology simply because it exists. Instead, make sure that the technology adds value to your course content and delivery. Carefully think out what enhancements you want to make to your teaching. Once you have decided what changes are needed, you will be in a position to determine how technology can help you attain your goals. At that point, answering the following questions may help you see more clearly how elearning can improve your students' learning. The answers may also assist you in setting realistic elearning expectations. If you are a novice instructor, answer the questions by recalling your own responses to teaching methods you encountered during your education.

- What do students like about my teaching?
- What do students dislike about my teaching?
- Is there a high dropout rate or a retention problem in courses I teach?
- Am I satisfied that my students are learning from my teaching?
- Are there specific improvements that are needed in my teaching?
- Why should I change the way I teach?
- Why do I want to implement elearning?
- Do I lecture too much?
- Is there anything about my teaching that creates difficulties for my department or institution?
- Is there anything about my teaching that creates difficulties for students?
- Do I need help in reducing my administrative workload?
- Am I ready for a new challenge?
- How can elearning help me improve my teaching?
- How can the subjects I teach be enhanced by elearning?

Step Four—Determine the Resources Available to You

It is important to take advantage of any resources your institution may provide in terms of hardware, software, technical support, and elearning expertise. It is also very important to have a realistic view of the limitations of the resources available to you. For example, it doesn't make sense to plan to use high-end elearning resources such as simulations if the technology to create and display them is not available to you and your students. One way to determine available resources is to talk with colleagues who are experienced elearning users, and discuss with them how they got started and what resources they are aware of at your institution. You can also communicate with personnel in your institution's Department of Instructional Technology or Department of Educational Technology, if one exists.

Step Five—Acquire New Technology Skills and Develop New Instructional Methods

There is no escaping one salient fact. In order to use elearning to bring about positive changes in your instructional environment, you must learn new skills, develop new teaching methods, and devise new ways of designing courses. And—to reiterate—you must be willing to invest the time it takes to accomplish these goals. Mastering the LMS from both a faculty and student perspective is critical, since doing so enables you to take advantage of the functions of the LMS and to develop the proper LMS orientation for your students. For instructors who are technology novices, a mastery of basic computer technology—operating system skills, word processing skills, and presentation graphics skills, for example—is also essential.

At least two noted educational organizations have identified recommended technology skills and standards for educators. These two organizations are the ▪ISTE (International Society for Technology in Education) and ▪NCATE (National Council for Accreditation of Teacher Education). ISTE's website provides access to information about the National Educational Technology Standards (NETS) Project, which recommends that technology become an integral part of the teaching and learning process in every setting that supports the preparation of teachers, and describes what teachers should know about and be able to do with technology. NETS standards recommend that teachers learn to use technology themselves, as opposed to having someone create elearning resources for them; that the learning of technology skills be an ongoing process to ensure that teachers remain current; and that the effective use of technology become a component of their teaching strategies. NCATE standards require that educational institutions seeking initial or renewed accreditation provide faculty and students adequate access to computers and other technologies, and that they ensure that faculty and students are able to use technology successfully.

Another example is the list of competencies developed by the ▪Educational Technology Department at Embry-Riddle Aeronautical University. A checklist of over 200 recommended faculty technology competencies are posted on the departmental website. The checklist is a way for faculty to determine what they already know about technology as well as the technical competencies they lack. The department in turn provides numerous training programs, both online and face-to-face, to help faculty develop all recommended technology competencies on the checklist. A visit to this website would provide you with the checklist to use to distinguish the technology skills you already have as well as those you need to develop.

Step Six—Plan

Planning is critical to the success of elearning. Your elearning resources and supporting coursesite will be more effective—and take you less time to develop—if you plan very carefully before you begin to execute. Your plan should be based on your instructional goals, your skills, the time you have available, the technology tools at hand, and the support your institution can give you. It should include developing instructional resources, designing the coursesite, creating getting-started activities for student success, and envisioning an assessment process. Effective elearning planning is an extensive undertaking. Chapter 3 addresses the subject at length.

REFERENCES

Arabasz, P., Pirani, J., & Fawcett, D. (2003, March). Supporting e-learning in higher education. *EDUCAUSE Center for Applied Research*. Retrieved December 1, 2003, from www.educause.edu/ir/library/pdf/ecar_so/ers/ERS0303/EKF0303.pdf

Birchard, K. (2001, May 8). British web site teaches users how to find online information in their disciplines. *The Chronicle of Higher Education*. Retrieved October 22, 2001, from http://chronicle.com/free/2001/05/2001050801u.htm

Boettcher, J. V. (2003a, July). Course management systems and learning principles: Getting to know each other. *Syllabus, 16*(12), 33–34, 36.

Boettcher, J. V. (2003b, July). Course management systems in perspective: A conversation with Carl Berger. *Syllabus, 16*(12), 12–14, 16, 49.

Brandao, C. (2002, May). Teaching online: Harnessing technology's power at Florida Virtual School. *T.H.E. Journal, 29*(10), 37–43.

Brown, D. G. (2000). *Interactive learning: Vignettes from America's most wired campuses.* Bolton, MA: Anker Publishing Company.

Carmean, C., & Haefner, J. (2003). Next-generation course management systems. *EDUCAUSE Quarterly, 26*(1), 10–13.

Carnevale, D. (2003, May 13). Texas legislature is set to create an online charter school with universities' help. *The Chronicle of Higher Education.* Retrieved May 13, 2003, from http://chronicle.com/daily/2003/05/2003051303t.htm

Cerny, M. G., & Heines, J. M. (2001, February). Evaluating distance education across twelve time zones. *T.H.E. Journal, 28*(7), 21–25.

Charp, S. (2002, May). Changes to traditional teaching. *T.H.E. Journal, 29*(10), 10–12.

Chizmar, J. F., & Williams, D. B. (2001). What do faculty want? *EDUCAUSE Quarterly, 24*(1), 18–24.

Crawford, K., & Geith, C. (2003, February/March). Technology in engagement, research, and instruction: The TERI index. *Converge: Visions & Trends for Higher Education, 6*(1), 18–19.

Creighton, J. V., & Buchanan, P. (2001, March/April). Toward the e-campus: Using the Internet to strengthen, rather than replace, the campus experience. *EDUCAUSE Review, 36*(2), 12–13.

Csapo, N. (2002, August). Certification of computer literacy. *T.H.E. Journal, 30*(1), 46–51.

Duderstadt, J. J. (2001, January/February). Technology. *EDUCAUSE Review, 36*(1), 48–56.

Epper, R. M., & Garn, M. (2004, March/April). Virtual universities: Real possibilities. *EDUCAUSE Review, 39*(2), 28–30, 32, 34–36, 38–39.

Fink, M. L. (2002, February). Faculty on the move: Rethinking faculty support services. *Syllabus, 15*(7), 27–29.

Foster, A. L. (2004, January 22). Four colleges collaborate on open-source courseware. *The Chronicle of Higher Education.* Retrieved May 10, 2004, from http://chronicle.com/prm/daily/2004/01/2004012204n.htm

Gallagher, S. R. (2003, May 13). The new landscape for course management systems. *ECAR (EDUCAUSE Center for Applied Research) Research Bulletin, 2003*(10).

Garofoli, E., & Woodell, J. (2003, January). Faculty development and the diffusion of innovations. *Syllabus, 16*(6), 15–17.

Gray, S. (2002, August). A moving target: Elearning vendors take aim in a changing environment. *Syllabus, 16*(1), 28, 30–32.

Green, K. C. (2001a, March/April). Mark Hopkins and the digital log. *EDUCAUSE Review, 36*(2), 34–45.

Green, K. C. (2001b, October). The 2001 national survey of information technology in U.S. higher education. *The Campus Computing Project.* Retrieved September 16, 2002, from www.campuscomputing.net

Green, K. C. (2003a, May). Chapter two: New beginnings. *Syllabus, 16*(10), 14, 41.

Green, K. C. (2003b, December). Tracking the digital puck into 2004. *Syllabus, 17*(5), 10–13.

Green, K. C. (2004, March). Digital tweed: Sakai and the four Cs of open source. *Syllabus, 17*(8), 16, 18.

Greenberg, M. (2004, March/April). A university is not a business (and other fantasies). *EDUCAUSE Review, 39*(2), 10–16.

Hagner, P. R. (2000, September/October). Faculty engagement and support in the new learning environment. *EDUCAUSE Review, 35*(5), 27–28, 30–32, 34–37.

Hanley, G. (2003, June). MERLOT: Peer-to-peer pedagogy. *Syllabus, 16*(11), 36–37.

Hanley, G. L., & Thomas, C. (2000, October). MERLOT: Peer review of instructional technology. *Syllabus, 14*(3), 16–18, 20.

Hermida, A. (2003, July 15). World's poor to get own search engine. *BBC News World Edition.* Retrieved July 17, 2003, from http://news.bbc.co.uk/2/hi/technology/3065063.stm

Hesemeier, S., Kuivi, M., & Sosteric, M. (2003, January/February). The Bazaar online conference system: Athabasca University's alternative to proprietary online course delivery platforms. *The Technology Source.* Retrieved January 6, 2003, from http://ts.mivu.org/default.asp?show=article&id=1037

Heterick, B., & Twigg, C. (2003, February 1). *The Learning MarketSpace.* Retrieved November 19, 2003, from www.center.rpi.edu/LForum/LM/Feb03.html

Islam, K. A. (2002, May). Is e-learning floundering? Identifying shortcomings and preparing for success. *e-learning, 3*(5), 22–24, 26.

Jones, C. (2001, January). Ain't got time to teach. *Onlinelearning, 5*(1), 62, 66, 68.

Kalmon, S. (2003, January/February). Principles for creating a statewide online learning organization: The process and decisions underlying the creation of Colorado Online Learning. *The Technology Source.* Retrieved January 6, 2003, from http://ts.mivu.org/default.asp?show=article&id=1010

Keats, D. (2003, January/February). Knowledge environment for web-based learning (KEWL): An open source learning management system suited for the developing world. *The Technology Source.* Retrieved January 6, 2003, from http://ts.mivu.org/default.asp?show=article&id=1021

Knowles, M. S. (1980). *The modern practice of adult education: From pedagogy to andragogy.* Chicago: Association Press/Follett.

Knowles, M. (1984). *Andragogy in action.* San Francisco: Jossey-Bass.

Lane-Maher, M., & Ashar, H. (2001). Students.edu: Guidelines for online education programs. *EDUCAUSE Quarterly, 24*(1), 26–31.

Lembke, R. L., Rudy, J. A., & the EDUCAUSE Current Issues Committee. (2001). Top campus IT challenges for 2001. *EDUCAUSE Quarterly, 24*(2), 4–19.

Lockee, B., Moore, M., & Burton, J. (2001). Old concerns with new distance education research. *EDUCAUSE Quarterly, 24*(2), 60–62.

Long, P. D. (2002, January). OpenCourseWare: Simple idea, profound implications. *Syllabus, 15*(6), 12–15, 16.

Lujan, H. D. (2002, March/April). Commonsense ideas from an online survivor. *EDUCAUSE Review, 37*(2), 29–33.

Margulies, A. H. (2003, March). Open access to world-class knowledge. *Syllabus, 16*(8), 16–18.

Martyn, M. (2003). The hybrid online model: Good practice. *EDUCAUSE Quarterly, 26*(1), 18–23.

Moore, A. H. (2002, September/October). Lens on the future: Open-source learning. *EDUCAUSE Review, 37*(5), 42–44, 46, 48, 50–51.

Morgan, B. M. (2000). Distance education at what price? *EDUCAUSE Quarterly, 23*(3), 44.

National Center for Education Statistics. (2002). The condition of education: Special analysis 2002. Retrieved August 27, 2003, from http://nces.ed.gov//programs/coe/2002/analyses/nontraditional/index.asp

Naughton, J. (2001). *A brief history of the future: From radio days to Internet years in a lifetime.* Woodstock, NY: Overlook Press.

NSSE. (2003). The 2003 national survey of student engagement. Retrieved May 10, 2004, from www.iub.edu/~nsse/html/overview_2003.htm

Oblinger, D. (2003, July/August). Boomers & gen-Xers millennials: Understanding the new students. *EDUCAUSE Review, 38*(4), 37–46.

Olsen, F. (2002, December 6). MIT's open window: Putting course materials online, the university faces high expectations. *The Chronicle of Higher Education,* pp. A31–A35.

Pew Learning and Technology Program. (2002, June). *Pew Learning and Technology Program Newsletter.* Retrieved June 19, 2002, from www.center.rpi.edu/PewNews/PLTP12.html

Sheeran, M. R. (2001, July/August). Beyond the first five years: Lessons learned in transforming teaching and learning. *EDUCAUSE Review, 36*(4), 12–13.

Smith, N. (2002, May/June). Teaching as coaching: Helping students learn in a technological world. *EDUCAUSE Review, 37*(3), 38–47.

Strauss, H. (2002, May/June). The right train at the right station. *EDUCAUSE Review, 37*(3), 30–36.

Teles, L. (2002, May/June). The use of web instructional tools by online instructors. *The Technology Source.* Retrieved June 10, 2002, from http://ts.mivu.org/default.asp?show=article&id=966

Twigg, C. A. (2000, May/June). Course readiness criteria: Identifying targets of opportunity for large-scale redesign. *EDUCAUSE Review, 35*(3), 41–49.

Twigg, C. (2003, September/October). Improving learning and reducing costs: New models for online learning. *EDUCAUSE Review, 38*(5), 28–38.

Waterhouse, S., & Harris, R. (2001). *A 10-step guide to establishing instructional technology.* Washington, DC: Executive Leadership Foundation.

Wilson, C. (2001). Faculty attitudes about distance learning. *EDUCAUSE Quarterly, 24*(2), 70–71.

Young, J. (2003, April 20). Virtual classroom: Education evolution has begun. *Daytona Beach News-Journal,* pp. 3D–4D.

Young, J. R. (2002a, February 22). Ever so slowly, colleges start to count work with technology in tenure decisions. *The Chronicle of Higher Education.* Retrieved December 2, 2003, from http://chronicle.com/prm/weekly/v48/i24/24a02501.htm

Young, J. R. (2002b, March 11). Research group to release technical standards for its free course-management software. *The Chronicle of Higher Education.* Retrieved March 11, 2002, from http://chronicle.com/free/2002/03/2002031101u.htm

URL REFERENCES

Angel: www.cyberlearninglabs.com
Bazaar: http://klaatu.pc.athabascau.ca
Blackboard: www.blackboard.com
Campus Computing Project: www.campuscomputing.net
Desire2Learn: www.desire2learn.com/welcome.html
eCollege: http://elearning.ecollege.com
Educational Technology Department, Embry-Riddle Aeronautical University: http://edtech.erau.edu
Educator: http://ucompass.com
Edutools Comparisons of Course Management Systems: www.edutools.info
FirstClass: www.firstclass.com
Florida Virtual School: www.flvs.net
Froguts.com: www.froguts.com
ISTE: www.iste.org
KEWL: http://kewlforge.uwc.ac.za

LearningSpace: www.lotus.com/home.nsf/welcome/
   learnspace
Math Emporium: www.emporium.vt.edu/emporium/
   newVisitor/index.html
MentorNet: www.mentornet.net
MERLOT: http://merlot.org
MIT OpenCourseWare: http://ocw.mit.edu
NCATE: www.ncate.org
NCES: http://nces.ed.gov
NSSE: www.indiana.edu/~nsse
OKI (Open Knowledge Initiative): http://web.mit.edu/oki

Program in Course Redesign: www.center.rpi.edu/
   PewGrant.html
Sakai Project: www.sakaiproject.org
TEK: http://tek.sourceforge.net
THRO: http://homepages.uc.edu/thro
WebCT: www.webct.com
Webstars: http://online.fsu.edu/webstars
Wired for Books: http://wiredforbooks.org
World Lecture Hall: www.utexas.edu/world/lecture/index.
   html

CHAPTER TWO

ELEARNING PEDAGOGY

As defined in Chapter 1, *pedagogy* is the art and science of teaching, and an *elearning resource* is a component of an elearning course that students access for learning. To design effective elearning resources, you should have a basic understanding of common pedagogical principles. Pedagogy has been studied at least since history began, and providing an authoritative summary of pedagogical principles is far beyond the scope of this book. Nevertheless, this chapter summarizes a few popular pedagogical principles that are relevant to elearning. The basic information on effective elearning teaching principles presented here is intended to provide you with a frame of reference when you begin the process of elearning course planning, addressed in Chapter 3.

This chapter is organized into three sections. The first section summarizes three pedagogical works that are frequently cited in articles about elearning. These three works—by Chickering and Gamson; Bloom; and Gagne—present important principles of effective instruction. Although the works in fact predate the current widespread interest in elearning, the concepts they articulate are directly applicable to creating elearning modules. The second section of the chapter addresses the subject of student-centered learning, perhaps the most important of all pedagogical concepts, and one that elearning technology makes easier to apply. Many instructors have concluded that student-centered elearning leads to dramatic improvements in teaching and learning. The third and final section of Chapter 2 addresses the need to develop a vocabulary related to elearning pedagogy. It explains terms related to elearning delivery modes.

THREE NOTED PEDAGOGICAL WORKS
RELATED TO ELEARNING

Many pedagogical theories have been advanced in numerous scholarly works, and those of you who have studied education formally most likely have your favorites. For those of you who have not, the following three works are intended to serve as an introduction to pedagogy and to provide you with guidelines to use in planning elearning resources for your courses. The three works are:

- Chickering and Gamson's *Seven Principles for Good Practice in Undergraduate Education*
- Bloom's *Taxonomy of Intellectual Behaviors*
- Gagne's *Nine Events of Instruction*

As previously indicated, none of these works was written with elearning in mind. However, taken together they provide an excellent overview of pedagogical principles useful in designing effective elearning courses. The summaries that follow explain how the ideas in these works apply to teaching in an elearning environment.

The Seven Principles for Good Practice in Undergraduate Education

In 1986, the ▪AAHE (American Association for Higher Education), in collaboration with the Education Commission of the States and the Johnson Foundation, Inc., initiated a project to summarize the findings from decades of research on the undergraduate experience. The goal of the project was to promote good undergraduate teaching. One of its most notable outcomes was ▪Chickering and Gamson's *Seven Principles for Good Practice in Undergraduate Education,* instructional guidelines applicable to the creation of individual learning activities, complete courses of instruction, and even entire academic programs (Chickering & Gamson, 1987). It is generally agreed that the Seven Principles represent fundamentally sound practices that, when followed, lead toward high-quality teaching. Hundreds of two- and four-year colleges in the United States and Canada use the principles as a pedagogical model (Chickering & Ehrmann, 1996). One noted example is Winona State University's adoption of the principles as a university pedagogical model. On a website containing a message from the president of ▪Winona State University, the use of the principles to promote high-quality education is described.

The Seven Principles apply to elearning as well as to a traditional instructional environment and in essence constitute a checklist of good instructional practices to follow when you design an elearning course. The principles are listed and described briefly here. Figure 2.1 provides examples of how the principles can be applied in an elearning environment.

- **Good practice encourages contact between students and faculty.** Frequent contact between students and instructor in class and outside of class is the most important factor contributing to student motivation.
- **Good practice develops reciprocity and cooperation among students.** Students learn better when they feel they belong to a group. Meaningful learning grows from collaborative and social interaction, rather than competitive and isolated learning. Sharing and discussing ideas deepens understanding and creates the opportunity for improved thinking.
- **Good practice uses active learning techniques.** Learning improves when students become actively involved in their studies. Activities that best promote learning are those through which students can talk and write about what they are studying, as well as relate newly acquired knowledge to their experiences and lives.
- **Good practice gives students prompt feedback.** In order to focus their study efforts, students need to understand what they know about a subject and what they don't know. They need prompt feedback that provides adequate information about what they did correctly and the areas in which they need to improve. Feedback should occur in a timely fashion to ensure gradual and continuous student development. Students also need to be able to assess and evaluate their own learning and progress.

FIGURE 2.1   Seven Principles for Good Practice in Undergraduate Education Applied to Elearning

PRINCIPLE	APPLICATION OF PRINCIPLE TO ELEARNING
1. Encourage Contact between Students and Faculty	■ Online announcements ■ Electronic discussions ■ Online tutoring ■ Online office hours ■ Online chats ■ Email ■ Online faculty bios and staff information ■ Online student bios
2. Develop Reciprocity and Cooperation among Students	■ Online team projects and study groups ■ Online forums and chats ■ Online group tests ■ Email ■ Online peer evaluations
3. Use Active Learning Techniques	■ Online research ■ Online field trips ■ Online experiments ■ Online simulations ■ Online case studies ■ Online role playing ■ Online discussion of internships and field experiences ■ Online self-tests
4. Give Students Prompt Feedback	■ Online pretests, self-tests, and exams and instantaneous grades ■ Online access to gradebook and individual grades ■ Virtual office hours ■ Online tutoring ■ Electronic feedback from instructor and peers
5. Emphasize Time on Task	■ Online resources ■ Electronic tracking of student activity ■ Online discussions to document student participation ■ Online calendars to prompt students on course events
6. Communicate High Expectations	■ Online syllabus with course goals clearly stated ■ Online contract or code of conduct to establish an agreement between instructor and student on expected performance ■ Online announcements to encourage students to set high standards ■ Online discussions to have students participate in goal setting ■ Online instructor comments that set an example of effective communications for students to emulate ■ Online portfolios to publicly display examples of student work
7. Respect Diverse Talents and Ways of Learning	■ Policies posted online that address respect for diversity ■ Online assignments that promote interaction with content, address a variety of learning styles, and provide students with choices ■ Online surveys to determine students' special needs and learning styles

- **Good practice emphasizes time on task.** In order to learn, students must invest an appropriate amount of time studying course content and applying what they are learning to real-world situations. Also, they must learn to use time productively and must establish effective time management skills.
- **Good practice communicates high expectations.** Setting appropriate goals contributes to successful learning. Students need to be challenged and encouraged to try harder, to learn more, and to focus on the importance of a high-quality education. Expecting students to perform well often becomes a self-fulfilling prophecy.
- **Good practice respects diverse talents and ways of learning.** Students hail from many diverse cultures, all of which are to be respected and celebrated. Their behavior—and the way they learn—reflects both the norms of these various cultures and individual differences within the cultural norms. Whenever possible, a variety of learning strategies should be used to address cultural differences and differences in the ways individual students learn.

Bloom's Taxonomy of Intellectual Behaviors

In 1956, Benjamin Bloom headed a group of educational psychologists tasked with classifying levels of intellectual behavior important in the learning process. Their work resulted in three learning domain categories:

- The *cognitive domain,* addressing intellectual skills and the acquisition of knowledge;
- The *affective domain,* addressing feelings, preferences, values, and attitudes; and
- The *psychomotor domain,* addressing physical skills.

Bloom's *Taxonomy of Intellectual Behaviors* has become one of the most important pedagogical works in the history of education. His ideas are often used to guide the construction of learning activities, courses, and comprehensive academic programs. The premise of Bloom's Taxonomy is that mastery of a concept is defined by the ability to exhibit six increasingly sophisticated levels of cognitive behavior relative to the concept (1969). The six behaviors are:

- **Knowledge**—ability to recall learned material
- **Comprehension**—ability to explain and restate ideas
- **Application**—ability to use learned material in new situations
- **Analysis**—ability to categorize, distinguish, compare, or contrast material
- **Synthesis**—ability to design, formulate, plan, or devise material
- **Evaluation**—ability to judge the worth of material against stated criteria

▪Bloom's Taxonomy can help elearning instructors conceive student-centered learning resources and activities that promote involvement with course content and encourage critical thinking. As an example, suppose you want to teach students how to discriminate high-quality websites from those that are of a lesser quality. You might design resources leading to sequential learning activities that systematically advance students through Bloom's six behaviors. The first two behaviors, *knowledge* and *comprehension,* might be achieved by a brief lecture and demonstration in which you access a few websites—some of higher and some of lesser quality—and explain what makes the good ones useful and the bad ones less useful. The lecture could be followed by an online self-test on the characteristics of quality websites. To address *application,* students could be asked to identify and comment on the good and bad characteristics of two other websites you select. To address *analysis,* you could divide your students into small groups and require each group to find a number of websites it considers to be valuable on a specified subject and rank the sites they discover from best to least excellent. The fifth behavior, *synthesis,* could be encouraged by requiring each group to report its findings in a class presentation or short paper posted on the coursesite that explains the criteria used to rank the sites. Finally, stressing the last behavior, *evaluation,* could involve having students—individually, in their small groups, or as a class—create a generic form or checklist for evaluating the quality of any arbitrary website.

Figure 2.2 illustrates how to incorporate the five learning activities described in the previous paragraph into a single assignment to be completed by an individual student. This approach would be useful for distance-learning students or when you are dealing with accomplished or mature students who can learn without close supervision. The assignment is for students in an Introduction to Elearning course. Note that the assignment instructions in Figure 2.2 are both straightforward and detailed. Clarity and completeness in elearning instructions decrease the frustration students experience when they do not understand exactly what is expected of them, especially if they are distance learners who cannot easily obtain clarification. There is another benefit to writing clear and appropriately detailed assignment instructions. The time you spend doing this will save time later when fewer students need to contact you personally for clarification about the assignment.

Gagne's Nine Events of Instruction

Robert Gagne is a well-known, widely respected researcher and writer in the field of systematic approaches to learning. The Gagne nine-step instructional process—called the Nine Events of Instruction—defines instructional circumstances that improve learning when they occur sequentially (1985). Like Chickering and Gamson's Seven Principles, ▪Gagne's Nine Events can be used as a checklist to promote the effective design of elearning resources. These events are especially relevant when you are developing strategies for presenting new concepts to students in an elearning environment. The nine events are:

- **Gain attention.** Capture students' attention before proceeding with a learning activity to promote learning.
- **Inform students of the objectives.** Advise students of the learning objectives at the beginning of the learning activity to help set direction and motivate students to complete the learning activity.
- **Use recall.** Associate new information with prior knowledge to help students focus on the material. When students are able to link new knowledge to personal experiences and prior knowledge, they can relate to the material, and it becomes easier to understand new information.
- **Present the material.** Present new content using a meaningful organization, perhaps in chunks of information to help students learn. Presenting the new content in ways that address students' preferred learning styles is highly desirable.

FIGURE 2.2   Bloom's Taxonomy Applied to a Website Evaluation Assignment

OVERVIEW AND PURPOSE OF ASSIGNMENT

This assignment will focus on two important topics: (1) the characteristics of a well-constructed website and (2) rubric evaluation instruments. The ability to distinguish well-constructed websites from those that are not well constructed will help you in your future web research in this course, in future courses, and in nonacademic web research.

Rubrics are instruments used in evaluation and assessment processes. Knowledge of how to construct an effective rubric will help you whenever you undertake to evaluate something, whether it be a website, your students' performances, the effectiveness of an elearning resource, the overall effectiveness of your teaching, or something else.

This assignment has three parts. The first part is designed to familiarize you with the characteristics of well-constructed websites as well as the characteristics of poorly constructed websites. The second part will give you practice in finding information on a website. You will go to two designated websites and search for specified information, after which you will comment in an online discussion about your experiences in conducting these two searches. In part 3, you will use the knowledge you have gained to search the web for information about *rubrics* and use the information you find to create a rubric to evaluate websites.

ASSIGNMENT OBJECTIVES—STUDENTS WILL BE ABLE TO

1. Evaluate the quality of websites
2. Describe the purpose of a rubric
3. Design a website evaluation rubric

IMPORTANT NOTES ABOUT THIS ASSIGNMENT

1. Several components of this assignment must be emailed to your instructor. Follow the "Emailing Assignments" procedures located in the Course Information section of the coursesite. Failure to comply with these procedures on any assignment component will result in a grade of 0 points for that component.
2. The form referred to in this assignment is located in the Forms component of Course Information in the coursesite.
3. The discussion forums referenced in this assignment are explained in the Discussion section of the coursesite.
4. Each assignment component must be submitted by midnight, Eastern Standard Time (EST), on the due date specified in the Component Due Dates and Grading table below.

COMPONENT DUE DATES AND GRADING—A MAXIMUM OF 18 POINTS IS POSSIBLE

COMPONENT	DUE DATE	POINTS
Part 1		
Score of 80 or Higher on Self-Test	September 22	0–2
Part 2		
Completed Information Sheet on Two Websites	September 24	0–2
Lists of Good and Bad Characteristics of the Two Websites	September 24	0–2
Two Original Postings in Discussion	September 26	0–4
Reply to Postings of Two Classmates	September 28	0–4

(continued)

FIGURE 2.2   Continued

COMPONENT	DUE DATE	POINTS
Part 3		
Rubric	September 29	0–4

ASSIGNMENT INSTRUCTIONS

Part 1

1. Review the presentation entitled "Quality Websites" listed in the Course Content section of the coursesite.
2. When you have completed the review of the presentation, take the corresponding "Quality Websites" self-test listed in the Quizzes and Test component of the coursesite. If you score below 80, review the presentation and take the self-test again. Keep trying until you have received a score of 80 or better on the self-test. The test must be completed successfully by September 22.
3. Visit the http://amazon.com website and the http://whitehouse.gov website.

Part 2

1. In order to become familiar with each site, complete a "Website Information Form" on each. Also, make a list of what you consider to be the good characteristics and the poor characteristics of each site. Send the two forms and two lists (with brief related comments as you wish) to your instructor via email no later than September 24.
2. Learn what a rubric is and how to create one by performing a web search on "rubric." Locate at least one site of high quality on the subject of rubrics, and one that is not of high quality. In a later portion of this assignment, you will be asked to create a rubric to use to evaluate websites. Consequently, locating quality sites on the subject is very important.
3. In the discussion forum named "Rubrics—Best Website," share the site name and URL you chose to be in the "best" category, and explain in one brief paragraph the characteristics of the site and why you selected it. In the discussion forum named "Rubrics—Worst Website," share the site name and URL you selected and explain in one brief paragraph the characteristics of the site and why you selected it. Enter both of your postings by September 26.
4. After students have had a chance to post information about the "Best" sites and the "Worst" sites (after midnight EST September 26), read as many of the student responses as you wish. In each forum, select at least one other student's response. Visit the website that student reported on, form your own impressions of the site, and report on this impression in a forum response by September 28. Include in your response whether you agree or disagree with the student's choice, and explain why in a brief sentence or two. Note that you must make two such responses—one for the "Best Website" forum, and one for the "Worst Website" forum.

Part 3

Using the knowledge you have gained about rubrics and the characteristics of quality websites, design a one-page rubric (evaluation instrument) for evaluating websites. The rubric must include at least four ratings and four categories to be rated. Create the rubric in Word. Email your rubric to your instructor by September 29.

- **Provide learning guidance.** Reinforce new concepts by providing examples, having students engage in case studies, using graphical representations and analogies, and similar active-learning approaches.
- **Elicit performance.** Elicit performance through practice and the application of new concepts. Providing learners with an opportunity to confirm their understanding increases the likelihood they will retain acquired knowledge.
- **Provide feedback.** Give prompt feedback to help students understand what they know and what they don't know about a subject. Students feel encouraged when they receive positive feedback. Constructive feedback on deficiencies helps them see where improvements are needed.
- **Assess performance.** Assess whether students have learned the material and met the specific objectives of the learning activity. Assessment processes help motivate students and should be incorporated into each major learning activity.
- **Enhance retention and transfer.** Afford students opportunities to apply new knowledge to real-world scenarios. Retaining knowledge is improved when students are required to apply information they have gained.

Figure 2.3—an outgrowth of Figure 2.2—illustrates how Gagne's Nine Events can be applied to an instructional module on website evaluation. The instructional module assumes a hybrid delivery mode whereby students meet face-to-face and have access to an LMS. In addition to Gagne's Nine Events, the activities described in Figure 2.3 also adhere to Bloom's Taxonomy. Students begin working on the *knowledge* behavior and advance to the *evaluation* behavior. Figure 2.3 also illustrates the application of elearning strategies designed to provide student interaction with course content.

STUDENT-CENTERED INSTRUCTION AND ELEARNING

Lecturing—a *teacher-centered* activity—has for a long time been the preferred method of instruction in secondary schools and universities worldwide. Many contemporary instructors argue, however, that learning increases dramatically when the instructional milieu is transformed from a teacher-centered to a *student-centered* environment, one where students take on more of the responsibility of learning and become more actively engaged in the learning process. Elearning makes this pedagogical approach even more attractive because it is more easily implemented. Recall the David Brown study, discussed in Chapter 1, involving the 42 institutions identified as "America's most wired campuses." When instructors at these institutions were surveyed about what they liked best about elearning, an overwhelming majority cited student-centered learning practices. They identified activities such as interactive learning, collaborative learning, learning by doing, role playing, and other student-centered activities as the major reasons they use elearning (Brown, 2000).

Perhaps you are one of many instructors accustomed to a traditional teacher-centered lecture environment. You have lectured—or been lectured to, if you are a novice instructor—for a number of years, without thinking very much about whether this is the best way to teach and/or learn. If so, now may be the right time to use elearning to include student-centered learning in your instructional environment. Your challenge is to understand how elearning

FIGURE 2.3   Gagne's Nine Events and Supporting Elearning Activities Applied to a Website Evaluation Module in a Hybrid Delivery Mode

EVENT	ELEARNING STRATEGIES
1. Gain Attention	■ Open class with a very poor website in view to dramatically illustrate poor website quality. "Busy" websites with distracting movement and numerous colors will gain students' attention.
2. Inform Students of the Objectives	■ State the objective of the learning activity at the beginning of the presentation and in the assignment instructions.
3. Use Recall	■ Have students recall websites they have used that are especially good, as well as those that are not good. Show some of their examples to the entire class.
4. Present the Material	■ Explain each characteristic of the poorly designed websites shown students in class. ■ Provide students with a "checklist" of items that illustrate a quality website. ■ Show students examples of quality websites that illustrate points on the checklist.
5. Provide Learning Guidance	■ Provide students with the URLs of websites that produce ratings and descriptions of other websites that are considered to be of high quality. ■ Provide students with the URLs of websites that produce ratings and descriptions of other websites that are considered to be of poor quality. ■ Have students revisit some of their favorite websites and use the checklist of Event 4 to evaluate each. ■ Have students review a few instructors-specified websites in each category and complete the checklist on each. ■ Review some of the students' evaluations in class. ■ Provide feedback to students on their evaluations.
6. Elicit Performance	■ Divide students into groups and ask them to identify websites on the subject of "rubrics" that are of good quality, and websites on the same subject that are of poor quality, using the checklist as a guide. ■ Ask groups to report to the class on their findings.
7. Provide Feedback	■ Have students take an online self-test on the characteristics of quality websites. ■ Provide feedback on individual assignment. ■ Provide feedback on group assignment. ■ Have students complete a self-evaluation of their rubrics. ■ Have students complete a peer evaluation of another student's rubric.
8. Assess Performance	■ Administer self-tests. ■ Conduct peer reviews. ■ Conduct self-evaluation. ■ Provide instructor feedback.
9. Enhance Retention and Transfer	■ Use the rubric evaluation form in future web research assignments in this course and other courses.

helps make this transformation possible. Start by understanding some of the teaching results of student-centered learning and how these results can be achieved using elearning. Some typical results of student-centered learning are listed and explained next.

- The lecture delivery format is revised.
- The instructor becomes a facilitator.
- Learning styles are addressed.
- Students are provided choices.
- Web-based interaction with content is implemented.
- Student communication and collaboration are increased.
- Problem-based learning is implemented.
- Self-assessment is used as a learning activity.
- Portfolio assessment is implemented.

The Lecture Delivery Format Is Revised

One of the major differences between student-centered and teacher-centered learning is the extent to which lectures are used to promote learning. In a student-centered environment, the amount of time spent on lectures typically decreases. Sometimes lectures are eliminated entirely. Why? Lectures typically place the instructor at the center of attention, creating a passive learning environment that allows students to remain uninvolved and intellectually aloof. Of course, some instructors are in fact excellent lecturers. Many more, however, believe—perhaps without much corroborative evidence—that when students take notes while listening to lectures, they are in fact interacting with the course content and hence learning. However, surveys show that students tend to have a negative view of courses that consist entirely of lectures, particularly large lectures delivered to captive audiences of hundreds. The lecture environment especially falls short of the expectations of many students raised on the Internet and interactive games. On the other hand, students relish engaging in challenging exercises wherein they discuss course content in groups with other students or have more opportunity to interact personally with the instructor and the course content. And it is a well-established fact that learning tends to occur when students are intellectually engaged in a subject they are studying.

Why Do Instructors Lecture So Much?   If it is true that most students would prefer not to have a steady diet of lectures, why do we lecture so much? One reason may be that lectures are the way we ourselves were taught when we were students. Another reason is that many instructors like to "perform" for student audiences. A few are even accomplished entertainers. Lectures abound as well because it is cost effective to lecture to large numbers of students (Kerns, 2002). Also, institutional schedules often mandate that classes be of a certain length, begin and end at specific times, and be conducted on specific days. In view of scheduling limitations, lectures may represent the least taxing method for you to deliver course content, especially if you have taught the course many times before and the lectures are already prepared.

What Are the Alternatives to Lectures?   In a student-centered elearning environment, students typically engage in activities in which they are actively involved with the course content as well as with each other. This does not mean that lectures must be eliminated as a pedagogical strategy. They may be used to cover or clarify major course topics or as a preview of concepts that will be reinforced by in-class or out-of-class activities. For example, after a lecture in which the instructor demonstrates how to evaluate information on a website, students working individually or in teams might be asked to search a website for answers to important questions, evaluate the information found, and report back about what they discovered at the end of the class period. Another activity reinforcing such a lecture might be to send students on an out-of-class electronic field trip to gather information on an assigned subject, then have them report their findings in an electronic discussion before the next scheduled class period.

Another approach to making lectures more interactive is the use of wireless keypads linked to a computer. Each student, using an individual keypad, clicker, or student response system as they are often called, can answer questions about the lecture information just delivered. Using a keypad, students would not respond by raising their hands, but would punch buttons instead. Results appear on a screen in the front of the room almost instantaneously. Educators who use them report that their classrooms come alive as never before (Hafner, 2004).

The Instructor Becomes a Facilitator

As a teacher in a student-centered learning environment, your role is to create elearning resources that guide and direct students, oftentimes working without direct instructor supervision, toward a desired learning goal. Consequently, the time you spend preparing and delivering lectures may decrease, and the time you spend creating interactive learning activities may increase. As a facilitator, you set the pace for the course and monitor the progress of individual students and groups, helping them get back on track if they stray away from the main objectives of an elearning activity. Often, instructors changing to a student-centered delivery mode find they must make major changes in their teaching philosophy. For many, the transition is very gradual. Changes in an individual's basic approaches to teaching ordinarily do not occur easily or quickly.

Learning Styles Are Addressed

Experienced instructors know that not all students learn in exactly the same way. This fact gives rise to the concept of an individual's *learning style*. One of the best-known learning style theories groups learners into three categories: auditory learners, visual learners, and tactile/kinesthetic learners (Sarasin, 1999). The majority of individuals appear to be visual learners, followed by auditory learners, then tactile/kinesthetic learners.

Auditory learners learn best when content is delivered orally or in written format, as in lectures, articles, and books. They prefer content to be presented as a series of specific ideas and facts, leading ultimately to a broader understanding of an entire concept. Also, auditory learners tend to prefer learning sequentially. Because auditory learners like lectures, if your instructional environment is largely student centered, you might create audio or video recordings of lecture information and post it to your course website where auditory learners can access it as desired. If creating audio or video components is not practical, another alternative is to use student teaching assistants to provide the kind of help auditory learners need. The assistants can use LMS electronic communications tools to conduct online help and tutoring sessions, increasing opportunities for auditory learners to obtain verbal feedback.

Visual learners learn best through visual aids such as images, diagrams, drawings, charts, pictures, or any other approach that helps them form a visual image. They often prefer to develop an overview of a subject before examining its component details. They tend *not* to enjoy lengthy lectures to which they must sit and listen intently for a half hour or more. In fact, visual learners often prefer to take detailed notes during lectures to help them absorb lecture information. Example learning strategies that typically appeal to visual learners are role playing, working with models, and seeing demonstrations. Elearning resources attractive to visual learners are movies and other multimedia presentations, animations, and text or lecture presentations that make extensive use of pictures, images, and diagrams.

Tactile/kinesthetic learners learn best when they are actively involved in the learning process. These learners prefer a student-centered learning environment where they are *doing* something to learn course content. They tend to dislike lectures and often fail to pay attention. For example, if you lecture in a classroom where each student station has a computer, the tactile learners are likely to be the ones reading their email while ignoring what you are saying. Tactile learners have a tendency to be very creative, and they like to have learning resources readily at hand. They thrive in a student-centered environment. A few examples of elearning activities enjoyed by tactile learners are team projects, web-based research, online experiments, online expeditions, simulations, and similar activities that actively engage them.

There is increasing evidence that today's youth will need and expect a very different learning environment from the one their parents and teachers experienced. In fact, a new classification of students has recently emerged that provides insight. *Millennials* are students who were born after 1982 and who most likely favor a tactile learning environment. Some of the characteristics of millennials are that (1) they are cooperative team players; (2) they spend more time doing homework and housework and less time watching TV; (3) they believe "it's cool to be smart"; (4) they are fascinated by new technologies; (5) they are racially and ethnically diverse; (6) they identify with their parents' values and feel close to their parents; and (7) they often (one in five) have at least one immigrant parent (Howe & Strauss, 2000). These characteristics indicate that they will thrive in learning environments that emphasize teamwork, experiential activities, and the use of technology (Raines, 2002).

The traditional teacher-centered environment tends to serve auditory learners well, do little for visual learners, and ignore tactile learners entirely. In a student-centered environment, by contrast, one consciously employs varying kinds of learning activities—discussions, group projects, lectures, demonstrations, films and audio recordings, lab experiments, practice tests, self- and peer evaluation, for example—which accommodate different learning styles. Although it may not be practical for most instructors to address each student's learning style individually, one successful approach is to provide a mix of elearning resources that accommodate learners in each of the three learning style categories. With this approach, at least some of the time students are learning according to their preferred learning styles.

The technology of elearning provides powerful support for developing student-centered resources. Summarizing the many theories of learning styles is far beyond the scope of this book. URL References at the end of this chapter provide further information on learning styles, including how to obtain web access to learning style inventories.

Students Are Provided Choices

In the student-centered environment, students are empowered to make choices about how they will learn. Sometimes they are even invited to participate in the construction of the learning environment based on their personal interests and goals. To better understand why giving students choices about learning might be desirable, consider the *constructivist*—as opposed to the *objectivist*—approach to delivering instruction. Constructivist practices encourage students to undertake activities that engage their interests and to build on their experiences. The constructivist approach also allows students to participate in constructing the learning path by choosing between learning alternatives and to discover principles by themselves through doing so. This approach helps students learn how to seek knowledge and find answers, invaluable skills they will exercise in the task of lifelong learning. Seymour Papert, a noted MIT professor and the creator of the Logo Language, is an early constructivist, along with Bruner, Vygotsky, and Dewey. Perhaps Papert best sums up the essence of this active approach to learning in his statement about children, which is also very applicable to adults: "The kind of knowledge children most need is the knowledge that will help them get more knowledge" (1993, p. 139). Elearning facilitates constructivist principles by providing a framework—the coursesite—by which students can select the type and ordering of their learning activities from a variety of equivalent elearning resources and by providing numerous technology-enhanced learning resources. For example, if your subject is dissecting a frog, your coursesite resources might include textual information on the subject, a film showing the process, and a link to the Froguts website, which uses computer simulation to allow a student to dissect a frog virtually, as illustrated in Chapter 1.

The constructivist approach is not equally appropriate for all disciplines, especially those requiring that a specific foundation of knowledge be mastered before moving to the next concept, such as learning to fly an airplane or how to design and build one. For such subjects, the objectivist approach may be more appropriate. In the *objectivist* approach, the instructor outlines a specific path of learning, and students are guided sequentially through the learning content. Elearning can also facilitate the objectivist learning approach. One example is the use of self-assessment activities that provide students a means of testing their knowledge and obtaining feedback before moving to the next topic. Also, an elearning coursesite facilitates access to specific documents, instructions, and other important course materials that provide the readily available guidance and instructions needed in an objectivist environment.

Many instructors combine constructivist and objectivist practices, incorporating the principles of both in student-centered learning. For example, the objectivist approach can be used initially to introduce foundation material sequentially. Later, after the foundation knowledge is mastered, a constructivist approach may be followed whereby students participate in selecting and determining the types of assignments they will work on to build on the knowledge they gained during the initial portion of a course.

Web-Based Interaction with Content Is Implemented

Web-based elearning resources and activities can greatly enhance a student-centered learning environment. For example, web-based research assignments involve students with course content and encourage critical thinking skills. Activities such as online field trips and virtual experiments involving visual simulations, among many others, increase student interaction with course content significantly. Also, elearning allows students to interact online with mentors. Chapters 5 through 7 provide an in-depth discussion of web-based learning strategies and resources appropriate for a student-centered environment.

Student Communication and Collaboration Are Increased

Elearning dramatically increases opportunities for students to communicate with each other and with the instructor, and these opportunities promote student-centered learning. Documents and other forms of information can be posted on a coursesite for students to access at their convenience. LMS capabilities allow setting up discussion groups whereby students can collaborate on assignments, gaining in the process the valuable experience of teamwork (Buckley, 2002). In addition, using elearning communications in this manner helps students master technology tools they will likely use one day in workplace collaboration. Chapters 5 and 6 address electronic communications in detail.

Problem-Based Learning Is Implemented

Problem-based learning, often called *project-based learning,* is a learning strategy that focuses on resolving real-world problems. In project-based learning, students typically apply the knowledge they are learning, engage in critical thinking, and work on practical real-world scenarios—all of which help them develop learning skills transferable to the workplace and to their personal lives. Students typically are challenged to explain "why" a fact is true or an idea is valid, and to justify their answers with supporting references and research. One of the most important outcomes of problem-based learning is that students have opportunities to "learn to learn," a skill that will be needed throughout life, as emphasized previously in this chapter (Watson, 2002). Elearning can dramatically improve project-based learning because electronic communications and collaborations, file sharing, and other web-based activities facilitate teamwork in such projects.

Self-Assessment Is Used as a Learning Activity

Self-assessment through self-testing is an excellent active learning activity, especially when students are provided immediate feedback on why they missed a question. Although elearning instructors may be leery of using online testing for grades due to the increased possibilities of cheating in an unproctored environment, online testing is excellent for self-assessment. Also, online testing tools can facilitate assessment surveys. For example, online assessment tools provide instructors with a simple method of collecting feedback on how well students have learned a concept (Byers, 2002). An electronic quiz can be administered quickly after a lecture, a reading assignment, or any other activity about which immediate feedback on student learning is desired. The student response systems discussed earlier could also help students assess their knowledge.

Portfolio Assessment Is Implemented

In a student-centered learning environment, student assessment does not have to be dependent on test grades alone. Rather, a variety of assessment methodologies can be utilized. One common alternative method is portfolio assessment. A portfolio is simply a collection of samples of completed work that provides practical evidence of the student's accomplishments in a course. Elearning technology affords students the opportunity to post their portfolios on a coursesite for review by the instructor, their classmates, and potential employers. Digital repositories of portfolios can include text, graphics, video, audio, photos, and animation.

The trend toward electronic portfolios may have a tremendous impact not only on the way instructors assess students but also on how both instructors and academic programs are assessed (Batson, 2002). As instructional documents and other materials migrate from paper to electronic files that can be web accessed, searched, reviewed, and commented on in digital format, the potential for change in the way teaching and learning are assessed increases dramatically.

TERMS TO DESCRIBE ELEARNING DELIVERY MODES

A jargon exists to describe instructional delivery modes, and more terms are evolving every day. Unfortunately—as with most jargon—the terms that describe elearning delivery modes are not always clearly defined and hence are sometimes used imprecisely. What follows to conclude Chapter 2 defines elearning delivery mode terms as understood in the context of this book. We believe that our definitions are accurate within the larger context of elearning as well.

Distance Learning

Distance learning is learning whereby students and instructors are engaged in learning activities in different locations and typically do not come face-to-face with each other. The terms *distance education* and *distributed learning* are also used to describe distance learning. Courses delivered totally online or via videoconferencing are examples of modern-day distance learning. TV-based courses and videotaped courses are examples of early distance-learning programs facilitated by technology.

Online Learning

The term *online learning* describes learning that is delivered solely via the web. Online learning may refer to entire courses or to learning activities conducted using individual elearning resources. Examples of online learning are when a student accesses information on a coursesite, participates in computer-based simulations, takes an online field trip, takes a test online, or uses LMS communication tools for group collaboration and other instructional activities enabled by the web. An *online course*—sometimes referred to as a *totally online course*—is one delivered entirely on the web. Online courses are also sometimes referred to as *virtual courses*. Institutions delivering courses totally online are often referred to as *virtual universities* or *virtual institutions*.

The term *distance-learning course* is not infrequently used as a synonym for *online course*. However, such a use seems imprecise: *Online learning* refers precisely to any elearning *activity*, whether it is an entirely online course or simply a resource in a course in which instructors and students sometimes meet face-to-face. Distance learning, on the other hand, most properly refers to any course delivery mode by which students and instructor do not meet face-to-face, regardless of whether elearning technology is used.

Hybrid eLearning Delivery Mode

A *hybrid* elearning delivery mode—also referred to as a *blended* delivery mode—uses the web to enhance face-to-face learning and in many cases decreases the number of face-to-face class sessions needed. In the hybrid delivery mode, a coursesite is typically used to distribute course information, conduct online assessment, and facilitate electronic discussions and web-based interaction with content, among other elearning activities. Instructors hesitant to engage in totally online course delivery find hybrid delivery methods less controversial and adopt them more readily (Young, 2002). The ▪MathOnline system at the University of Colorado at Colorado Springs reflects a hybrid course delivery approach combining traditional mathematics instruction with online learning activities. Surveys illustrate that students are very satisfied with this hybrid mode of delivery. One major reason is that individual learning styles are addressed, among other advantages (Abrams & Haefner, 2002).

Another variation of the hybrid concept is the *web-enhanced* delivery mode. In web-enhanced instruction, elearning resources are used to supplement face-to-face class sessions. Examples are in-class activities used to reinforce a lecture or presentation such as teams working on web research or the administration of online self-tests to determine whether students have grasped the concepts discussed in the class.

Synchronous versus Asynchronous Learning and Communications

A *synchronous* learning environment is one in which students and instructors engage each other at the same time, but not necessarily at the same location. Traditional classroom-based learning is a common form of synchronous learning. A videoconferenced class, whereby one or more groups of students are gathered in individual classrooms and are taught by an instructor at a remote location, also exemplifies the synchronous delivery mode. A telephone conversation is an example of synchronous communications.

An *asynchronous* learning environment is one in which students and instructors are engaged in "anytime-anyplace" learning. Students do not have to be in the same room with other students or their instructor, nor do they all have to be engaged in a learning activity at the same time. Taking a course by correspondence is a traditional form of asynchronous learning. As opposed to a telephone conversation, the exchange of email exemplifies asynchronous two-way communications: Individuals send and receive messages anytime that doing so is convenient. Chapter 6 explains electronic discussions, another form of two-way communication used in elearning. Electronic discussions fall into two categories, forums and chats. Typically, forums are asynchronous and chats are synchronous.

REFERENCES

Abdulezer, S. (2000, November). Breaking out. *Converge.* Retrieved November 19, 2003, from www.converge mag.com/magazine/story.phtml?id=3339

Abrams, G., & Haefner, J. (2002, September/October). Blending online and traditional instruction in the mathematics classroom. *The Technology Source.* Retrieved September 3, 2002, from http://ts.mivu. org/default.asp?show=article&id=970

Anderson, L. W., Krathwohl, D. R., & Bloom, B. S. (2000). *Taxonomy for learning, teaching, and assessing: A revision of Bloom's taxonomy of educational objectives.* White Plains, NY: Longman.

Batson, T. (2002, December). The electronic portfolio boom: What's it all about? *Syllabus, 16*(5), 14–20.

Bleed, R. (2001, January/February). A hybrid campus for the new millennium. *EDUCAUSE Review, 36*(1), 16–20, 22, 24.

Bloom, B. S. (1969). *Taxonomy of educational objectives: The classification of educational goals.* White Plains, NY: Longman.

Brown, D. (2000). *Interactive learning: Vignettes from America's most wired campuses.* Bolton, MA: Anker Publishing Company.

Brown, D. (2003a, March). Enhancing the seven practices. *Syllabus, 16*(8), 20.

Brown, D. (2003b, September). Faculty practice: Leveraging technology for learning. *Syllabus, 17*(2), 14.

Buckley, D. P. (2002, January/February). In pursuit of the learning paradigm: Coupling faculty transformation and institutional change. *EDUCAUSE Review, 37*(1), 29–30, 32–36, 38.

Byers, C. (2002, May/June). Interactive assessment and course transformation using web-based tools. *The Technology Source.* Retrieved June 10, 2002, from http://ts.mivu.org/default.asp?show=article&id=928

Chamberlin, W. S. (2001, December). Face-to-face vs. cyberspace: Finding the middle ground. *Syllabus, 15*(5), 10–11, 32.

Chickering, A., & Ehrmann, S. C. (1996, October). Implementing the seven principles: Technology as lever. *AAHE Bulletin.* Retrieved September 1, 2003, from http://aahebulletin.com/public/archive/seven principles.asp

Chickering, A. W., & Gamson, Z. F. (1987, March). Seven principles for good practice in undergraduate education. *AAHE Bulletin.* Retrieved September 1, 2003, from http://aahebulletin.com/public/archive/ sevenprinciples1987.asp

Chickering, A. W., & Gamson, Z. F. (1991). *Applying the seven principles for good practice in undergraduate education.* San Francisco: Jossey-Bass.

Frand, J. L. (2000, September/October). The information-age mindset: Changes in students and implications for higher education. *EDUCAUSE Review, 35*(5), 15–18, 22, 24.

Gagne, R. (1985). *The conditions of learning* (4th ed.). New York: Holt, Rinehart & Winston.

Graham, C., Cagiltay, K., Lim, B., Craner, J., & Duffy, T. (2001, March/April). Seven principles of effective teaching: A practical lens for evaluating online courses. *The Technology Source.* Retrieved December 18, 2003, from http://ts.mivu.org/default.asp? show=article&id=839

Green, D. W., & O'Brien, T. (2002, June). The Internet's impact on teacher practice and classroom culture. *T.H.E. Journal, 29*(11), 44, 46, 48, 50–51.

Hafner, K. (2004, April 29). In class, the audience weighs in. *The New York Times.* Retrieved May 10, 2004, from http://query.nytimes.com/gst/abstract.html? res=F60A10F7345E0C7A8EDDAD0894DC404482

Harley, D., Maher, M., Henke, J., & Lawrence, S. (2003). An analysis of technology enhancements in a large lecture course. *EDUCAUSE Quarterly, 26*(3), 26–33.

Howe, N., & Strauss, W. (2000). *Millennials rising: The next great generation.* New York: Vintage Books.

Interview: Lippman on learning fundamental changes [Editorial]. (2002, February). *Syllabus, 15*(7), 12–13.

Johnstone, S. M. (2004, March). Distance learning: Are you ready for laptop high grads? *Syllabus, 17*(8), 20.

Kassop, M. (2003, May/June). Ten ways online education matches, or surpasses, face-to-face learning. *The Technology Source.* Retrieved December 4, 2003, from http://ts.mivu.org/default.asp?show=article &id=1059

Keane, J. (2002, August). Teacher vs. computer: Where educators stand in the technology revolution. *T.H.E. Journal, 30*(1), 38–40.

Kerns, C. (2002, May/June). Constellations for learning. *EDUCAUSE Review, 37*(3), 20–24, 26, 28.

Lago, M. E. (2000, November). The hybrid experience: How sweet it is! *Converge.* Retrieved November 19, 2003, from www.convergemag.com/magazine/ story.phtml?id=3340

Laurillard, D. (2002, January/February). Rethinking teaching for the knowledge society. *EDUCAUSE Review, 37*(1), 16–20, 22–25.

Mangan, K. (2002, October 9). Colleges in sixteen countries work to create virtual medical school. *The Chronicle of Higher Education.* Retrieved December 4, 2003, from http://chronicle.com/free/2002/ 10/2002100901t.htm

Papert, S. (1993). *The children's machine: Rethinking school in the age of computers.* New York: Basic Books.

Raines, C. (2002). Managing millennials. *Generations at Work.* Retrieved August 31, 2003, from www. generationsatwork.com/articles/millenials.htm

Rogers, E. M. (1995). *Diffusion of innovations* (4th ed.). New York: Free Press.

Sarasin, L. C. (1999). *Learning style perspectives: Impact in the classroom.* Madison, WI: Atwood Publishing.

Watson, G. (2002, May/June). Using technology to promote success in PBL courses. *The Technology Source.* Retrieved June 10, 2002, from http://ts.mivu.org/ default.asp?show=article&id=969

Wingard, R. G. (2004). Classroom teaching changes in web-enhanced courses: A multi-institutional study. *EDUCAUSE Quarterly, 27*(1), 26–35.

Young, J. R. (2002, March 22). "Hybrid" teaching seeks to end the divide between traditional and online instruction. *The Chronicle of Higher Education.* Retrieved December 2, 2003, from http://chronicle. com/prm/weekly/v48/i28/28a03301.htm

URL REFERENCES

AAHE: www.aahe.org

Abiator's Online Learning Style Inventory: http://berghuis. co.nz/abiator/lsi/lsiframe.html

Bloom: Major Categories in the Taxonomy of Educational Objectives: http://faculty.washington.edu/ krumme/guides/bloom.html

Bloom's Taxonomy: OfficePort Resources: www.office port.com/edu/blooms.htm

Chickering and Gamson Seven Principles for Good Practice in Undergraduate Education Application: www. msu.edu/user/coddejos/seven.htm

DVC Online: www.metamath.com/lsweb/dvclearn.htm

Felder and Solomon Learning Styles Survey: www. engr.ncsu.edu/learningstyles/ilsweb.html

Felder Resources on Learning Styles: www2.ncsu.edu/ unity/lockers/users/f/felder/public/RMF.html

Gagne's Nine Events of Instruction: Resources and Strategies: http://ide.ed.psu.edu/idde/9events.htm

Jester Learning Style Survey: www.metamath.com/multiple/ multiple_choice_questions.cgi

Kearsley Explorations in Learning and Instruction: The Theory into Practice Database: www.gwu.edu/~tip

Learning Styles Chart on Auditory, Visual, or Kinestic Learners: www.chaminade.org/inspire/learnstl.htm

MathOnline: www.math.uccs.edu/mathonline

Myers-Briggs Type Interpretation and Student Learning Styles: www.gsu.edu/~dschjb/wwwmbti.html

Penn State Royer Center for Learning and Academic Technologies—Learning Styles Inventory: www. clat.psu.edu/gems/Other/LSI/LSI.htm

VARK: A Guide to Learning Styles: www.vark-learn. com/english/index.asp

Winona State University President's Message on the Seven Principles: www.winona.msus.edu/president/seven. htm

....

CHAPTER THREE

THE ELEARNING
PLANNING PROCESS

This chapter discusses elearning planning, a crucially important part of creating an elearning course. It is organized into five sections. The first briefly indicates why elearning planning is important. The second explains a seven-phase *course instruction cycle* called VPODDDA. Understanding VPODDDA is important because all seven of its stages must be considered in the elearning planning process. The third section develops an *elearning planning model* based on the first five stages of the VPODDDA course instruction cycle. The fourth briefly explains the importance of *iterative refinement* in the planning process, while the fifth and last section introduces the concept of *reusable elearning resources,* that is, resources that have the potential to be used in more than one elearning course.

THE IMPORTANCE OF ELEARNING PLANNING

If your goal is to use elearning to improve your instructional environment and help your students learn better, you must create your course and its elearning resources to take full advantage of elearning's power. A good course results in turn from a good planning process, making it more likely that elearning activities will result in a meaningful learning experience for your students. In short, planning is a crucially important phase in creating an elearning course. And planning requires a planning procedure.

What exactly is an elearning instructional plan, and why should you devise and follow such a plan? It is a guide to lead you through the major phases of designing an effective elearning course. To better understand the concept of planning, consider the process a construction engineering firm undertakes before ground is actually broken in constructing a building, whether it be a five-room country cottage, a five-bedroom luxury home, or even a fifty-story apartment building in a major metropolitan area. First, information must be gathered to determine the needs of the customer commissioning the building and the individuals who will use it, the space available to build it, when it must be finished, what building materials will be available, and so forth. Next, architects must produce building plans that meet the needs and constraints reflected in this information. The plans are then reviewed with the customer to assure they describe the desired building and then revised to meet any objections the customer may raise. Care must also be taken to assure the plans reflect a proposed structure that can in fact be realized. One cannot, for example, build a marble-fronted building unless marble is available. Next, the contractor who will oversee physical construction of the building must be furnished copies of the plans, and he or she must ensure that required resources—building materials and subcontractors, for example—will actually be available at the building site when they are needed. Finally, before the contractor actually begins construction, the plans must be rechecked—and revised as needed—to assure they meet all applicable building regulations and codes. After all, building inspectors at each stage of the building's implementation will assess whether it is being constructed correctly before they ultimately issue a certificate of occupancy. In other words, an integral part of planning a building is an understanding of the procedures that will be used—*at every stage of its construction, from conception to occupancy*—to assure that the final product will be sound, usable, and aesthetically pleasing.

When you build—that is, create—an elearning course, you need a detailed instructional plan analogous to the building construction plan described in the previous paragraph. As the construction example implies, you must plan for both the delivery and assessment of the course before you begin to develop it. Such a plan fulfills at least two very important purposes. First, it provides you a frame of reference for considering all the important elements needed in an effective elearning course. Second, it helps you focus on elearning pedagogy and improved learning, and not on technology alone. The goal of the elearning planning model presented in this chapter is to help you create a plan that will result in an effective elearning course. To be sure, planning is a time-consuming process. However, a good plan— by minimizing the need to correct mistakes—can actually shorten the total time you spend developing an elearning course. Also, well-structured elearning content improves your students' ability to learn (Boettcher, 2003).

Planning will help you set realistic elearning goals. However, it is important to realize and accept that creating an elearning course may take longer than you originally anticipate, especially if you are an elearning novice. It is entirely realistic to assume that creating a robust elearning environment takes at least as much time as preparing a new traditional course. As reported by Ronald Cohen, the American Society for Training and Development estimates that an hour of classroom instruction takes about 25 hours of development time, and that it isn't uncommon for the ratio to increase to as much as 300 hours of development time for one hour of totally online asynchronous elearning instruction (Cohen, 2002). However, this ratio is already decreasing as learning management tools improve, and it will undoubtedly continue to decrease in the future. Moreover, because you probably will not be developing the very extensive materials required to support a totally online course, it is very unlikely that you'll experience anything like the development time ratio Cohen reports.

Nevertheless, you should allow as much time as possible between the start of planning your course and the time your course actually begins. Always assume that the undertaking of preparing an elearning course will take longer than you anticipate, because it probably will. Also, do not overlook the possibility of using student assistants to help you develop a course. Many students are highly computer literate, and many relish the chance to work closely with faculty members and to help their student peers by improving a course. In the K–12 environment perhaps individuals serving as instructional aides can help you develop elearning modules. Finally, you must accept the fact that your course's elearning resources and coursesite will need to be refined from time to time, just as conventional courses require periodic refinement. In fact, many instructors report that the more experience they gain, the more elearning resources they want to add to their courses.

One of the hardest concepts to master in elearning planning—or in any field—is that orderly and systematic effort at every stage of a task is the best and most time-efficient approach to accomplishing a long-range goal. It is human nature to rush into examining details before seeing the big picture. However, this approach can result finally in spending more time to accomplish a goal, not less. Before you wander into the trees without determining the extent of the elearning forest, tell yourself that much of the time you spend implementing an imperfectly planned elearning course may well turn out to be time wasted. The rest of this chapter is to help you plan carefully to avoid ultimately wasting time.

THE VPODDDA COURSE INSTRUCTION CYCLE

In this section we discuss a seven-phase process of creating a course of instruction, a process equally applicable to a traditional or to an elearning course. The process is important because all seven phases must be considered in elearning planning. Depending on who is describing the process, the number of phases and their names may vary, but such a process always involves the major tasks of developing, delivering, and assessing a course. Although we present the phases of the process sequentially, we refer to the process as an instruction *cycle,* because after a course has been delivered and assessed, the process is repeated in order to *refine* the course. In fact, refinement is ongoing throughout the instruction cycle, rather than occurring only at its conclusion. We call this cyclical process *iterative refinement* and discuss it more thoroughly later in the chapter. The instruction cycle itself we call **VPODDDA,** an acronym formed from the first letter of each of its seven phases, which are Vision, Profile, Objectives, Design, Development, Delivery, and Assessment. What follows in the rest of this section briefly describes each phase in the cycle. Our goal is to establish a frame of reference for discussing the elearning planning model presented in the next section.

Vision Phase

The first phase in the course instruction cycle is the *vision* phase. Here you develop an overview of the course you are going to teach. Being a subject matter expert, you have a pretty good idea of the major topics you wish to cover, and you have some notion of how you will organize and present these topics. Also, there most likely is an existing course description that clearly states goals of the course. In the vision phase, you envision what subject matter and delivery mode you will use to achieve these goals.

Profile Phase

Next, you go through a process of discovery whereby you collect and assimilate information about the course you are planning. What prerequisite knowledge will your students have? How many hours of instruction will the course require? How many students will you teach at a time? What expertise do you need to teach the course that you presently do not have? Where will the course meet? Are laboratories required? These are among the many questions that arise during what we call the *profile* phase of the instruction cycle, because it involves profiling the instructor, the prospective students, and the instructional environment to collect information that will be used in subsequent phases.

Objectives Phase

In the third phase of the instruction cycle you formulate course *objectives*. Objectives are usually expressed as statements of measurable behaviors—called *student outcomes*—that an individual must be able to exhibit on successfully completing your course. For example, in a course about ancient western warfare, one outcome might require that students be able to compare and contrast the Greek city-state wars with Alexander the Great's wars of territorial acquisition. Many colleges and universities—urged on by accreditation bodies—require student outcomes to be stated in a course outline kept on file by administrators. Stating outcomes, of course, is desirable in any instructional or training environment, not only in higher education.

Design Phase

The fourth phase of the instruction cycle is the *design* phase. It is ordinarily the most time-consuming of the first four. Here you conceive the learning activities you want students to engage in, and design the resources they will use to engage in these activities. You also organize these resources into a coherent whole to the end of achieving the objectives you formulated in phase three. For example, if your course will involve traditional lectures followed by testing on lecture content, you break the course content down into individual units amenable to being treated within the time limits of a single class. Of course, the sequence of lectures—the course organization—must be coherent and logical. At some point, you outline—in your head, if not on paper—the contents of individual lectures. At another, you design—at least broadly—the assignments and tests you will give your students. You will also have to conceive a course syllabus and formulate policies about course conduct and student behavior.

Development Phase

The fifth phase of the instruction cycle involves developing the resources you have designed in phase four. We call this phase the *development* phase. In this phase you might, for example, prepare the lectures, assignments, tests, and other resources you conceived during the design phase. During the development phase, it is very likely that you will discover the need to make refinements, unless you have the ability to create a perfect course design on your first attempt. For example, you may realize that you left out a critical topic or that an assignment you designed needs to be expanded, and so on. Consequently, making refinements to your course design is usually a major part of course development.

Delivery Phase

The sixth phase of the instruction cycle is the *delivery* phase. At this point students are attending your course, and you are trying to help them learn. During the delivery phase, most instructors constantly process student *feedback* to determine whether the course is progressing satisfactorily. Such feedback can be *formal,* that is, explicitly solicited using an assessment instrument, or *informal,* that is, observed in passing during course delivery. For example, if you notice that students are becoming glassy-eyed in a lecture, you might stop and digress a moment, relate a relevant anecdote, or perhaps tell a joke. If students performed poorly on average in an exam, you might solicit feedback about why their performances weren't up to your expectations. In short, in course delivery—as in course development—refinement is an integral part of the instruction cycle.

Assessment Phase

There is currently an ongoing discussion among educators about appropriate uses of the terms *assessment* and *evaluation.* In this book, we use the term *assessment* to denote obtaining feedback on student performance, on instructor performance, and on the overall effectiveness of a course. In the *assessment* phase of the instruction cycle, the notion of obtaining feedback about a course and its instructor is formalized. Traditionally, feedback is obtained at the end of a course via a form students use to anonymously evaluate the course and its instructor. However, many equally suitable methods for obtaining feedback exist, as discussed later in the book, particularly in Chapter 11. The information obtained during assessment is then used to revise the course prior to delivering it the next time. This revision process restarts the instruction cycle.

THE VPODD ELEARNING PLANNING MODEL

This section describes the *VPODD Elearning Planning Model,* which is based on the first five phases of the VPODDDA course instruction cycle. Figure 3.1 illustrates graphically the relationship between VPODD and VPODDDA. Although development involves implementation, we view it as part of planning, because—as previously indicated—ordinarily the four preceding VPODD phases must be revisited during development. Another important point about the VPODD Elearning Planning Model is that work done during the planning cycle must include plans for course delivery and assessment, even though these phases are not actually included in the five-phase planning model. Anticipating what will happen during these two instructional phases is an important part of elearning planning. In particular, planning for assessment plays a much larger role in elearning planning than in planning a traditional course.

The VPODD model represents a simple although we hope not simplistic approach to elearning planning. For individuals seeking a more sophisticated view of the much discussed subject of instructional planning, the end-of-chapter references identify a number of addi-

FIGURE 3.1   Relationship of VPODD to VPODDDA

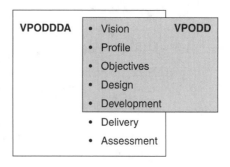

tional URL resources on instructional design models including ADDIE and the Dick and Carey Model, among others. VPODD is intended for instructors new to elearning, as well as for those more experienced instructors who wish to employ a more formal planning process than the one they presently use. The model is useful at any elearning planning level, from the high-level process of creating a course or battery of courses down to the task of creating just one elearning module or a single elearning resource. It is also well suited for use by instructional design teams composed of educators, instructional designers, and/or support personnel such as educational or instructional technologists.

We make four assumptions about an individual who will use the VPODD planning model. First, we assume that you are a subject matter expert in your own field—though not in the field of elearning—and that you have already developed a traditional version of your course or can do so on your own. Second, we assume you have an LMS available to help you create your elearning coursesite and know how to use it. Third, we assume you have the requisite computer skills for creating an elearning course; that is, that you know how to use word processor and presentation graphics software, can browse the web without guidance, know how the operating system on your computer works, and have any other basic computer skills needed for creating your course. Fourth, we assume you will plan and develop your own instructional environment. Although a few institutions may provide elearning design and development services to instructors, ordinarily the burden of creating elearning modules falls solely on instructors themselves.

Vision Planning Phase

The first phase in creating effective elearning, and one of the most important, is to create a vision for how you want to use elearning in your course. As discussed in Chapter 1, this may require that you rethink your course by imagining what you would like for it to become. Some instructors avoid thinking about how elearning can improve a traditional course. Instead, they try to re-create the traditional course by posting existing course materials online, as mentioned earlier. It is true that posting information online does provide many advantages; but if this is the only use you make of elearning, you and your students are missing out on the powerful, student-centered learning environment that elearning makes possible.

In the visioning process, ask yourself why you want to use elearning and what you want to accomplish. Many instructors desire to create an active learning environment. Others want to use elearning because students are expecting it and because they deserve no less (Lynch, 2002). Consider how you conduct your course currently. Are there problems that you would like to overcome? Think about available elearning tools and how they can help you incorporate learning strategies not easily realized without technology, such as electronic discussions, online team projects, or online self-assessment. Can elearning enhance your current teaching practices? For example, could you reinforce the ideas presented in lectures and textbook assignments by devising web-based research projects related to these ideas? Do you want to lecture less, to use more student-centered learning activities? Would you like to incorporate project-based learning in your course? Team collaborations?

When you engage in the visioning process, also think about your personal teaching strengths and weaknesses. How can you embellish your strengths and overcome your weaknesses in the elearning environment you create? Elearning is merely a means to an end, not an end in itself. In fact, it has been determined that technology in the hands of good teachers has the potential to make them even better, whereas technology in the hands of incompetent teachers often makes them even less effective (Holden, 2002).

Another question worth pondering in the visioning process is current attitudes about the meaning of the term *school*. In the past, school was often conceived as a place where courses are taught according to a set schedule. Elearning allows educators the opportunity to consider school as a method—as opposed to a place—of learning. When this happens, asynchronous learning tends to assume equal importance with conventional synchronous learning that for many years has represented the notion of school. When school is defined in such a way, the actual time and place where educational activities occur becomes far less critical (Karnovsky & Warner, 2002). However, elearning can also enhance classroom-oriented synchronous learning. As a consequence, many institutions have invested heavily in classroom technology that—properly taken advantage of—can dramatically enhance synchronous teaching and learning (Brown & Lippincott, 2003). To help you see how to create an elearning vision for your course, Figure 3.2 presents a vision statement for an Introduction to Elearning course. Note that the vision is similar to a course description but emphasizes how technology will be used to enhance the course.

Profile Planning Phase

The profile phase of elearning planning is a discovery process. You collect and process information about yourself as the instructor, about the students you will teach, and about the environment in which you will deliver your course. Instructor profiling helps you understand your own degree of readiness to engage in elearning. Student profiling allows you to identify the special needs of your students. Finally, environmental profiling allows you to determine what technology will be available in the instructional environment where you will teach and where your students will learn.

Instructor Profiling.   Instructor profiling is little more than self-examination, although instructor profiling should also include student and teaching assistants if such individuals will be available to help with the course. First of all, you must honestly evaluate whether you have complete command of the subject matter of your course. For the purposes of this discussion,

FIGURE 3.2   Vision Statement for an Introduction to Elearning Course

Introduction to Elearning presents the basic principles of elearning pedagogy and identifies and explains the types of resources desirable in effective elearning courses. The course also addresses how to use the functionality of a learning management system (LMS). It will implement a student-centered learning environment that provides students with many learning choices. Students will work on projects and assignments that will enable them to apply critical thinking skills and to interact with the ideas and content of the course.

Student teams will use the elearning principles they learn in the course to design and develop a training module relevant to their chosen fields of endeavor. They will learn how to use technology tools that will help them succeed in their professions and personal lives. The course will make extensive use of elearning technology including online testing, online communications, online team collaborations, and web-based research.

subject matter expertise is assumed. However, if you are teaching a course for the first time, or if the course subject is peripheral to or outside of your area of expertise, you will probably have to devote more effort to becoming a subject matter expert than you would otherwise. This is an important factor to consider when you construct a time schedule for course development.

You must also carefully assess your knowledge of elearning and assure that it is adequate to plan and develop the course you have envisioned. Your decision to read this book was probably motivated by a desire to increase your knowledge about elearning. Learning about elearning is a time-consuming activity, but one that can result in significantly improving your performance as an instructor. Be aware that obtaining knowledge about the power of elearning is an ongoing rather than a one-time activity. As technology changes, LMS capabilities can be expected to improve dramatically. You must keep abreast of new LMS functionality and learn how to use it. Moreover, related elearning technology will become more readily available and easier to use. For example, if you currently wish to make a streaming video, you will probably have to take a videotape in digital or analog format to your institution's educational technology department and have personnel there create the streaming video for you using expensive hardware and software that is time-consuming and somewhat challenging to operate. In the near future, equipment to accomplish this task will become cheaper and more highly automated—hence easier and faster to use. Thus it is more likely to be available for your convenient personal use.

Figure 3.3 presents a checklist for profiling the instructor of an Introduction to Elearning course. A similar checklist would serve to profile student assistants and teaching assistants.

Student Profiling.   Profiling students involves collecting information about them that will help you in your role as elearning instructor. You cannot, of course, profile students until your course actually starts. However, it is possible in the profile planning phase to make estimates about the kinds of students you will teach and to devise instruments for gathering profile information from students once your course begins. If you are likely to encounter students with sight, hearing, or other disabilities, you can take steps ahead of time to ensure that your coursesite and its resources are designed to accommodate their needs or at least provide them with other options for accessing and using course materials. A visually or hearing impaired student may excel in a traditional teacher-centered environment and yet experience difficulty in an interactive computer-based elearning course in which it is mandatory to view coursesite materials and use audio and video files. Chapter 8 provides more information on this subject.

You can also anticipate the demographics of your class before it begins and plan your elearning course accordingly. If your class will be comprised of adult learners or graduate students, you can probably expect them to be more self-motivated than younger learners and to adjust more rapidly and respond more enthusiastically to a student-centered elearning environment. In this case, you can probably include more subject matter content in your course. If your class is mostly college undergraduates—and especially if they are freshmen—you may have to devote extra class time to helping them adjust to elearning and a student-centered environment that may require them to be self-motivated. Under such circumstances, you may need to devote less time to course content and more to the mechanics of the elearning environment. Students will not perform well if they are uncomfortable in their learning environment.

During elearning planning, it is wise to create profiling instruments and procedures to determine—once your course begins—whether your students have the required prerequisite

FIGURE 3.3   Instructor Profile Checklist for an Introduction to Elearning Course

**SUBJECT MATTER EXPERTISE—
MAJOR COURSE TOPICS**

- ☐ Elearning overview
- ☐ Elearning pedagogy
- ☐ Elearning planning and instructional design
- ☐ Overview of LMS functionality
- ☐ Coursesite design and development
- ☐ Coursesite maintenance
- ☐ The distribution of information via the web
- ☐ Online communications facilitation
- ☐ Elearning policies and procedures
- ☐ Managing students in the elearning environment
- ☐ Elearning assessment

BASIC TECHNOLOGY SKILLS

- ☐ Operating system
- ☐ Word processing software (MSWord)
- ☐ Email utility
- ☐ Presentation graphics software (PowerPoint)
- ☐ Fundamentals of web research
- ☐ Spreadsheets software (Excel)
- ☐ Digital imaging software (Adobe Elements)

LMS FUNCTIONALITY SKILLS

- ☐ Using LMS functionality from student perspective
- ☐ Posting announcements
- ☐ Posting documents
- ☐ Posting electronic forum topics
- ☐ Facilitating chats
- ☐ Archiving forums and chats
- ☐ Using the whiteboard
- ☐ Creating online tests
- ☐ Creating online surveys
- ☐ Using the gradebook
- ☐ Receiving assignments electronically
- ☐ Returning assignments with feedback electronically
- ☐ Archiving and backing up the coursesite
- ☐ Collecting coursesite statistics

knowledge and technical skills to undertake your course. Students who lack technology skills may become frustrated and lag behind in your course. Those who lack writing expertise may experience frustration when expected to respond in electronic discussions and chats, in which everyone in the class can see their weakness. Poor typists may also be at a disadvantage. Different levels of prerequisite knowledge among students in the same course will definitely influence the ease with which they learn, even when all are presented the same information in the same manner (Shank, 2001a). It is also a good idea to determine whether work or family responsibilities will limit the amount of time a student can devote to your course. In the K–12 environment, it may be easier to determine students' workloads such as what other courses they are taking and the anticipated workload that will be generated from those courses, especially what other online courses your students may be taking.

You should use the student profiling instruments you create very early in course delivery. One approach is to assign ungraded basic technology tasks that allow you to evaluate a students' technology, typing, and written communications skills. Another approach is to conduct an online survey by which students report their feelings about elearning and student-centered learning, and perhaps answer questions about their prerequisite knowledge. This would enable you to assess their proficiency in written communications, evaluate their technology skills, and determine their prerequisite knowledge. If you use this second approach, be mindful of the student privacy policies of your institution and, if necessary, make answering personal questions optional. Chapter 10 addresses course delivery and provides an example student profile survey recommended for use at the beginning of a course.

If student profiling leads to your discovering students who are at a disadvantage, you may be able to help them overcome their difficulties. For example, you can advise technology novices of the specific skills they need in your course, and recommend tutors, books, or other approaches to assist them in gaining these skills. Another approach—it is easier to implement in a hybrid elearning environment than in a totally online course—is to establish a "buddy system" that pairs technology novices with students who have advanced technology skills. The novices can ask their buddies for help as necessary. If you identify students who lack the required course content prerequisite knowledge, you may be able to help them by pairing them with better-prepared students. In the extreme, however, students lacking prerequisite skills must be advised to withdraw from your course and enroll in the course or courses that will prepare them for the subject that you are teaching. Such students sometimes "poison the well" of elearning by blaming their insufficiencies on the elearning environment.

Student profiling should also involve determining your students' learning styles. As explained in Chapter 2, one of the most important facts you must accept to be an effective teacher is that different students learn in different ways. The more you know about your students' learning preferences, the easier it will be for you to create an effective elearning environment where they can thrive. Of course, you cannot determine the learning preferences of individual students during elearning planning. Rather, you ordinarily assume that your class will have the same distribution of learning styles as exists in the overall population of learners. However, once your class begins, you can have students take one of the several web-based learning style inventories referenced in Chapter 2 and then report their learning styles to you. If you find that your class is atypical, you can make adjustments during course delivery. In the best of all possible worlds, you would have planned ahead of time for such an adjustment. For example, suppose you find that you have a very small percentage of auditory learners in your class. You might choose to deliver shortened versions of the lectures you have planned and to address the topics they cover using slide shows, in-class team activities, web-based research activities, and many other resources more appropriate for visual or tactile learners.

The following list summarizes information relevant to profiling students:

- Prerequisite knowledge
- Technology skills, including typing skills
- Hearing, visual, or other impairments
- Communication skills
- Work responsibilities
- Family responsibilities
- The workload resulting from the other courses they are taking
- Class demographics
- Learning styles

Environmental Profiling.   In environmental profiling, you collect information about your elearning instructional environment that is critical to the successful delivery of your course. For instance, you should determine the anticipated size of your class; what computer technology is available to support the development and delivery of your course; whether your course will be presented totally online or in a hybrid delivery mode; classroom size if a classroom will be used; the computer labs available for your students' use and how they are equipped; how much time you have available to prepare your course; what help you may have in preparing and delivering your course; and other information appropriate to your environment. As an example of the importance of such information, it would be unwise to plan to use online videos if your institution does not have the technology needed to support them. As another example, consider that as class size increases, it becomes increasingly difficult to engage in one-on-one contact with students. Consequently, if you anticipate large class sizes, you must conceive elearning resources that reinforce student learning but at the same time allow you to keep your workload at an acceptable level. In general, the time you have to develop a course and the assistance you anticipate having when you prepare or teach it are factors of great importance in choosing how to plan an elearning course. Such assistance includes the help you receive from teaching and/or student assistants or from educational or instructional technology experts at your institution.

The following list summarizes information relevant to profiling the environment:

- Anticipated number of students
- Available assistance such as student and graduate assistants
- Course delivery mode
- Course start and end dates
- For a hybrid course, available classroom technology (computer, software, Internet connectivity, projection system) and furnishings (facilities for small group work)
- Laboratory support (number of computers, software, Internet connectivity, lab assistants, facilities for small group work)
- Classroom and laboratory computer login procedures
- Technical assistance available for instructors and students (Help Desk, procedures for getting technical help)
- Educational technology assistance for instructors (Educational Technology Department policies, kinds of assistance provided, kinds of assistance *not* provided)

Objectives Planning Phase

Objectives you should formulate in the elearning planning phase fall into two categories, *course content objectives* and *general knowledge objectives.*

Course Content Objectives.   Course content objectives for an elearning course should be very specific and stated in measurable terms, just as is necessary in the traditional course delivery mode. To cite two examples, if you are teaching the course Introduction to Computer Algorithms, you might require that students be able to write—on the final exam—pseudocode for three recursive sorting algorithms and to explain the relative advantages and drawbacks of each of the three. If you are teaching a hybrid course in Mark Twain's Fiction, you might expect students on their final exam to be able to recapitulate ideas delivered in lectures about the similarities and differences in Twain's treatment of the child heroes in *Tom Sawyer, Huck Finn,* and *Pudd'nhead Wilson.* Figure 3.4 lists the course content objectives for an Introduction to Elearning course.

General Knowledge Objectives.   General knowledge objectives address the pursuit of knowledge not specifically related to course content. Desirable categories of general

FIGURE 3.4   Course Content Objectives for an Introduction to Elearning Course

On completing the course, students will be able to:

- Define elearning.
- Define elearning pedagogy.
- Describe at least five advantages of student-centered learning.
- Construct an elearning instructional design plan for a course they may teach.
- Construct an instructional module that utilizes elearning.
- Design a coursesite.
- Write a discussion question to promote critical thinking.
- Create a web-based research assignment for a course they will teach.
- Design a course syllabus for web access.
- Design a PowerPoint presentation suitable for web access.
- Design an online team project.
- Use the functionality of an LMS from a student's perspective.
- Use the functionality of an LMS from an instructor's perspective.
- Write policies appropriate for an elearning course.
- Write procedures appropriate for an elearning course.
- Create an assessment plan for assessing student performance in elearning.
- Create an instrument for assessing the overall effectiveness of an elearning course.

knowledge ensuing from any course of instruction include critical thinking skills (analysis, synthesis, evaluation, abstract thinking, etc.); both verbal and written communication skills; workplace skills including ability to cooperate with peers and superiors and to work in teams; lifelong learning skills such as finding and evaluating information; and technology skills such as the ability to engage in web research or to participate in online forums and chats.

The way you realize course content objectives to some extent determines the kinds of general knowledge objectives you can accomplish. As an example, consider the course content objective for the Mark Twain course mentioned in the previous subsection. Because the objective requires students to hear or read ideas and recapitulate them in writing, it presumably will improve students' written communication skills. If you had asked your students to pursue the same objective by reading your lecture notes and then participating in small team forums, you might have also achieved general knowledge objectives involving technology and teamwork skills. As this example makes clear, elearning makes possible achieving general knowledge objectives that are typically difficult to pursue in a traditional course delivery mode.

You promote general knowledge objectives whenever you create a student-centered learning environment, use a computer to increase student-to-student communication and student-to-instructor communication, or provide your students with online mentoring, among many others activities. Figure 3.5 lists the course general knowledge objectives for an Introduction to Elearning course. Of course, these general knowledge objectives would be suitable for many if not most elearning courses. Some of the general knowledge student outcomes in Figure 3.5 are more difficult to measure objectively than many course content outcomes, for the same reasons that it is more difficult to grade a student essay than a calculus exam objectively. Indeed, the importance of many general knowledge objectives is succinctly implied by a nice observation about life borrowed from the well-known author Eudora Welty: *The end is nothing; the road is all.*

FIGURE 3.5   General Knowledge Objectives for an Introduction to Elearning Course

On completing the course, students will be able to:

- Perform web research.
- Evaluate the quality of websites.
- Write entries that reflect critical thinking when participating in online discussions.
- Synthesize instructor and peer comments in online discussions and respond appropriately.
- Communicate and collaborate with team members in online discussions.
- Display appropriate netiquette in electronic communication.
- Construct a personal web page and eportfolio.

Design and Development Planning Phases

Because elearning development so often leads to revisiting earlier VPODD phases, including particularly the design phase, we discuss the design and development planning phases together. In the design phase of elearning planning, you conceive and design the individual resources of your course, whereas in the development phase you create and implement these resources and organize them on your coursesite. However, implementation of a design often leads to discovering design flaws, hence to redesign. Development also involves the time-consuming task of obtaining all materials you need to create your resources. These materials include but are not limited to graphical images, drawings, photographs, videos, audios, and information from books and articles and from the Internet.

This section presents an overview of the types of resources you might design and develop for your elearning course. Resources are difficult to group logically, with the result that our four categories for them are not always mutually exclusive. Our goal is simply to introduce you to the variety of resources that make up a typical elearning course. The four categories are *getting-started* resources, *course content* resources, *policy and procedures* resources, and *course and coursesite assessment* resources. We defer discussing coursesite design until Chapter 8, which is devoted entirely to this important subject.

Getting-Started Resources.   Getting started smoothly in an elearning course helps your students form an initial favorable attitude toward elearning. However, achieving a smooth start can be more difficult than you might at first imagine. You may encounter some students who lack familiarity with the computer technology you plan to use. Others may not have personal access to an Internet connection or may have a very slow Internet connection. Technology failures may occur that threaten to turn students new to elearning against it entirely. Also, you will have to ensure that your students know how to use your coursesite. And these are just a few of the potential problems you may experience.

To forestall such difficulties, you should prepare "getting-started" resources and post them to your coursesite before your course begins. This will make it more likely that your course will get off to a good start. One of the most important of these resources is of course the course syllabus. It will contain the information students need to know about course content and schedules, grading criteria, file format standards, and other relevant information. Other appropriate getting-started resources include a welcome message posted as an announcement, staff information, and an introductory electronic discussion to get students comfortable with the elearning environment and to help them get to know you and their classmates. You should also develop reusable "how to" tutorials on coursesite orientation, including instructions on the use of electronic discussions (forums, chats, whiteboards), how students should access and use the gradebook, and so forth. Finally, if you plan to conduct student profiling when your course starts, you will need to design profiling resources to collect the information you desire.

In addition to these considerations, you should also plan to check that the classroom and laboratory technology you will use in your course is in proper working order. This check should of course be accomplished immediately prior to commencing course delivery. You must also advise students of the personal computer technology they will need for your course and urge them to perform a personal technology check. Figure 3.6 is a checklist of getting-started resources for an Introduction to Elearning course. The contents of the figure may help you determine the getting-started activities you must plan for your own course. Chapter 10 contains more information on getting-started activities.

Course Content Resources.   Course content resources can be categorized as content *delivery* resources, *assignment* resources, and *student assessment* resources. Delivery resources include lecture notes, presentation graphics slide shows, multimedia—audio and/or video—presentations, third-party websites, and guest speaker presentations, among others. The types of resources you design will of course be determined by the course content objectives and general knowledge objectives you conceived in the VPODD objectives planning stage. In a hybrid course, you will probably use delivery resources to present course content in class, although you may expect students to process some delivery resources independently, for example, videos. If your class is totally online, then students will invariably use delivery resources for independent learning.

Assignment resources—typically listed in the course syllabus as assignments—are ordinarily related directly to delivery resources. For example, if you post lecture notes or slide

FIGURE 3.6   Getting-Started Checklist for an Introduction to Elearning Course

GENERAL

☐ Welcome announcement
☐ Course syllabus
☐ Course orientation
☐ Staff information
☐ Survey form to profile students
☐ Coursesite orientation

GETTING TO KNOW EACH OTHER EXERCISES

☐ Getting to know each other discussion question
☐ Student biography exercise

HOW-TO TUTORIALS AND EXERCISES ON LMS FUNCTIONALITY

☐ Access the coursesite
☐ Navigate the coursesite

☐ Discussion forums
☐ Chats
☐ Whiteboard
☐ Online tests
☐ Online gradebook
☐ Create a homepage
☐ Send email to instructor and other students
☐ Send an assignment via the LMS
☐ Use tools and settings

TECHNOLOGY CHECKOUT PROCESS

☐ Classrooms
☐ Laboratories
☐ Student's personal technology systems

shows to your coursesite, you may assign students to preview such a resource and take an online self-assessment test on it before you present the resource in class. If you want to promote improved student written communication and group collaboration skills, you will probably choose to develop assignment resources that involve online discussions and team projects. Such assignments require students to exhibit critical thinking about the subject of a delivery resource. Remember that you will have to prepare and post clear instructions that explicitly state what you expect students to do to complete an assignment successfully. These instructions are especially important for totally online courses, because in these courses it may be difficult for students to contact you for clarification about an assignment.

Elearning assessment resources are more various than assessment resources in a traditional course. Of course, many assessment resources perform a dual role. For example, if you choose to have students compile online portfolios that you evaluate, the portfolios thereby become both assignment and assessment resources. If you do plan to evaluate student portfolios, you will have to prepare instructions explaining what documents must be in the portfolios and how the portfolios will be evaluated. You may also choose to assess students in a conventional manner by testing them online or in a proctored classroom. Other means of student assessment include self- and peer evaluation, or grading student participation in online discussions, group projects, and similar assignments. Although it is tempting to put off preparing student assessment resources until shortly before they are required, you will serve yourself well if you design and develop all such resources during VPODD planning, well before your elearning course starts.

Figure 3.7 provides a checklist of the course content resources for an Introduction to Elearning course. The checklist is intended to help you determine the course content resources you must plan for your course. Chapters 5, 6, 7, and 10 provide more information about various course content resources. Chapter 11 discusses student assessment.

Policy and Procedures Resources.   Policy resources must be posted on your coursesite to explain to students what is expected of them and what they can expect of you. Appropriate subjects for policy resources include—among others—how to submit assignments electronically; what to expect when a technology failure occurs and an assignment is due; what kind of student email you will answer and how promptly; what you will and won't do for students who need help; how you plan to deal with students who appear in the course without the required prerequisite knowledge; the extent to which you intend to participate in online discussions; and what constitutes appropriate and inappropriate behavior in email and online discussions. Formulating precise and appropriate policies and posting them conspicuously on your coursesite is of the utmost importance. It enables students to understand what their responsibilities are in your course and exactly what your role is in helping them fulfill these responsibilities. If your policy resources are nonexistent, imprecise, or unfair to students, you will find yourself spending—we should say *wasting*—a lot of time dealing with confused, unhappy, and disgruntled students. You are only one person who must communicate electronically with many. Because the teacher–student relationship is a win-win game, if you don't set up the rules of the game correctly, you will lose, and so will your students.

Policies are resources in the sense that students read them to learn about their learning environment. By contrast, procedures are not precisely course resources but rather are plans for dealing with foreseeable events that will affect your students' use of course resources. They differ from policies in that ordinarily students need not be aware they exist until an un-

FIGURE 3.7   Course Content Checklist for Introduction to Elearning Course

CONTENT DELIVERY—PRESENTATIONS

☐ Elearning overview
☐ Elearning pedagogy
☐ Elearning instructional design plan
☐ Elearning technology
☐ Distributing information electronically
☐ Electronic forums and chats
☐ Website research and evaluation techniques
☐ Coursesite design
☐ Intellectual property rights and policies
☐ Elearning course delivery techniques
☐ Elearning assessment

CONTENT DELIVERY—GUEST SPEAKERS

☐ Dr. Pedersen on elearning instructional design
☐ Dr. Johnson on distributing information for web viewing
☐ Dr. Rogers on coursesite design

ASSIGNMENT INSTRUCTIONS

☐ Website evaluation
☐ Discussion on best website
☐ Discussion on worst website
☐ Web-based research techniques
☐ Web research project on learning styles
☐ Web research project on Gagne and Bloom
☐ Web research project on web resources
☐ Book report
☐ Personal website
☐ Team project on course redesign
☐ Individual project on creating an elearning instructional module

ASSESSMENT RESOURCES

☐ Unit 1 Quiz—Elearning Overview and Planning
☐ Unit 2 Quiz—Elearning Technology
☐ Unit 3 Quiz—Elearning Strategies
☐ Unit 4 Quiz—Elearning Delivery and Assessment
☐ Portfolio of work samples
☐ Self-evaluation form to evaluate performance in course
☐ Peer evaluation form to evaluate performance in team projects
☐ Coursesite assessment form
☐ Course assessment form

---

usual circumstance arises. However, students will be affected when you apply these procedures. Procedures include but are not limited to what you will do if you are teaching a class and the technology you need to conduct it fails; how to deal with students who have very weak communication skills; how to deal with students who have little or no knowledge about how to use a computer at the level required by the course; and what to do when unforeseen eventualities prohibit your keeping the schedule planned in the course syllabus. A number of coursesite management procedures are also needed including coursesite backup, saving end-of-course grades, rolling old course content over into new course sections, keeping the coursesite updated, organizing student assignments submitted electronically, and others.

Figure 3.8 is a checklist of policies and procedures needed for an Introduction to Elearning course. The checklist—applicable to most elearning courses—is intended to help you identify the policies and procedures you must plan for your own courses. Chapter 9 provides additional information about course policies and procedures.

Course and Coursesite Assessment Resources.   Instruments are needed to assess the success of your course and the usability of your coursesite. Such instruments are called course and coursesite assessment resources. These resources allow you to collect formal feedback to determine how easy it is to use your coursesite and related resources, whether the learning activity associated with a resource led to obtaining related course objectives, how good

FIGURE 3.8   Policies and Procedures Checklist for Introduction to Elearning Course

POLICIES	PROCEDURES
☐ Reading announcements and checking email	☐ Dealing with the Problem Student Behaviors
☐ File formats and virus-free files	▪ Quiet, loud, disgruntled, domineering, and so on
☐ How to email assignments to instructor	▪ Poor written English
☐ Email etiquette	▪ Poor typing
☐ Email instructor will and will NOT respond to	▪ Poor technology skills
☐ Behavior required in forums and chats	▪ Lack of prerequisite knowledge
☐ Instructor's participation in forums and chats	☐ Dealing with the Technology Failures
☐ What to do in the event of a personal technology failure	▪ Student's technology
☐ What to do in the event of an institutional technology failure	▪ Classroom technology
☐ Intellectual property rights guidelines	▪ Laboratory technology
☐ Institutional student privacy policies	▪ Technical problems with the LMS
☐ Institutional technology use policies	☐ Coursesite Management
☐ How to obtain help	▪ Coursesite backup
☐ Assignment policies	▪ Backing up grades
☐ Student code of conduct policies	▪ Saving end-of-course grades
	▪ Rolling course resource into new LMS course sections
	▪ Organizing student assignments submitted electronically

a job you did as a course instructor, and what actions you can take to improve the overall effectiveness of the course. You can obtain formal feedback about your course from peers and student reviewers before delivery begins. After your course starts, students are the primary source of formal feedback. During VPODD planning, you should design and develop the resources you plan to use to collect formal feedback on your course and coursesite. Early and continuous feedback during course delivery is especially important in an elearning course.

Examples of course and coursesite assessment resources are coursesite usability forms completed by student reviewers and peer reviewers before "going live" with the coursesite; an anonymous online discussion forum whereby students are encouraged to post feedback on the course on an ongoing basis; a teacher evaluation form students complete at the conclusion of a course; and a short anonymous survey conducted in the online testing component of the LMS. Short surveys make it easy to obtain immediate feedback on course activities such as presentations, guest speakers, team projects, and an individual assignment, among other aspects of a course. Chapter 11 provides more information about course and coursesite assessment.

ITERATIVE REFINEMENT

Unless you never make a mistake or an omission when you create your course, you will need to make refinements to the work you accomplish during elearning planning. As you progress systematically through the VPODD planning process, it is not uncommon to "loop back" to an earlier phase to refine work that seemed complete initially but that, in retrospect, needs to be improved. In fact, in any phase of the VPODDDA instruction cycle—including delivery and assessment—you can return to one of the VPODD *planning* phases to effect an improvement to your elearning course. This returning process results in what we call *iterative refinement.* For instance, suppose in the development phase—or during course delivery or assessment— you realize that you have omitted an important course objective. The process for addressing the needed revision would be to backtrack to the objectives phase of VPODD, formulate the new objective, and then to proceed to the design and development phases to create the resource or resources that support it, as illustrated in the iterative refinement paths in Figure 3.9.

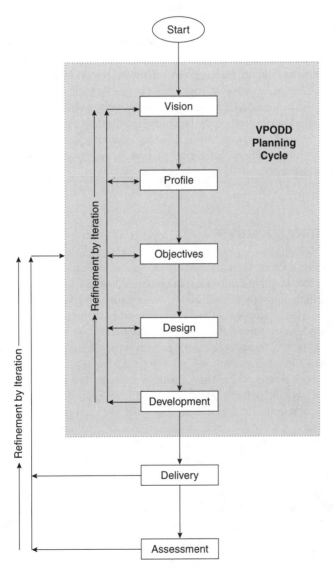

FIGURE 3.9   Iterative Refinement Paths in the Instruction Cycle

You may want to formalize the process of iterative refinement by conducting a *formative evaluation* of your elearning course, a process frequently used by instructional designers and instructors to obtain information needed to revise instructional resources *before* they are delivered. A formative evaluation typically includes up to three stages. In the first stage, designers observe individual learners at learning tasks to determine which resources if any require revision. In the second stage, designers administer the revised resources to a small group of students representative of the target audience. These students are then tested and surveyed to collect data about the effectiveness of the resources. The third stage involves a field trial in which the resources are tested is a situation similar to the real-world use of the resources. It is unlikely that instructors working alone to develop an elearning course will have the time to conduct a detailed formative evaluation. However, a basic understanding of the concept may motivate you to devise an abridged evaluation process to help you determine the refinements your course needs.

A related refinement process—one you are probably familiar with—is the *summative evaluation,* used to determine instructional effectiveness after course delivery has been completed. In a summative evaluation, each student's individual performance and the overall effectiveness of the course are assessed. If the course is an elearning course, the coursesite's effectiveness must also be assessed. The results of a summative evaluation lead to needed refinements in the instructional plan before the course is taught again. From this description, it is obvious that a summative assessment is a formal approach to the assessment phase of VPODDDA. As previously indicated, Chapter 11 provides suggestions to help you assess your course and its resources.

REUSABLE ELEARNING RESOURCES

A *learning object* is a specific learning activity or "chunk" of instruction. In other words, any object used for learning that can be used in elearning—in digital format or otherwise—is considered a learning object (McGreal, 2001). As explained in Chapter 1, we call such objects *elearning resources.* Examples of elearning resources are web research assignments, discussion questions for electronic forums, lectures, simulations, videos, presentation graphics slide shows, online collaboration activities, team projects, case studies, course documents, videos, audio clips, animations, and photographs, among others.

This section explains the concept of a *reusable elearning resource.* Properly designed elearning resources have the potential to be reused and repurposed, thus increasing the return on the investment required to create them. They can, for example, be used by a number of instructors teaching the same course or by instructors teaching different but related courses. Because creating elearning resources is time-consuming, it seems wise during course planning to consider whether you can design a resource or instructional module so it can be reused. Moreover, there is growing interest in creating central repositories of learning resources allowing objects to be searched for and retrieved, much like a catalog in a library pointing to books and articles on a specific subject. During elearning planning, you should be aware of the existence of such repositories. They contain resources you can use when you construct your elearning course.

One metaphor that has been used to describe a repository of reusable resources is the dictionary—an organized set of words that can be easily combined and recombined into sentences (Acker, Pearl, & Rissing, 2003). Another way to understand reusable elearning resources is to consider the analogy of a popular children's construction toy, LEGO building blocks. A child can fit together LEGO blocks, which come in several discrete shapes and sizes, to construct a virtually infinite variety of shapes. Similarly, elearning instructors potentially can create many different courses using resources from existing libraries containing quizzes, virtual labs, video clips, and similar elemental components of course content (Gnagni, 2001). Such resources are of course the analogue of basic LEGO construction blocks.

As more emphasis is placed on reusing learning resources, the need for standards becomes critical. For example, if you search a database of resources and find several appropriate for your course, you will certainly want to be able to use them in your coursesite, whether your proprietary learning management software comes from Blackboard, WebCT, Desire2Learn, or some other company. Furthermore, if you change organizations and need to move your course materials from one LMS to another, it would be more convenient if these materials were compatible with the new LMS. *Organizational standards* lead to libraries that focus on a specific discipline or on closely related disciplines, making it easier for instructors to find resources relevant to elearning courses in their disciplines. For example, a learning resource library might be organized to appeal to instructors of undergraduate mathematics, of meteorology, or of aerospace engineering.

Current LMS technology makes it difficult to port resources created in one LMS to the environment of a different LMS. Solutions to address this "interoperability problem" among learning technologies are needed (Long, Merriman, Kumar, & Walker, 2003). In response to such needs, design and *implementation standards* for learning objects are emerging. These standards make it easier to organize, categorize, access, and retrieve learning objects in libraries, and in the process ensure resource compatibility between different LMSs. Three important learning objects standards are ▪SCORM, ▪IMS, and ▪SIF. *SCORM* is an acronym for the *Sharable Courseware Object Reference Model* for learning objects. SCORM standards provide guidelines for organization and retrieval methods related to learning objects. They are a product of joint efforts involving the United States Department of Defense, the White House Office of Science and Technology Policy (OSTP), and the Advanced Distributive Learning Project (ADL).

IMS standards are a set of specifications prescribing how to use metadata tags to facilitate a search for learning objects. *Metadata* tags are descriptors that can be placed with learning objects to identify specific information. For example, a tag may include the type of learning object, its author, copyright information, the level of difficulty of the learning object, and related information. Being able to search this metadata helps instructors as well as students locate and retrieve needed learning objects. A third example of interoperability standards is *SIF* (Schools Interoperability Framework), an initiative to develop open specifications for K–12 instructional and administrative applications (Tansey, 2003). In the future, as more content libraries and repositories of learning objects are created, standards such as SCORM, IMS, and SIF will support instructors and learners who must be able to access resources they want from thousands or millions of files on the web.

Notable work on learning object repositories is now in progress. MIT's ▪DSpace project provides free software—available on the Internet— for making unpublished texts, lecture notes, and other learning objects available online. Also, DSpace software allows an institution to harness and organize its own intellectual output by creating "institutional repositories" of the work its members produce (Marx, 2003). ▪CAREO (Campus Alberta Repository of Educational Objects) is a searchable, web-based collection of multidisciplinary teaching materials for educators. ▪MERLOT, discussed in Chapter 1, is a free website with links to online learning materials and related information such as peer reviews of the materials. The ▪NLII (National Learning Infrastructure Initiative) Learning Objects Program, sponsored by ▪EDUCAUSE, is another example of a learning object repository.

Finally, LMSs are now appearing with content management capabilities for creating and managing reusable learning objects. A notable example is Blackboard's Content Management System, which allows users to share content objects stored in a repository. Assuming permissions on an object are properly set, many different instructors can link to the same object in the repository from a coursesite developed using Blackboard, regardless of who created the object. A repository interface tool allows authorized users to browse, access, and share content created by themselves and others.

REFERENCES

Accetta, R. (2002, June). Clearing the fog: Seven questions to help you cut through the e-learning haze. *e-learning, (3)*6, 30–32.

Acker, S. R., Pearl, D. K., & Rissing, S. (2003, July). Is the academy ready for learning objects? *Syllabus, 16*(12), 28–32.

Alley, L. R. (2001, November). What makes a good online course? The administrator's role in quality assurance of online learning. *Converge.* Retrieved November 19, 2003, from www.convergemag.com/magazine/story.phtml?id=9054

Augustine, F. K., Oliphant, G., & Amiri, S. (2000, April). Planning for information technology: A cornerstone for the university. *Syllabus, 13*(8), 48, 52–53.

Boettcher, J. V. (2003, January). Designing for learning: The pursuit of well-structured content. *Syllabus, 16*(6), 10–13.

Brown, M. B., & Lippincott, J. K. (2003). Learning spaces: More than meets the eye. *EDUCAUSE Quarterly, 26*(1), 14–16.

Carnevale, D. (2003, January 30). Six institutions will help fine-tune a popular new archiving program. *The Chronicle of Higher Education.* Retrieved December 4, 2003, from http://chronicle.com/free/2003/01/2003013001t.htm

Cohen, R. (2002, October 29). How many hours? *OLNews.* Retrieved October 28, 2002, from www.vnulearning.com/archive/oln102902.htm

Dalziel, J. (2003). Open standards versus open source in e-learning. *EDUCAUSE Quarterly, 26*(4), 4–7.

Daughenbaugh, R., Daughenbaugh, L., Surry, D., & Islam, M. (2002). Personality type and online versus in-class course satisfaction. *EDUCAUSE Quarterly, 25*(3), 71–72.

Downes, S. (2002, May/June). The Centre for Educational Technology interoperability standards. *The Technology Source.* Retrieved June 10, 2002, from http://ts.mivu.org/default.asp?show=article&id=1007

Gnagni, S. (2001, February). Building blocks: How the standards movement plans to revolutionize electronic learning. *University Business.* Retrieved January 22, 2002, from web.archive.org/web/20010405124052 and www.universitybusiness.com/0101/cover_building.html

Holden, D. (2002, September). The litany: Investigating the organizational changes needed to make technology effective in the classroom and create an environment where no child is left behind. *T.H.E. Journal, 30*(2), 68–72.

Jacobsen, P. (2001, November). Reusable learning objects: What does the future hold? *e-learning, 2*(11), 24–26.

Johnstone, S. M. (2002, September). Does the academic calendar still work? *Syllabus, 16*(2), 10.

Karnovsky, S. D., & Warner, C. (2002, June/July). John Bailey: Conversation in the key of B. *Converge.* Retrieved November 19, 2003, from www.convergemag.com/magazine/story.phtml?id=14674

Katz, R. N. (2002, July/August). The ICT infrastructure: A driver of change. *EDUCAUSE Review, 37*(4), 50, 52, 54, 56, 58–61.

Lick, D. W. (2001, December). Leading change: Creating the future for education technology. *Syllabus, 15*(5), 22–24.

Long, P. D., Merriman, J. W., Kumar, V., & Walker, E. C. T. (2003, July). Education plugs into standards: Data and service specifications for interoperability. *Syllabus, 16*(12), 25–27, 49.

Looney, M. (2003, March). The need for digital archiving standards. *Syllabus.* Retrieved December 4, 2003, from www.syllabus.com/article.asp?id=7362

Lynch, D. (2002, January 18). Professors should embrace technology in courses. *The Chronicle of Higher Education.* Retrieved December 2, 2003, from http://chronicle.com/prm/weekly/v48/i19/19b01501.htm

Marx, V. (2003, August 3). In DSpace, ideas are forever. *New York Times,* p. 4A8.

McGreal, R., & Roberts, T. (2001, October). A primer on metadata for learning objects. *e-learning, 2*(10), 26–29.

Murphy, C. (2002, September). ABCs of smart classrooms. *Syllabus, 16*(2), 24–26.

Shank, P. (2001a, June). Urban (training) legends: Six common myths about learners and learning debunked. *OnlineLearning, 5*(6), 54, 56, 58.

Shank, P. (2001b, September). Out with the old: Is it time to rethink instructional design? *OnlineLearning, 5*(8), 64–69.

Sonwalkar, N. (2001, December). The sharp edge of the cube: Pedagogically driven instructional design for online education. *Syllabus, 15*(5), 12–16.

Sonwalkar, N. (2002a, March). Demystifying learning technology standards part I; Development and evolution. *Syllabus.* Retrieved September 17, 2002, from www.syllabus.com/article.asp?id=6134

Sonwalkar, N. (2002b, April). Demystifying learning technology standards part II: Acceptance and implementation. *Syllabus, 15*(9), 14–16.

Strauss, H. (2002, September). New learning spaces: Smart learners, not smart classrooms. *Syllabus, 16*(2), 12–17.

Tansey, F. (2003, March). The standard bearers close ranks. *Syllabus, 16*(8), 13–16.

Troha, F. J. (2002, June). The right mix: A bulletproof model for designing blended learning. *e-learning, 3*(6), 34–37.

Valenti, M. S. (2002, September/October). The black box theater and AV/IT convergence: Creating the classroom of the future. *EDUCAUSE Review, 37*(5), 52–54, 56, 58, 60, 62.

Wang, A. Y., & Newlin, M. H. (2002, May). Predictors of performance in the virtual classroom: Identifying and helping at-risk cyber-students. *T.H.E. Journal, 29*(10), 21–28.

Warger, T. (2002). The open-source movement. *EDUCAUSE Quarterly, 25*(3), 18–20.

Zvacek, S. M. (2001). Confessions of a guerilla technologist. *EDUCAUSE Quarterly, 24*(2), 40–45.

U R L   R E F E R E N C E S

ASTD: www.astd.org
CAREO: www.careo.org
DSpace: www.dspace.org
EDUCAUSE: www.educause.edu
Idaho State University College of Education on ADDIE: http://ed.isu.edu/addie/research/Research.html
IMS: www.imsglobal.org

MERLOT: http://merlot.org
NLII: www.educause.edu/nlii
Ryder on Instructional Design including Dick and Carey: http://carbon.cudenver.edu/~mryder/itc_data/idmodels.html
SCORM: www.adlnet.org
SIF: www.sifinfo.org

PART II

TOOLS AND RESOURCES

CHAPTER FOUR

ELEARNING TOOLS

This chapter discusses tools for creating, organizing, and accessing elearning resources. You create resources with a learning management system (LMS) and other software tools such as word processor and presentation graphics programs. You also use an LMS to create the coursesite that organizes your elearning resources. Students, of course, access the coursesite using a computer connected to the Internet. Our goal in this chapter is to describe the functionalities of elearning tools briefly. Subsequent chapters provide the details about organizing and using elearning resources created with these tools. However, if the resources a tool allows you to create can be explained in a paragraph or two, we give the explanation here rather than later.

The chapter is organized into three sections. The first section explains the capabilities of a typical LMS. The second treats two potential impediments to students' using resources on a coursesite—incompatible file formats and long download times. The third section identifies other software tools for creating elearning resources and discusses emerging hardware and software that will make it more convenient to access and use these resources.

LMS FUNCTIONALITY

This section describes the functionalities of a typical LMS. We divide these functionalities into three categories:

- Tools supporting one-way communication
- Tools supporting two-way communication
- Organizational tools for creating coursesite structure

The terms *one-way* and *two-way* communication are defined next. The LMS functionalities we mention are generic; that is, we are not describing any particular LMS.

One-Way Communication Tools

When a person writes or speaks to you, that person *sends* you a *message,* and you *receive* it. If you *reply* to the message, you in turn send a message that the other person receives. Not all messages, however, anticipate a reply. An uninterrupted talk—for example, a television newscast—sends messages to which immediate replies are not expected. We refer to such communication as *one-way* communication. In elearning, posting information to your coursesite for students to view at their convenience usually exemplifies one-way communication. *Two-way* communication involves sending messages and receiving replies to them. This subsection discusses LMS functionality that allows you to create elearning resources used primarily for one-way communication with students. The following subsection treats two-way communication.

Announcements and Documents Created Using the LMS.   An announcement differs from a document in that ordinarily it is brief and intended to endure on a coursesite for a limited period of time. Your LMS will likely allow you to create announcements and documents directly on the coursesite. Because the LMS software has limited functionality, these files will typically contain mainly text with unsophisticated formatting. Creating a more complex document currently requires using other software, as discussed in the third section of this chapter. Chapter 5 explains how to design announcements and documents.

To create an announcement, you type the text you want to post in a text box or similar window generated by the LMS. This is the equivalent of typing text into a word processor window. Your LMS will probably allow you to specify the date and time you want an announcement to be posted, and the date and time when you no longer want it to be visible on your coursesite. Typically, an announcement will appear on the top-level page of your coursesite, to maximize the chance that students will see and read it. Figure 1.1 illustrates an announcement on the homepage of a Blackboard coursesite.

You also create a document by typing or pasting information into a text box. Your LMS will also allow you to select the file folder in which you wish your document to be saved. When students access the document, they must enter the coursesite organizational section associated with this folder before they can open the document file. Creating file folders to organize coursesite resources is discussed later. (Here and throughout we use the term *file folder* as synonymous with *directory*.)

Figure 4.1 illustrates the text box used by an instructor to enter assignment instructions in a Blackboard coursesite. Figure 4.2 illustrates a student's view of the information.

Files Created Using Other Software.   In addition to allowing you to create announcement and document files, your LMS will allow you to upload to your coursesite files created using other software and to delete these files should you no longer desire students to access them. For instance, you can upload a file you created using Microsoft Office or Adobe Acrobat software—both of which are discussed in the third section of this chapter. As with a file created directly on the LMS, you will be able to choose which file folder you want the file to reside in and to name the link to the file that appears in the folder.

Posting files you create outside of the LMS allows you to design resources more sophisticated in content and layout than can be produced using LMS functionality. To access such files, however, your students must have software compatible with the software you used to create them. Large resources such as multimedia files can be uploaded, but because of their size, your students may have trouble downloading them on a slow Internet connection. In addition, your LMS provider will probably limit the storage space you are allocated on its servers. In this case, a single multimedia file can use most or all of your allocated storage. Chapter 5 provides an overview of multimedia. The two difficulties alluded to here—incompatible file formats and slow downloads—are discussed later in this chapter.

① Content Information

Name: [Assignments   ▼]

or specify your own name: [Boeing Questions   ]

Choose Color of Name: [■] (🎨 Pick)

Text:

[Normal ▼] [3 ▼] [Times New Roman ▼] **B** *I* <u>U</u> ≡ ≡ ≡ ⋮≡ ⋮≡ ⋭ ⋲

[🔍 ᴬᴮᶜ ✂ 📋 📋 ↶ ↷ 🔗 ▦ ✏ ✐ 🖍 A̲ √x̄ ‹❖› <html> Preview ⑦]

[📄 🖼 🗂 📑 📎 ƒ]

Recall the Boeing case that was discussed in Thursday's lecture. Consider the following
questions and be prepared to discuss in our next session.

1. What should Boeing have done differently?

2. Are its future outlooks reasonable?

3. Is it taking a global outlook?

FIGURE 4.1   Entering Text in a Blackboard Text Box

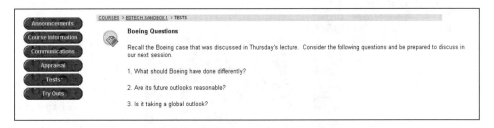

COURSES › EDTECH SANDBOX 1 › TESTS

Boeing Questions

Recall the Boeing case that was discussed in Thursday's lecture. Consider the following questions and be prepared to discuss in
our next session.

1. What should Boeing have done differently?

2. Are its future outlooks reasonable?

3. Is it taking a global outlook?

Announcements
Course Information
Communications
Appraisal
Tests
Try Outs

FIGURE 4.2   A Student View of Text in a Blackboard Coursesite

Figure 4.3 illustrates how an instructor uploads a PowerPoint presentation to a Blackboard coursesite. Figure 4.4 illustrates a student's view of the file.

Gradebooks.   Your LMS will provide a gradebook, perhaps with the names of students entered automatically when they register for your course. When you access the gradebook, you see information for every student; students, however, see only their own grades. As discussed later, you can create and administer an online test and—if the test is objective—have the LMS automatically grade it and record the grades in your gradebook. To record grades manually, you simply type the data into the gradebook when it appears. Students, of course, can read the LMS gradebook, but not modify it. Figure 4.5 illustrates the instructor view of a gradebook associated with a Blackboard coursesite.

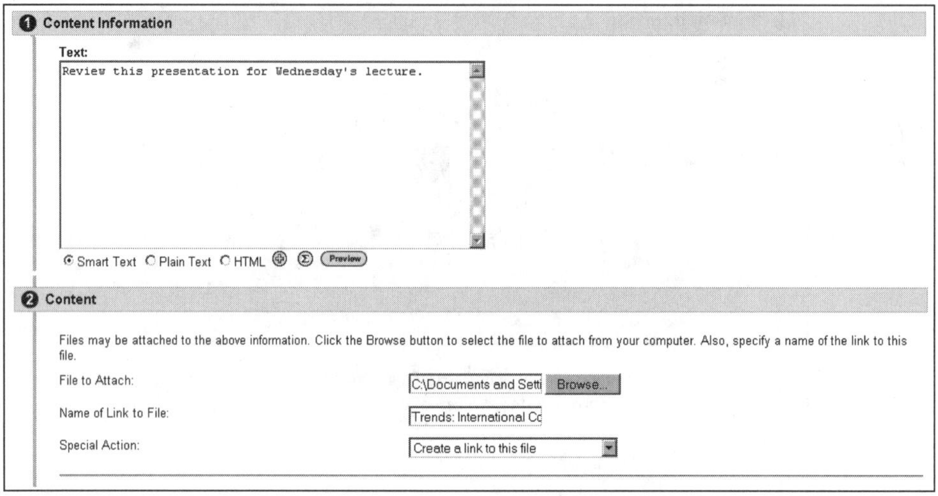

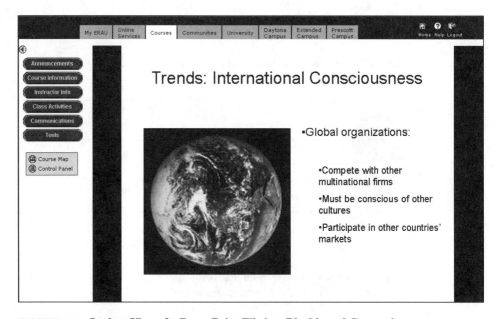

FIGURE 4.3   Uploading a PowerPoint File to a Blackboard Coursesite

FIGURE 4.4   Student View of a PowerPoint File in a Blackboard Coursesite

A distinct advantage of LMS gradebooks is that scores resulting from online examinations are automatically posted to the gradebook file. As a consequence, students can view
their performance in an online test or quiz immediately on completing it. However, some
LMS gradebooks are unsophisticated compared with gradebooks maintained using a spreadsheet program, for example, Microsoft Excel. Chapter 5 has information about how you can

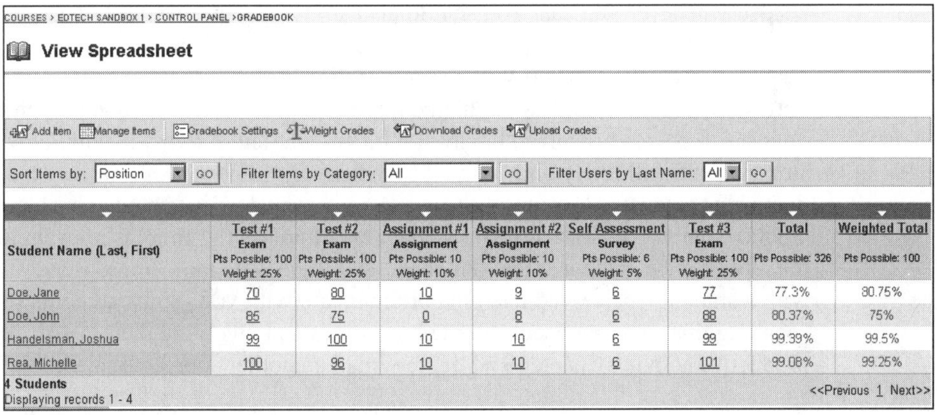

Student Name (Last, First)	Test #1 Exam Pts Possible: 100 Weight: 25%	Test #2 Exam Pts Possible: 100 Weight: 25%	Assignment #1 Assignment Pts Possible: 10 Weight: 10%	Assignment #2 Assignment Pts Possible: 10 Weight: 10%	Self Assessment Survey Pts Possible: 6 Weight: 5%	Test #3 Exam Pts Possible: 100 Weight: 25%	Total Pts Possible: 326	Weighted Total Pts Possible: 100
Doe, Jane	70	80	10	9	6	77	77.3%	80.75%
Doe, John	85	75	0	8	6	88	80.37%	75%
Handelsman, Joshua	99	100	10	10	6	99	99.39%	99.5%
Rea, Michelle	100	96	10	10	6	101	99.08%	99.25%

4 Students
Displaying records 1 - 4 <<Previous 1 Next>>

FIGURE 4.5 A Gradebook in a Blackboard Coursesite

create an Excel gradebook on your personal computer and post its contents to your coursesite without revealing the names of individual students who achieved the grades. However, if you are unwilling to have each student see the grades for every student in your class (without associated names, of course), then you cannot use this approach. On the other hand, if you are unwilling to have students see the average of grades you award, then perhaps you should examine your grading procedures to see why you would want to keep this kind of information secret. We have found that posting grades for an entire class is likely to reinforce high achievers and motivate low achievers.

Email. Your LMS will allow you to compose an email message and send it to your entire class or to any subset of the class. If you are not emailing the entire class, you will be asked to pick the recipients you want to receive your message from a list of students in the class. Depending on what LMS you use, the email accounts may be private to the LMS, or the LMS may require course participants to have existing Internet email accounts.

Email is an alternative to using an announcement to convey timely information to an entire class. However, when your LMS sends email to your students, it will use either LMS email addresses created for each user or the users' institutional email addresses. Many students—especially university students—maintain private email accounts with their Internet providers or by using Microsoft mail or Hotmail. In this case, they are more likely to read their private email more frequently than their LMS or institutional email. For this reason, announcements may be preferable to email as a method of communicating brief messages to students.

Your LMS may allow students to change the address to which the LMS sends them email. However, some commercial email accounts view mass mailings as spam, in which case the danger exists that email sent by the LMS to students' private email addresses will not be delivered. The obvious solution to this problem is to require students to visit your coursesite daily to view announcements and to read email sent to their institutional accounts. However, if a student is taking a number of elearning courses, visiting each coursesite daily can become a time-consuming activity. This consideration suggests you should send students information—whether by announcement or email—well in advance of the time it is needed whenever you can. You should also advise students to check announcements and email immediately whenever something unexpected occurs in your course.

Email serves as a two-way communication tool when you exchange email messages with students or when they exchange them with one another. However, once you allow yourself to become involved in any significant amount of two-way email exchanges with students, you will likely find yourself spending large amounts of time that could more productively be devoted to your other duties as an instructor. You should consider establishing a policy that you will not reply to student email unless the email is relevant to the course, the reply can be made in a few sentences, and there is no more appropriate way of dealing with a student's perceived need to communicate with you. Some students seem to enjoy spending time sending needless email messages and involving their instructors in this unproductive activity. Chapter 9 addresses email and other course policies.

Calendars.   Your LMS is likely to have a calendar tool. If it does, you can use it to record course milestones and other important information—test dates, assignment due dates, and so on. A detailed calendar—one that shows daily activities in the course—can be a great assistance to students in planning their workloads and to you because it allows you to determine at a glance whether you are on schedule in delivering your course. Figure 4.6 illustrates a calendar created in a Desire2Learn coursesite.

Homepages.   Your LMS will likely set up a homepage area for everyone participating in an elearning course—instructors, staff, and students—on which a personal picture and biographical information can be posted. This information is useful in helping you and your students get to know each other. As explained later in the book, because of personal privacy rights, you may not require a student to post personal information on a coursesite. However, most students like the idea of publicizing themselves on the Internet, and preparing and posting a homepage early in an elearning course provides them a chance to orient themselves to the coursesite and begin to learn how to use its tools. Homepages will be referred to again in Chapter 10, and Figure 10.4 provides an example student homepage.

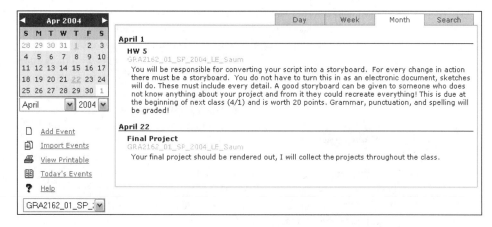

FIGURE 4.6   Course Calendar in a Desire2Learn Coursesite

External Links.   Your LMS will allow you to create and name links to external websites in any existing file directory. Of course, website links can also be embedded in the files you upload to your coursesite. These links facilitate one-way communication because the Internet files that the links point to can be used as course resources in the same way as files internal to the LMS. However, you must check external links regularly to be sure they are still current.

Two-Way Communication Tools

We have seen that one-way communication involves sending a message without provisions for receiving a reply, whereas two-way communication occurs when messages are both sent and received. In two-way elearning communication, students interact with their instructor or with each other. Discussions are the most common form of two-way communication using an LMS. However, your LMS will have additional functionalities that make two-way elearning communication easier.

Discussions.   Your LMS will allow you to set up electronic discussions that facilitate two-way communication. Typically it will support creating two categories of discussions, forums and chats. Forums are asynchronous discussions. You may be familiar with forums under another name—electronic bulletin boards. Chats are synchronous discussions. In the broader world of the Internet, chats are called chat rooms. Students participating in a forum or chat submit their contributions by typing or pasting them into a text box that the discussion interface allows them to invoke. Figure 4.7 illustrates the discussion board area in a Blackboard coursesite and four discussion forums.

Setting up forums and chats is not difficult, but because the procedures are LMS specific, you will have to learn on your own how to perform these tasks. You can involve your entire class in a discussion or limit the discussion to a specified subgroup of students. Chapter 6 explains how to use and facilitate discussions. Chapter 10 contains a section about the use of discussions in small group projects.

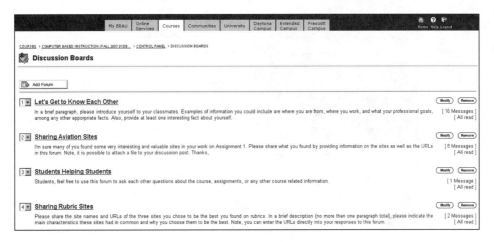

FIGURE 4.7   Discussion Board in a Blackboard Coursesite

Whiteboards.   Your LMS will likely feature a *whiteboard* that students in synchronous discussions can use to share information that cannot be typed into text boxes. For example, students can use the whiteboard to display mathematical equations, images including diagrams and drawings, and information from presentation graphics slide shows. Your whiteboard will probably also allow students to view an Internet site together and may have among other functionalities the ability to use mouse gestures within the whiteboard to create simple line drawings. Visual learners appreciate a whiteboard because it can provide a visual representation of a concept. For tactile learners, who prefer a hands-on approach to learning, the whiteboard provides an additional opportunity to become actively involved in online discussions.

Figure 4.8 illustrates students using a whiteboard and chat capabilities in a Blackboard coursesite. Displayed on the whiteboard is the website of a future guest speaker. The students are engaged in a chat and are brainstorming what topics they would like the speaker to address. Referring to the speaker's website on the whiteboard provides a convenient way for the students to review important information about the guest speaker during this brainstorming session.

Online Tests.   Your LMS will allow you to set up online tests and to specify the date and time a particular test should be made available to students. Currently LMS online testing tools seem to be most appropriate for constructing objective tests, that is, multiple-choice and true–false tests, or tests with short-answer questions. The LMS can grade such tests and enter

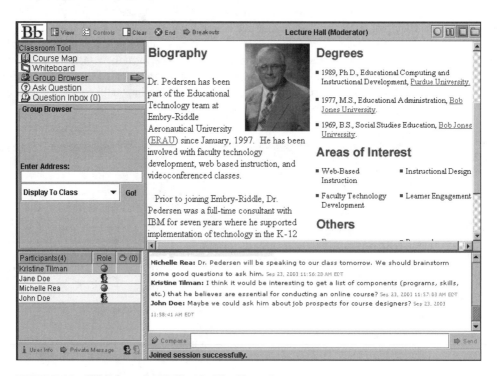

FIGURE 4.8   Whiteboard and Chat in Blackboard

the scores in the online course gradebook. Your LMS may allow you to provide automatic feedback to students when they answer a test question incorrectly. Such feedback can powerfully reinforce learning when students are using online testing as a self-assessment tool. Figure 4.9 illustrates the area used to construct a true–false test question in a WebCT coursesite. Note the area used to enter feedback for students who choose the incorrect answer.

The LMS testing functionality also allows you to construct tests whereby a student types answers to nonobjective questions into a text box. However, the LMS obviously cannot grade such a test. Moreover, regardless of whether your tests are objective or subjective, a number of difficulties arise when using online testing to determine a student's grade in a course. The most significant is that it can be difficult to determine who actually took a test administered by the LMS. Chapter 11 discusses online testing in more detail.

Private Storage Space.   Your LMS will probably allocate private storage space to you and to each student enrolled in your elearning course. In their private storage spaces, students can upload files that they create. They will probably also be able to request that a particular file—for example, an assignment file—be forwarded from their own storage spaces to the instructor's private storage space. This functionality provides a simple, graceful way for students to submit elearning assignments and for you to electronically return graded assignments to them.

Typically, this procedure for managing assignments is as easy for instructors to use as it is for students. Most, but not all, LMSs transparently organize individual student assignment files so that they can be accessed by a particular assignment. However, if your LMS lacks this feature, every assignment file may appear in the same LMS folder. When this happens, all too soon the folder contains a large number of files from different students and different assignments, especially if the class enrollment is large. In this case, you will need to organize the assignment files yourself, probably by transferring them to the hard drive of your personal computer. You can organize the assignment files on your hard drive by assignment number or alternately place all assignments submitted by a particular student

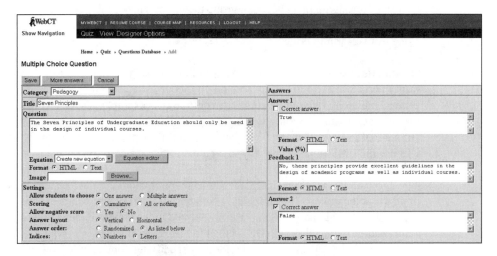

FIGURE 4.9   A True–False Test Question under Construction in WebCT

within a single directory associated with that student. When grading an individual assignment, grouping by assignment number is desirable. After an assignment has been graded, one would prefer that the organization be by students, in case you wish to review the totality of a student's work before deciding on a final course grade for that student or writing a letter of recommendation. You will have to decide which approach suits your needs better.

In any event, even if your LMS manages student assignment files gracefully, you should probably also store copies of assignment files on the hard drive of your personal computer, to guard against the unlikely circumstance that an LMS server failure results in an irretrievable loss of information stored on your coursesite. Chapter 10 provides additional information about managing assignment files submitted by students. This information is related to a discussion in Chapter 8 about the need to create backup copies of files stored on the LMS server.

Organizational Tools

LMS organizational tools allow you to constitute groups of course users with special privileges and to create a directory structure to organize elearning resources on your coursesite. Special privileges are automatically granted when you organize your class into small groups to work on team projects.

Granting Special Privileges.   When you as instructor access your coursesite using an LMS, you have capabilities denied to students. Some examples are the ability to create new course resources, delete resources no longer in use, modify the course calendar, post announcements, set up discussions, and so forth. Your LMS will probably allow you to delegate this authority to select members of your course such as teaching assistants or a student assistant. You should grant this capability with discretion, however, because by doing so you are creating a course user with many of the same powers you have to modify your coursesite.

Your LMS will also allow you to set up student groups with special privileges. These privileges may include a private discussion area, a group email list, and space for storing files and exchanging them between group members. This capability is very useful for organizing your elearning class into project teams. Chapter 10 provides information about managing team elearning projects.

Organizing Course Resources.   You will of course have specific ideas about how you want to organize elearning resources on your coursesite. This involves creating an organizational hierarchy for your resources. An outline is an example of such an organizational hierarchy familiar to everyone. When you use the file management system to create folders and subfolders for organizing files, you construct an electronic organizational hierarchy. You will use the LMS in a similar way to create a folder structure that organizes resources on your coursesite.

Your ability to create an organizational hierarchy for your coursesite resources may be limited to some extent by the graphical user interface (GUI) your LMS provides. Typically the top-level folders already exist and are represented in the GUI as buttons or tabs. Clicking on a link, button, or tab takes an LMS user to the corresponding contents. Your LMS may permit you to modify the existing top-level folders by specifying, for example, how many folders are visible and how they are named. In addition, you may be able to modify the attributes—color;

button, tab, or icon representation; button shape if buttons are chosen; and so on—associated with the graphical representations of top-level folders. Figure 4.10 shows the opening screen of the Multimedia Authoring II course created using Desire2Learn. The top-level folders shown at the top of the screen include content, glossary, links, and others.

Your LMS will also allow you to create subfolders of top-level folders and to name them appropriately. In this way, you can organize the resources you post to your coursesite logically, making it easy for students to find them. Figure 4.11 depicts a partial organizational hierarchy for an elearning course. Three of the top-level folders shown have subfolders that organize their contents according to course units. The course organization posts all external links in a single folder called "Resource Links." References to these links would occur in resources filed under "Topics," in which files containing course content information are stored and perhaps in files residing in other directories. This approach discourages students from interrupting their train of thought by impulsively following links when they first encounter them. Chapter 5 discusses the disadvantages of embedding URL links throughout

FIGURE 4.10   Multimedia Authoring II Coursesite Homepage

Dr. Robert Saum, Daytona Beach Community College. Created in Desire2Learn, used with permission.

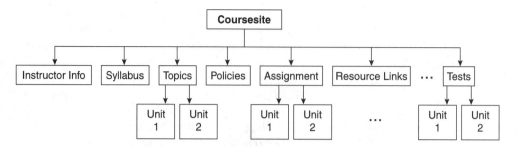

FIGURE 4.11   Partial Organizational Hierarchy for an Elearning Course

the contents of elearning resources. The sole purpose of Figure 4.11 is to illustrate the notion of an organizational hierarchy. Chapter 8 discusses the principles of good coursesite design.

Currently, not all LMS software provides an easy way to link from one resource file to a related resource file in the coursesite organizational hierarchy. For example, you might like to decompose one large file into a number of smaller files with links between them, thus allowing students to download—from a larger amount of related information—only the small portion that currently is needed. If your LMS doesn't allow you to do this gracefully, you might post the related files on a personal website supported by your institution and insert a link from your coursesite to the top-level page of the file. Linking between files stored on your personal website is easy. This solution may seem less than ideal for a novice elearning instructor, because it involves obtaining a login account from the manager of your institution's web server and then learning how to create and maintain your own personal website. However, as you become more experienced in elearning, you will discover that this process is not nearly as complicated as it sounds. Most people can master the basic concepts and become familiar with the software required to implement a personal website in a day or two. Later in this chapter we discuss HTML editors that make it easy to create sophisticated websites without knowing how to write HTML code.

You can expect LMS organizational tools to become increasingly sophisticated and powerful as learning management software develops in the future. In fact, when one recalls how rapidly word processors, presentation graphics programs, spreadsheets, and web editors have evolved over the past decade, it is exciting to think that in the future, LMSs may combine the current power of all four kinds of software, among other capabilities. In any event, it behooves you to become intimately familiar with the organizational functionality of your LMS because this functionality allows you to create an attractive, easily navigated coursesite. Like slow downloads, which we discuss in the next section, a poorly designed coursesite is a major turnoff to your elearning students, who will look only so long for what they want on your coursesite before they abandon the search entirely.

ELEARNING RESOURCE ACCESS PROBLEMS

In the previous section, we characterized the LMS as a tool for elearning communication. In this section, we discuss problems that can hinder such communication. Two potential difficulties may occur when students attempt to use the resources you store on a coursesite. First, the question arises as to whether students have the technology required to receive the electronic information you send them. If, for example, you post a document on your coursesite prepared using proprietary word processor software, your students must have this same software on their computers to open the document file. Second, even if your students have the appropriate software to read information you post, if the information is in a large file, the time to download it from the LMS server to their own computers may be excessive, especially if they are using dialup Internet connections. We call the first problem the *incompatible file format* problem and the second problem the *long download time* problem. In this section, we discuss ways to deal with these problems.

Incompatible File Formats

Computer software consists of instructions to process data. Very commonly, these data are stored in a file, for example, the word processor file containing data representing the contents of this chapter of our book. The conventions a software program uses to construct a data file determine the *format* of the file. Unfortunately, different software programs use different *file format* conventions for storing data. As a result, one software program may not be able to understand data another program stores in a file, leading to the notion of *incompatible file formats*. Incompatible file formats make it difficult or impossible for users of different proprietary software programs to interchange information using the Internet. For example, users of WordPerfect word processing software cannot easily read a sophisticated document file produced using Microsoft Word software, and vice versa. In short, to access a data file you place on your coursesite, your students must have software that knows how to decipher the file format your data are written in. Typically, but not always, this means they must have access to the same software program you used to create the file. Likewise, when a student sends you an assignment file, you must have the same software as the student to read it.

Describing the many and various file formats used in elearning software is beyond the scope of this book. However, we will mention a few of the more common formats and indicate why we believe elearning instructors should in most cases limit themselves to these few. HTML—hypertext markup language—is a common human-like language used to prepare documents for display on the web. Any web browser has the ability to read an HTML file, although depending on the sophistication of the file's contents, add-on software *plug-ins*— most are downloadable free on the Internet—may be required to display it successfully. Moreover, very sophisticated websites can be created using HTML. However, you cannot ensure exactly how an HTML file will appear on the screen of a student who accesses it, because the student's default browser settings and monitor resolution affect how the information in the file is displayed. For this reason, despite the obvious advantages of HTML, we believe this file format is suitable for elearning resources containing textual information primarily when the resource content is brief. HTML files can also be used as containers for embedded multimedia files. Chapter 5 discusses multimedia resources. The end-of-chapter URL References provide links to sites where browser plug-ins may be downloaded. Students need to be aware that plug-in software changes from time to time, so that one must visit download sites periodically to obtain the must current version of a browser plug-in.

For creating more sophisticated elearning resources, we suggest the use of proprietary file formats—specifically those used in the ▪Microsoft Office software package. Though not free, this software is available at a modest cost, and many institutions have purchased licenses that allow its use for all individuals associated with the institution, including the right to install it on home computers. To be sure, some individuals deplore Microsoft's ostensible "monopoly" in personal computer software, and the company of course has been prosecuted for restraint of trade—although not very rigorously—by the United States Department of Justice. Nevertheless, Microsoft's business practices—however questionable to some—have had at least one favorable outcome: Microsoft Office file formats have become *de facto* standards, allowing information to be shared among computer users worldwide. Both Intel-based and Apple personal computers can run Office software. In fact, it has been estimated that 90 percent of all personal computers in the world have Office software installed on them. Thus most students already have access to the relatively inexpensive Microsoft word processing, presentation graphics, spreadsheet, and database software—Word, PowerPoint, Excel, and Access. Establishing a policy that designates Office file formats as institutional standards will virtually assure that students can open the course resource files you create and that you will be able to open files students submit to you, and this will be further discussed in Chapter 9.

In addition to HTML and Office formats, there are at least two other file formats worth considering—*rich text format (RTF)* and ▪Adobe Acrobat's *Portable Document Format (PDF)*. Most word processing programs can read an RTF file and allow saving a file in RTF format. Thus RTF format enables users of different proprietary word processors to share files. However, RTF files cannot capture all the text formatting information contained in proprietary word processing files, for example, superscripts and subscripts, or mathematical equations. Moreover, RTF files do not support embedding complex objects such as audio or video clips in text documents. In short, RTF format is a least common denominator for sharing information among users of different proprietary word processing software. Along with HTML, it is a last resort for text files in the event you are unable or unwilling to establish proprietary file format standards.

By contrast, Adobe's PDF file format allows you to create extremely sophisticated documents, making it an excellent choice for resources containing complex text and graphics, such as brochures or newsletters. Moreover, the Adobe Reader for *viewing* PDF files is freeware downloadable on the web from the Adobe website. Another advantage of the PDF format is that Acrobat software allows you to control how the user of a PDF file can manipulate it. You can specify, for example, that students be able to view a PDF file but not to edit, copy, or print it. Finally, Acrobat can convert files created with word processor software into PDF format, allowing them to be accessed on any computer that has the free Adobe Reader installed on it.

Figure 4.12 summarizes the preceding discussion about file formats and identifies other common formats used in elearning. The file types fall into seven categories: text, presentation graphics, data (spreadsheet and databases), images, animations, audios, and videos. More than a dozen common image formats exists, from which we have chosen only three. Images, animations, audio, and video are discussed in Chapter 5 in an overview of using multimedia resources in elearning. Chapter 5 also discusses file streaming. Note that Microsoft Office files, like PDF files, can have objects of other types embedded in them, for example, images, URL hyperlinks, animations, and video and audio clips, among others.

Long Download Times

Even when students have the required software to read a file posted on a coursesite, before they can open it they still must wait for the file to download to their personal computers from

FIGURE 4.12   Common eLearning File Formats

TYPE	TYPICAL SOFTWARE TO CREATE/ACCESS FILE	COMMENTS
Text Files		
HTML	Text editor, word processor; HTML editor	Readable by any web browser
DOC	Microsoft Word	*De facto* word processor standard
PDF	Adobe Acrobat/Acrobat Reader	Acrobat Distiller can import MS Office files
RTF	Word processor	Use to counter word processor incompatibilities
Presentation Graphics Files		
PPT	Microsoft PowerPoint	*De facto* presentation graphics standard
Data (Spreadsheet and Database) Files		
XLS	Microsoft Excel	*De facto* spreadsheet standard
MDB	Microsoft Access	Database software bundled with Microsoft Office
Image Files		
GIF	Macromedia Fireworks, Adobe Photoshop, Microsoft Photo Editor	Use for drawings, line art, text, limited color
JPEG	See above	More suitable for color photographs than .gif
PNG	See above	Supports transparency
Animation Files		
GIF	Macromedia Fireworks, Adobe Photoshop	Animated GIF files are large; plug-in required
SWF	Macromedia Flash, Macromedia Shockwave	Plug-ins required; smaller file size than GIF animations; streamed downloading
Audio Files		
MID	Play with Windows Media Player, RealOne Player, Apple QuickTime plug-in	MIDI: Musical Instrument Digital Interface
MP3	See above	Emerging standard for music files
WAV	See above	Microsoft format
RA	See above	RealAudio format; streams with RealOne Player
Video Files		
AVI	Play with Windows Media Player, RealOne Player, Apple QuickTime plug-in	Microsoft format
MPEG	See above	High quality, large file sizes
RM	See above	RealAudio format; streams with RealOne Player
MOV	See above	Apple QuickTime Movie

the Internet server where it resides. If the file is large, the download time may be excessive, especially on a low-speed Internet connection. File download times as a function of file size are given in Figure 4.13. Times are computed assuming nine bits per byte (one parity bit) and are rounded to the nearest second. These are *best-case* times; that is, downloads can take significantly longer if network congestion exists. Note that a one-megabyte file—relatively small by Internet standards—takes over five minutes to download at a speed of 28.8K. Although

FIGURE 4.13   Computed Minimum File Download Times in Minutes and Seconds (MM:SS)

Connection Speed	Transfer Rate (bits/sec)	FILE SIZE					
		10Kb	50Kb	100Kb	500Kb	1Mb	10MB
28.8K	28,800	00:03	00:16	00:31	02:36	05:13	53:08
56K	56,000	00:02	00:08	00:16	01:20	02:41	26:47
ISDN/2b	112,000	00.01	00:04	00:08	00:40	01:20	13:24
T1	1,440,000	00:00	00.00	00.01	00.03	00:06	01:03
DSL	1,500,000	00:00	00:00	00:01	00:03	00:06	01:00
T3	4,473,600	00:00	00:00	00:00	00:01	00:02	00:20

this may not sound like a long time, it feels like an eternity to a student sitting in front of a computer waiting for the download to complete.

Long waits on file downloads are a major turnoff to students and can seriously hinder their performance in your course. It follows that you must be sensitive to download time when you create a file with the aim of communicating the information in it to your students via the Internet. File size is a notorious problem when you are using PowerPoint software, because PowerPoint files become very large very quickly. PowerPoint allows you to save a slide presentation as an HTML file. If you do so, the HTML file will download a slide a time, making it much easier for an Internet user with a slow connection to view the presentation. Another strategy is to convert presentation graphics files to Macromedia Flash format using software, which can decrease file size as much as an order of magnitude. PowerCONVERTER, a software program from ▪PresentationPro, is highly suited to this task. Conversion to Flash format also reduces file size for resource types such as animations and audios. Software from ▪Impatica turns a PowerPoint presentation into an HTML file that is much reduced in size—the company claims up to a 95 percent reduction. A fourth approach—explained earlier—is to decompose one large file into a number of smaller files with links between the files. This strategy works for any file format. Chapter 5 provides more information on this subject.

OTHER TOOLS FOR CREATING OR ACCESSING ELEARNING RESOURCES

This section discusses elearning tools other than the LMS. It is divided into two subsections. The first identifies additional tools for creating elearning resources. The second includes information about emerging technologies that will change—perhaps even revolutionize—the way students access elearning resources.

Tools for Creating eLearning Resources

Point-and-Click HTML Editors.   It is not necessary to learn how to write HTML code in order to create sophisticated HTML documents and even entire websites. Instead, you can use a free or proprietary HTML point-and-click editor to create these objects. Point-and-click HTML editors are WYSIWYG—"what you see is what you get"—editors. This means that what you see on your computer screen when you create a file is what students will see when they access it—bearing in mind of course that browser settings influence how an HTML file is displayed. The best of the point-and-click HTML editors rival word processors in power and sophistication, and they are as easy as word processors to learn how to use. Free HTML editors—for example, Netscape Composer—are useful for making relatively simple web files but have limited functionality in comparison to proprietary HTML editors. Three well-known and very excellent proprietary web editors are listed in alphabetical order:

- Adobe Go Live
- Macromedia Dreamweaver
- Microsoft Front Page

You may not want to bother about learning how to use an HTML editor early in your elearning career. However, as you become more experienced and more knowledgeable, you will probably realize that the effort you devote to learning this software is likely to be richly repaid. HTML editors are not inexpensive, but they are worth every penny you pay for them. Every institution seriously committed to elearning should make one or more of these products available to instructors who desire to use them. As previously explained, students require only a web connection to access any HTML file/website you create.

Microsoft Office and Adobe Acrobat.   We have already discussed the Microsoft Office Suite and Adobe Acrobat, but we will list these products here for the sake of completeness. Recall that to open a file created with any Office component, students must have the same software you used to create the file. Adobe PDF files can be read—but not created—using the free Acrobat Reader.

- Microsoft Office Suite: Word, PowerPoint, Excel, and Access
- Adobe Acrobat (students need only the Acrobat Reader)

The odds are very high that you will want to use one or both of these software products early in your elearning career.

Multimedia Software.   In the present context, multimedia resources include image, animation, audio, and video files. Although we will not attempt to provide details about tools for developing multimedia resources, we will mention several such tools. You will likely need to solicit the help of skilled professionals at your institution to create multimedia resources, because the equipment/software required is fairly complex and typically not inexpensive. Some common graphics/multimedia tools—most of which are mentioned in Figure 4.12—are listed here:

- Adobe Photoshop—a sophisticated photo editor
- Microsoft Photo Editor—basic photo editor
- Macromedia Fireworks—create images (GIFs, JPEGs, PNSs) for use on the web
- ▪Macromedia Flash—create web interfaces, basic simulations, and animations

The Adobe and Macromedia software are also available to Macintosh users, who in addition have access to a sophisticated suite of multimedia tools that we will not attempt to catalog. Common players/plug-ins that handle multimedia files are:

- Windows Media Player (for Microsoft Windows-based PCs only)
- ▪RealOne Player (works on both Windows-based and Apple PCs)
- ▪Apple Quicktime (runs Apple MOV files and many audio and video file types on either Microsoft or Apple platforms)

Miscellaneous Tools.   Other tools to facilitate elearning include proprietary online testing packages, desktop video conferencing packages, and freeware for conducting discussions and chats. An Internet search will provide information about these and related kinds of software.

Resource Access Tools

Students commonly access coursesites and other elearning resources using desktop or laptop computers with network and Internet connections supported by the wired transmission of digital data. By contrast, emerging technologies are making it increasingly possible to access elearning materials remotely via wireless networks and smaller computing devices such as handheld computers, ebooks, and tablet PCs. In addition, *portals* provide convenient, centralized access to many different kinds of elearning resources on a single subject. Finally, Internet2 shows promise as a support for the increased use of multimedia resources in elearning. What follows briefly discusses these various devices and technologies that one so frequently finds mentioned in the elearning literature.

Portals.   The word *portal* is a much-used term in articles about Internet access. To judge from the literature, it is used in at least two distinct ways. In one sense, a portal is a website tailored to an individual's or an organization's unique online needs. Rather than delivering information in the same format to every user, an *institutional portal*—called an *enterprise portal* in the business world—personalizes an individual's view of its web contents (Ateshian, 2004). The *Yahoo!* website, for example, allows registered users to design their opening screens to reflect the web services they are most interested in seeing.

In the world of education, institutional portals provide students, faculty, alumni, parents, staff, clubs, and other groups of campus constituents direct access to personalized information (Taggart, 2004). As an example, Figure 4.14 illustrates the *ERAU Online* portal page of an Embry-Riddle Aeronautical University (ERAU) graduate student whose first name is Kristine. The page is personalized to reflect Kristine's interests and current activities and commitments. All students in the university have a similar web page on which they can read announcements relevant to them personally, enter coursesites for elearning courses in which they currently are participating, view their academic transcripts, and access many other individualized university services. ERAU faculty and staff also have portals personalized for their special needs. In general the use of portals in higher education is on the rise, perhaps because administrators view them as a competitive advantage in recruiting students (Zazelenchuk & Boling, 2003). The 2003 Campus Computing Project Survey found that 28.4 percent of the campuses participating in the survey had a portal, up from 21.2 percent in 2002 (Green, 2003).

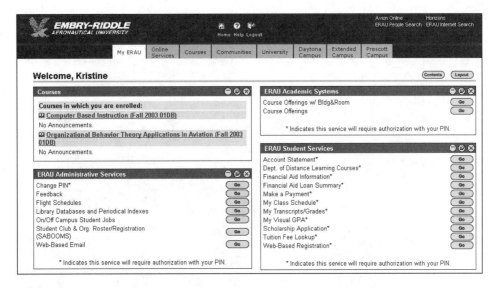

FIGURE 4.14   ERAU Online Student Portal Page

Kristine M. Tilman, used with permission.

A second meaning of the word *portal* is reflected in its use to describe websites that provide access to collections of information on subjects of special interest. An example of a portal in this sense is the ▪Nobel e-Museum website, depicted in Figure 4.15. This portal is a gateway to a wide variety of information about the Nobel Prize awards and individuals who have received them. Note that the Nobel site, in addition to textual information about the subject of the portal, provides access to related readings and multimedia resources such as computer games, audio recordings, and simulations.

One might fairly call the Nobel e-Museum website an *educational portal* in the sense that its contents comprise a course of instruction about the Nobel prizes and the disciplines in which they are awarded—physics, chemistry, medicine, literature, economics, and world peace. The site includes lectures in textual format (over 7,000 documents), labs (simulations), and library resources (readings and recordings)—all parts of a traditional course of instruction—with only quizzes and tests omitted. Educational portals are of particular interest to instructors and students engaged in elearning. As they now exist, elearning course-sites are rudimentary portals to information about the elearning courses they support. Chapter 7 provides examples of educational websites in various categories—digital library resources, online museums, virtual experiments, online expeditions, and textbook supplements, among others. When one imagines these kinds of elearning resources fully integrated with the resources of a well-developed current-day elearning coursesite, the sophisticated elearning world of tomorrow begins to come into focus. We predict that educational portals are the wave of the future for students engaging in elearning. In short, coursesites ultimately will become—at the world's best universities—"full-service" educational portals suitable for self-study and self-assessment.

Wireless Computing and Handheld Computers.   *Wireless networks* are by now a well-known part of the computing world. In an educational environment, wireless technology

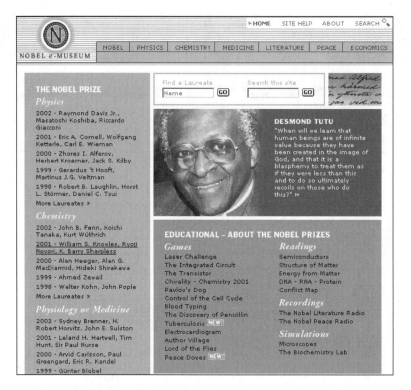

FIGURE 4.15   Nobel e-Museum

© The Nobel Foundation.

consists of strategically placed network computing devices called *access points* distributed throughout buildings on a campus. Interface hardware in students' laptops facilitates wireless connectivity to the institution's computing network when they are in the proximity of any one of these many access points. Students can use their computers in locations remote from the network server, such as the campus lawn, student union buildings, and older dorm rooms not wired for network access. When students can roam the campus freely without losing network and Internet connectivity, the entire campus becomes a classroom (Bowers, 2001). Wireless networks in the K–12 environment allow students to move about the classroom and facilitate, for example, group work requiring the use of a computer.

Wireless networks facilitate unconventional approaches to delivering elearning courses. For example, the Faculty of Education at Simon Fraser University in Canada uses wireless networking in hybrid professional development elearning workshops for teachers. Weekend workshop participants are divided into small groups equipped with wireless laptops. Wireless connectivity allows the groups to work together anywhere in the university's Education Building and—weather permitting—outside on decks and grassy lawns (Johnson, 2003).

Another approach to wireless computing is the use of cell phone technology. As everyone knows, cell phones are rapidly becoming handheld computers that can send and receive email, take and transmit digital pictures, connect to the Internet, and perform an increasingly large number of similar computing tasks. Although cell phones without interface hardware cannot be used to access network software, the fact that cell phone access points exist around the globe makes it likely that this technology will become an important supplement to wireless networking in the world of educational computing. In any event, it now seems reasonable to group cell phones with other handheld wireless computing devices such as personal digital assistants (PDAs) and ebooks.

Until recently, PDAs were small stand-alone computers used to organize appointments and maintain address lists, among other personal tasks. Today they have the capability of connecting wirelessly to a computer network. Students can use them, for example, to access course information such as announcements, assignment instructions and due dates, course schedules, and grades. Also, PDAs can be used to look up information about the faculty, campus, or community. Networked PDAs can introduce additional interactivity into a traditional classroom setting (Oliver, Eckel, & Ball, 2002). Much like student response systems, PDAs and similar handhelds make it possible to poll students and obtain virtually instantaneous responses (Bishop, Dinkins, & Dominick, 2003). For example, a brief quiz answered using handhelds and graded automatically might enable an instructor to determine whether additional clarification is required for a concept just presented in a lecture or other classroom activity. Medical schools in the United States are in the vanguard of users of handheld computers in education. In these schools, handheld computers are just about as common as stethoscopes (Fallon, 2002). Handhelds help ensure that medical students have access to up-to-date professional information as they move between classrooms, hospitals, libraries, and clinics.

Ebook readers are handheld computers with screens large enough to display pages of books, articles, and other lengthy documents. Many books are now available in digital format for viewing using an ebook reader. Ebook software supports interactivity with an ebook's content, such as the ability to click on a word to see its definition or on an image to learn more about what the image represents. Some of the readers also allow users to connect wirelessly to the Internet, in which case it would be possible to click on a URL link to visit a website for additional information relevant to the ebook a user is reading.

Ebook readers, PDAs, and laptop computers can be used to provide convenient access to information. For example, medical students can now refer to the lengthy *Physicians' Desk Reference* on a PDA while making their rounds. In Forney, Texas, 10- and 11-year-old students use notebook computers, instead of traditional textbooks, to access in digital format many of their math and science textbooks or to read American literary classics in digital format such as Mark Twain's *Adventures of Huckleberry Finn* or Stephen Crane's *The Red Badge of Courage* about the Civil War (Humer, 2004).

Like wired PDAs and student response systems, networked ebook readers facilitate getting timely feedback from a group. The theater department at Ball State University used ebook readers creatively in its production of *Blood Relation,* a play about Lizzie Borden, the Fall River, Massachusetts, woman who was acquitted of the notorious ax murders of her father and stepmother more than a century ago. More than half of the audience members accepted the offered loan of an ebook reader on entering the auditorium. Participants with ebooks could view historical photos of the Borden family and the crime scene, and read commentary about the play's subject written for the production. At the end of the play, audience members used their ebook readers to submit a verdict on Lizzie Borden's guilt (Carlson, 2002).

Tablet PCs.   A tablet PC is a computing device combining the portability of a pad of paper with the computing power of a laptop (Foster, 2003). Whereas screens of conventional laptops merely output data, the screen of a tablet PC is an input as well as an output device. Anything "written" on the screen with a stylus—notes, equations, drawings—is digitized and can be saved in a file. Thus tablet PCs are convenient for taking notes, particularly on technical subjects. In addition, character-recognition software can "learn" a user's handwriting, allowing notes preserved in digitized image format to be converted to word processor format, from which they can be edited and searched.

Tablet PCs also allow users to write directly onto documents displayed on their screens. This feature makes it easy for an instructor to grade a student's assignment submitted in electronic format via the Internet. The instructor can handwrite comments directly on a student's displayed assignment, save the handwriting over the text or request that it be converted to text, and send the graded assignment back to the student electronically. This functionality is equally useful to students, who can, for example, write personal observations on elearning lecture notes downloaded from a coursesite and displayed on the screen of a tablet PC (Herrmann & Popyack, 2003). Files created or modified using a tablet PC can be converted to an image or text format for display on computers that do not have tablet capabilities.

Most tablet PCs are laptop size, but one can anticipate that handheld computers with screen digitizers will become more common in the future.

Internet2. ▪Internet2 is a nonprofit consortium—initiated in 1996—involving over two hundred universities partnered with industry and government. The consortium's goal is to create a communication network supporting much higher data transfer rates than are possible using commercial Internet providers, and to make the network available and affordable to researchers and university instructors whose work requires its high-speed capabilities. By association, the term *Internet2* also denotes the network itself. At the heart of Internet2 is a backbone network called ▪Abilene. With nodes located in Seattle, San Francisco, Los Angeles, Denver, Houston, Chicago, Atlanta, Washington, DC, and New York, among other cities, Abilene spans the United States from coast to coast. One important use of the Internet2 network is scientific research. For example, astronomers at the Massachusetts Institute of Technology (MIT) are experimenting with moving data from remotely located radio telescopes to high-speed computers in Cambridge, Massachusetts, which have the ability to process the data in real time.

Predictably—because universities are a major part of the Internet2 consortium—the Internet2 network is already having a significant effect on elearning in higher education, mainly through its ability to support high-quality videoconferencing. At Kansas State University, the high-speed videoconferencing possible on Internet2 brings together three subject matter experts who conduct courses on plant pathology in a virtual classroom accessible at Kansas State in Manhattan, Kansas, the University of Nebraska at Lincoln, and Oregon State University in Corvallis, Oregon. At the National University of Singapore and Singapore's Nanyang Technological University, students take classes at MIT using videoconferencing supported by Internet2 and other international research networks. Under ideal conditions, video signals reach Cambridge from Singapore, half a world away, in less than a second. For some institutions, however, the cost of Internet2 may delay its widespread acceptance in elearning in the very near future. Even if Abilene becomes widely available and affordable, campus networks with low transmission speeds constitute an end-user bottleneck that slows data flow to rates unacceptable for videoconferencing. Such networks require a technology upgrade before an institution can participate in Internet2 (Olsen, 2003). Related to Internet2 is the ▪National LambdaRail initiative, a research project to engage scientists and researchers in developing high-speed networking technologies based on a fiber optic infrastructure.

As we have seen, the use of multimedia resources in elearning is limited by the fact that long download times currently make accessing them on the Internet impractical. Nevertheless, telecommunications—like elearning—is still in its infancy. The transmission of high-quality video and audio information over long-distance telecommunication networks will one day be possible. In addition, organizations associated with Internet2 are developing standards for sharing web-based materials. We believe that technology advances in the next few decades will make it possible to conduct virtual classes—whether live or recorded—that approximate current classrooms in realism and authenticity. When this happens, students around the globe will be able to study with the world's most accomplished subject matter experts despite the fact that these experts are remote to them in both time and space. Elearning will bring educational opportunities to people who otherwise would not have them; these learning opportunities will be facilitated by the world's best instructors; and the learning resources students use will allow them to see and hear their instructors with better clarity than is possible today using analog television transmissions.

In addition, it will be possible for educational institutions to use high-speed networks to share electronic information freely while protecting against unauthorized access of this information. An example of group effort toward this end is the ▪Shibboleth Project, overseen by the ▪Middleware Architecture Committee for Education (MACE). The Shibboleth Project team is developing architectures, policy structures, practical technologies, and an open source implementation to support interinstitutional sharing of web resources subject to access controls. Shibboleth will also develop a policy framework that will allow interoperation within the higher education community (Klingenstein, 2003).

REFERENCES

Ateshian, R. (2004, March). eLearning portals: You've come a long way baby. *Syllabus, 17*(8), 33–34, 39.

Barton, C., & Collura, K. (2003, November). Catalyst for change: Bishop Hartley becomes the first U.S. high school to furnish an entire class with tablet PCs. *T.H.E. Journal, 31*(4), 39–42.

Bishop, A., Dinkins, R., & Dominick, J. (2003). Good ideas: Programming handheld devices to enhance learning. *EDUCAUSE Quarterly, 26*(1), 50–53.

Boerner, G. (2002, October). The brave new world of wireless technologies: A primer for educators. *Syllabus, 16*(3), 19–20, 22.

Boettcher, J. (2001, January). Wireless teaching and learning: Mobile and untethered. *Syllabus.* Retrieved December 4, 2003, from www.syllabus.com/article. asp?id=436

Bowers, P. (2001, January). Discovery-based learning: Lessons in wireless teaching. *Syllabus, 14*(6), 38–40.

Bruce, J. (2003, January/February). Beyond bandwidth. *EDUCAUSE Review, 38*(1), 23–31.

Carlson, S. (2002, November 1). Electronic books have a supporting role in a play at Ball State U. play. *The Chronicle of Higher Education.* Retrieved November 29, 2003, from http://chronicle.com/prm/weekly/ v49/i10/10a03203.htm

Clark, D. R. (2003, September). Putting chemistry in the palm of your hand. *Syllabus, 17*(2), 22–25.

Dominick, J. (2002, September). Ready or not—PDAs in the classroom. *Syllabus.* Retrieved December 4, 2003, from www.syllabus.com/article.asp?id=6705

E-enabled textbooks: Lower cost, higher function [Editorial]. (2002, May). *Syllabus, 15*(10), 44.

Eisler, D. L. (2002, July). Campus portals: Future hope, past history, or more hype? *Syllabus, 15*(12), 12–16.

Fallon, M. (2002, November). Handheld devices: Toward a more mobile campus. *Syllabus, 16*(4), 10–15.

Foster, A. L. (2003, April 4). Tablets sneak up on laptops. *The Chronicle of Higher Education,* p. A33.

Green, K. C. (2002, October). The 2002 national survey of information technology in U.S. higher education. *The Campus Computing Project.* Retrieved January 10, 2003, from www.campuscomputing.net

Green, K. C. (2003, December). Tracking the digital puck into 2004. *Syllabus, 17*(5), 10–13, 38.

Herrmann, N., & Popyack, J. L. (2003, January). Electronic grading: When the tablet is mightier than the pen. *Syllabus, 16*(6), 19–21.

Humer, C. (2004, April 27). Students set to hit the latest e-books. *MSNBC: Technology & Science.* Retrieved May 10, 2004, from http://msnbc.msn.com/id/4846005/

Interview: Facing the portal: A conversation with Annie Stunden [Editorial]. (2004, March). *Syllabus, 17*(8), 8–10, 12, 14.

Johnson, W. (2003). Secure wireless networking at Simon Fraser University. *EDUCAUSE Quarterly, 26*(2), 28–33.

Karnovsky, S., & Warner, C. (2002, October/November). An instant feedback learning environment. *Converge, 5*(5), 20–22.

Katz, R. (2003, July/August). Balancing technology and tradition: The example of course management systems. *EDUCAUSE Review, 38*(4), 48–59.

Klingenstein, K. (2003, July/August). The rise of collaborative tools. *EDUCAUSE Review, 38*(4), 60–61.

Levinson, E., & Grohe, B. (2001, September). At ease in the handheld world. *Converge, 4*(9), 58–59.

Lindsey, S. (2003, November). On-demand lectures create an effective distributed education experience. *T.H.E. Journal, 31*(4), 16–20.

Long, P. (2003, November). Trends: Document formats for the web: PDF, DWF, and CMS. *Syllabus, 17*(4), 6–8.

Looney, M. (2001, January). E-books: Enhancing the educational experience. *Syllabus, 14*(6), 48–49.

Looney, M. A., & Sheehan, M. (2001, July/August). Digitizing education: A primer on ebooks. *EDUCAUSE Review, 36*(4), 38–46.

McCloskey, P. (2002, December). Tablet PCs stake out higher ed. *Syllabus.* Retrieved December 4, 2003, from www.syllabus.com/article.asp?id=6985

Moriarty, L. J. (2001). The wireless war dance: Why and when should you begin to take wireless seriously? *EDUCAUSE Quarterly, 24*(1), 4–6.

Oliver, K. M., Eckel, C. C., & Ball, S. B. (2002, October). Wireless interactive teaching simulations. *Syllabus, 16*(3), 33–36.

Olsen, F. (2003, May 16). Internet2 at a crossroads. *The Chronicle of Higher Education,* p. A32.

Penley, L. E. (2004, March/April). Bringing technology into the laboratory. *EDUCAUSE Review, 39*(2), 10–16.

Peterson, D. (2002, November). Implementing PDAs in a college course: One professor's perspective. *Syllabus.* Retrieved December 4, 2003, from www.syllabus.com/article.asp?id=6897.

Respondent survey: Wireless networking in higher education in the U.S. and Canada. (2002, June). *EDUCAUSE Center for Applied Research.* Retrieved December 1, 2003, from www.educause.edu/ecar

Scott, L. A. (2003, October). Wireless tots: Primrose school launches first wireless technology program for preschoolers. *T.H.E. Journal, 31*(3), 16–22.

Strauss, H. (2003, July). An enterprise portal: Essential or indispensable? *Syllabus, 16*(12), 49–50.

Taggart, B. M. (2004, February). Portal integration and a scalable, flexible enterprise system. *Syllabus, 17*(7), 20, 22, 24.

Wangemann, P., Lewis, N., & Squires, D. (2003, November). Portable technology comes of age: The utilization of handhelds in a pilot teacher education program. *T.H.E. Journal, 31*(4), 26–32.

Zazelenchuk, T. W., & Boling, E. (2003). Considering user satisfaction in designing web-based portals. *EDUCAUSE Quarterly, 26*(1), 35–40.

URL REFERENCES

Abilene: http://abilene.internet2.edu

Adobe: www.adobe.com

Apple QuickTime Plugins: www.apple.com

Edutools—Comparisons of Course Management Systems: www.edutools.info/course/compare/compare.jsp?produce=144,160

Impatica: www.impatica.com

Internet2: www.internet2.edu/about/aboutinternet2.html

Macromedia for Flash and Shockware Plugins: http://macromedia.com/

Microsoft: www.microsoft.com

Middleware Architecture Committee for Education (MACE): http://middleware.internet2.edu/MACE

National LambdaRail: www.nationallambdarail.org

Nobel e-museum: www.nobel.se/index.html

Presentation Pro PowerCONVERTER: http://www.presentationpro.com/products/PowerCONVERTER.asp

Real: www.real.com

Shibboleth Project: http://shibboleth.internet2.edu/

■ ■ ■ ■ ■ ━━━

CHAPTER FIVE

ONE-WAY COMMUNICATION: DISTRIBUTING INFORMATION ELECTRONICALLY

Recall that one-way communication involves your sending information and students receiving it. This chapter identifies different categories of information you can distribute using the web and explains how to format the most common kinds. Every elearning resource posted on a coursesite will be viewed—initially at least—on a computer. Hence we focus on how to design information for a computer display. This chapter is organized into six sections. The first briefly explains why electronic distribution of information can be preferable to the conventional means of distribution. The second section identifies four categories of electronic information that make up elearning resources. The third and fourth sections explain, respectively, how to format announcements and documents, two forms of textual information. The fifth section of the chapter discusses how to design presentation graphics slide shows. The sixth and last section provides an overview of the use of multimedia in elearning. Chapter 7, a detailed discussion of web-based resources, provides examples of multimedia resources.

ELECTRONIC VERSUS PAPER DISTRIBUTION

The ability to distribute information via the web is a major advantage of elearning. It enormously simplifies one-way communication with students. Consider, for example, how you distribute information in a conventional learning environment. First you create a file on your computer, then print a copy for each student. Time-consuming collation of pages and stapling may be involved. Next, you take the document to class and manually distribute it or alternately mail it to distance learners. Providing a copy to a student who misses class often requires a face-to-face meeting.

By contrast, disseminating information electronically is much more efficient and convenient, hence also less costly. When you use electronic distribution, each student performs a small fraction of the total work you would have to accomplish to disseminate a paper document. After the document file is created, you simply upload it to your coursesite, a process that can be completed in a few seconds. Then students access the document on the web when it is convenient for them to do so. Revision of information is also more efficient when materials are distributed electronically. One simply modifies the associated file and uploads it to the coursesite, then posts an announcement to inform students that the revised materials are available. In fact, when you consider the work required to prepare—or revise—and distribute the paper handouts so often used in traditional classes, it is hard to imagine why anyone would prefer this method to the electronic distribution of information.

FOUR CATEGORIES OF ELECTRONIC INFORMATION

A computer allows you to represent information in many different ways, for example, as text, slide show presentations, audios and videos, or still and animated graphics. This section groups electronic information into four categories and briefly discusses the characteristics of each. The four categories are textual information, presentation graphics slide shows, spreadsheets and databases, and multimedia objects. As explained in Chapter 4, we recommend using the Microsoft Office Suite—Word, PowerPoint, Excel, and Access—to create information files, because doing so makes it extremely likely that students will be able to access the information you distribute to them.

Textual Information

As the name implies, textual information consists mainly of words, as opposed to electronic objects such as photos, animations, videos and audios, and the like. Traditionally, textual information has been read on paper in written or printed form, for example, as in a letter, newspaper, magazine, or book. In elearning courses, however, text is commonly viewed—initially, at least—on a computer monitor. This consideration affects the way such information must be formatted, as discussed in later sections.

We subdivide textual information into *announcements* and *documents*. An announcement is characterized by its brevity and—ordinarily—its temporality. An announcement is prepared using the LMS software. A document differs from an announcement in that it is longer and addresses its subject in more detail. Course outlines, course notes, policies, and assignment instructions are examples of documents. Like announcements, documents can be created using an LMS. However, we recommend using a word processor to prepare documents, because a word processor allows much easier and more powerful control of document layout than does LMS software. In addition, because students use the same word processor software to view a document that you used to prepare it, you can be sure that students who access the document will see it exactly as you laid it out. This is not true of HTML files, because a user's web browser preferences and screen resolution to a significant extent determine how an HTML document appears on the computer display.

Presentation Graphics Slide Shows

In contrast to textual information, which can be viewed either on a computer monitor or in printed form, presentation graphics slide shows—despite the fact that ordinarily they consist primarily of text—convey information visually. Slide shows will be viewed on a computer screen, or on a projection of a computer screen, and must be designed accordingly. Perhaps because presentation graphics is a text-based medium popularized by the desktop computer, design of slide shows is not a well-understood concept. A later section addresses this subject. One should bear in mind, however, that not all slide shows are textual. Very dramatic effects can be achieved by making slide shows that consist primarily or entirely of digital images.

Spreadsheets and Databases

Spreadsheets and databases provide two common ways of representing data. As explained in Chapter 4, LMS functionality also allows posting data in a calendar. Although some instructors will wish to disseminate course information in spreadsheet or database format, we will not attempt to explain how these formats can be used in elearning. We would like to point out, however, that Excel allows posting student grades in a most useful way. Currently, LMS gradebooks have not achieved a high level of sophistication. If you design your Excel gradebook properly and post it to your coursesite as a read-only file, students who access it can play "what if" with the recorded grades to date. For example, suppose only a final exam remains to complete course grades. A student can enter different numeric values in the blank final exam cell and see how a certain grade on the final will affect his or her final course grade. Alternately, you can save and post an Excel gradebook as an HTML file. Of course, when you post Excel files in either format, you must be careful not to identify students by name. Instead, use an appropriate ID number or similar pseudonym.

Multimedia Objects

We use the term *multimedia objects* to describe elearning resources that consist primarily of still pictures, moving pictures, or sound, or some combination of these three. Still pictures include images, drawings, and graphs. Videos and animations are examples of moving pictures. Pictures and sound are often combined in a single multimedia object, but of course sound resources such as music and recorded voices exist independently of still or moving pictures. Although multimedia objects can be embedded in documents, presentation graphics slide shows, or spreadsheets and databases, it seems appropriate to treat this crucially important aspect of elearning in a category of its own. Although it is beyond the scope of this book to treat multimedia in detail, a later section provides an overview of the subject. File formats associated with multimedia objects are discussed in Chapter 4.

ANNOUNCEMENTS

The announcement component of an LMS makes it easy for you to distribute up-to-the minute information to students. In this section, we identify potential uses for announcements and explain—mainly by example—how to format an announcement.

Uses of Announcements

Electronic announcements can help reduce your workload. For example, when several students send you email inquiring about the same subject, you can respond via an announcement, rather than having to send an email response to each student. In fact an announcement is preferable to individual responses in such cases, because several students asking the same question implies the existence of other students who want the same information but who are reluctant to request it. As another example, announcements can help you facilitate electronic discussions more efficiently. Whereas it can be very time-consuming to respond to numerous individual student or team discussion comments, you can review all these comments online and post an announcement containing your summary observations. However, bear in mind that unless you establish a course policy requiring students to visit your course website daily, you may find that announcements will not be read in a timely fashion.

The following list identifies additional uses of announcements:

- Clarification on course issues
- Reminders of important dates of assignments, quizzes, and tests
- Motivational words of encouragement
- Congratulations to class on course milestones
- Changes in course syllabus or course assignments
- Previews of course topics
- Summaries of course topics
- Congratulations to students on important accomplishments
- Information on technical difficulties
- Introduction of a guest speaker
- Current events or special-interest facts related to course topics
- News about students in the course

Formatting Announcements

Most effective announcements are concise and can be created in less than a minute or two and read in a few seconds. For subjects requiring more detail, post the information in a longer document in a convenient location in the coursesite, and direct students to it with an announcement. It is a good idea to save announcements if your LMS allows doing so. You may need to document that you in fact posted an announcement affecting grades or student performance such as a revised test date, or a modification or clarification of the requirements for an assignment. Figure 5.1 provides five example announcements.

In addition to posting announcements, most LMSs enable you to send the same email message to every student in your course, much as a listserv does. When using email to send a general announcement, keep the message simple. If details are needed, prepare a document, and attach it to the email or post it to the coursesite, rather than requiring students to read a lengthy email message. Also, realize that unless your course policies require students to read email every day, the information in email messages may not reach its recipients when you want it to.

DOCUMENT DESIGN

In the present context, a document contains information, mostly textual, that will be viewed on a computer. In this section we focus on designing documents for a computer display. It turns out that web design techniques also work well in a traditional print environment.

FIGURE 5.1   Examples of Announcements

Clarify a Course Issue: There seems to be some confusion on how to select the book for the book report that is due on October 25. You may select ANY of the books listed in the course syllabus in the "Recommended Reading List" category. The choice is up to you.

Reminder on Assignment Due Date: Reminder! Assignment 3 is due on November 5 at 11:00 P.M. Eastern Standard Time. I'm looking forward to seeing your excellent work!

Congratulations on Course Milestone: Congratulations students! We have just passed the halfway mark for this semester. I am very pleased with your dedication and your enthusiasm for our course. Please take a moment to complete the survey posted in the Tests & Surveys section of the coursesite marked "Midterm Evaluation." Your feedback will be anonymous and hopefully will help me make the course better for you. Thanks.

News about Students: Congratulations to the former Ms. Marsha Rollins, who is now Mrs. Josh Bennett (Marsha Bennett). Marsha and Josh were married in a hot air balloon last Saturday.

Information on Technical Difficulties: I apologize for the recent difficulties you have had accessing the coursesite. The Information Technology Department assures me that the problem has been resolved. I have extended the deadline date for the completion of Quiz 3 by three days. The new deadline is midnight EST on December 4. To ensure that you know how to access the quiz, please review the detailed login procedures I have posted in the Course Information section. Thank you for your patience.

When they access it from your coursesite, students typically will quickly peruse a document and decide whether to print it based on how easy it is for them to understand what they see on the computer screen. When a document contains line after line of closely interspersed text, it is hard to read on a computer screen. In that case, a hard copy will probably be required. A good online document strives to preclude this eventuality. Ideally, students will be able to make full use of a course document without having to engage in the time-consuming and expensive process of printing it on paper. Of course, lengthy documents, or documents that are continually reused, may well deserve printing. Course notes are a good example. Nevertheless, in most cases your students' time potentially will be wasted if an electronic document is not designed to accommodate the medium—a computer screen—in which they will view it.

The following list cites some of the most important design techniques that facilitate making documents screen-readable. Following the list, a subsection describes each technique individually. As previously indicated, you need not be concerned that good practices for designing documents for the computer screen will prove unsuitable for documents some students may choose to view in print. These design methods also promote readability in printed documents:

- Chunk information.
- Use white space, bulleted lists, and other text attributes.
- Use URL links appropriately.
- Use text links within documents.
- Address user viewing preferences.
- Require standard file formats.

Chunk Information

Chunking text makes it easier for a reader to process information on a computer screen as well as in paper format. In chunking, lines and lines of text are studiously avoided. Information is organized so that the most important ideas are presented first. An overview or "top-level" page allows readers to view the contents of the entire document, then navigate as appropriate to relevant portions of the document for further information. Chunking often involves putting discrete segments of information in separate files that are accessed sequentially from a top-level file, with each file containing no more information than can be viewed on a single computer screen. An alternative method to achieve chunking involves using text links within documents, as described below. Microsoft Word supports chunking using internal hyperlinks.

For most people, reading from a computer screen is not as comfortable as reading printed matter. In fact, most students will not read as much information from their computer screens as they are willing to read from hard copy, in part because access to electronic material is essentially sequential as opposed to random. Consider, for example, the difficulty of comparing two widely separated pages of a book when the book is viewed on a computer screen. In addition, differing screen sizes significantly affect how much information is visible at any one time, potentially requiring students to scroll horizontally or vertically to access what they want to see. This process interrupts information flow for most students and may in fact disturb their thought processes. In short, scrolling is a turnoff for many students and may even cause students to miss important information, simply because it wasn't easy to access. Chunking is a technique that strives to avoid the necessity of scrolling. Note, in particular, that horizontal scrolling ideally should *never* be required.

Use White Space, Bulleted Lists, and
Text Attributes to Simplify Textual Display

The use of ample white space and bulleted lists greatly improves students' ability to process text quickly on their computer screens. Labels and headings that are carefully worded help students identify major topics. Related visual clues such as italics, bolding, and color can be applied for further clarification. Also, font sizes and types—carefully and consistently employed—can assist a reader in distinguishing between major topics and related subtopics. The extensive use of multiple fonts should be avoided.

Use URL Links Appropriately

Because web resources provide valuable reference information, they are frequently cited in course documents. Such a citation typically provides a *URL (uniform resource locater) link* or *web address* that when clicked on will take students directly to the website presenting the reference information. Consider, however, that this common and useful practice has a significant potential drawback: Links often break, change, move, or become outdated. Consequently, they require constant updating and maintenance. In fact, in one recent study of the web links in three courses, one-half of the links were no longer available within 55 months of their initial posting (Kiernan, 2002). Consequently, you should embed in a document only those URL links absolutely needed to support the concept you are addressing.

The effective placement of URL links is also a very important consideration in document design, because students are curious by nature, and many are easily distracted. The blue highlighting that denotes a URL link is often irresistible to students, who, on encountering one, will click on it and visit the related website immediately. This practice disrupts students' concentration and disturbs their processing of the information on the same subject in your own document. It follows that you should place URLs in documents in ways that do not distract students. For example, you may choose to avoid colored or bolded links that draw the reader's eye to them. Some instructors favor placing URL links in a centralized location such as the end of a document section or the end of the entire document. Another option is to place all links in a centralized external links section of the coursesite. In either of these cases, you can insert a symbol such as ▪ into the text to indicate that a relevant link on the subject is available elsewhere in the document or on the coursesite.

Figures 5.2 and 5.3 illustrate contrasting methods of arranging information in a document. In Figure 5.2, URL links are inappropriately placed and the text is difficult to read. Figure 5.3 illustrates the same information displayed using chunking, bulleted lists, and white space to enable students to process information quickly on their computer screens. Also, in Figure 5.3, URL links are positioned to facilitate convenient website access without interrupting the flow of ideas in the text.

Use Text Links within Documents

A *text link* is a mouse-selected *button*—typically a portion of the text itself—that causes a "jump" from one section of a document to a related subsection. In Microsoft Word, a text link is called a *hyperlink*. Such links facilitate accessing a document in a nonsequential fashion. Text links are an excellent time-saving way to organize a lengthy document for screen viewing. For example, you might list the major topics denoting overall organization on an overview screen at the beginning of a document, with associated links from each major topic to the related information in a subsection of the document. When using text links, be sure to

FIGURE 5.2   A Confusing Display of URL Links and Text for Computer Screen Viewing

A Summary of Three Important Pedagogical Works

Various pedagogical theories have been advanced in numerous scholarly works. Three of the most popular are Chickering and Gamson's *Seven Principles for Good Practice in Undergraduate Education* (visit www.msu.edu/user/coddejos/seven.htm); Bloom's *Taxonomy of Intellectual Behavior* (visit www.officeport.com/edu/blooms.htm); and Gagne's *Nine Events of Instruction* (visit http://ide.ed.psu.edu/idde/9events.htm).

The following is a summary of the major elements of each of these three works. The seven principles for Good Practice in Undergraduate Education are good practice encourages contact between students and faculty, good practice develops reciprocity and cooperation among students, good practice uses active learning techniques, good practice gives students prompt feedback, good practice emphasizes time on task, good practice communicates high expectations, and good practice respects diverse talents and ways of learning. Bloom's Taxonomy of Intellectual Behavior includes knowledge, comprehension, application, analysis, synthesis, and evaluation. Gagne's Nine Events are gain attention, inform students of the objectives, use recall, present the material, provide learning guidance, elicit performance, provide feedback, assess performance, and enhance retention and transfer.

FIGURE 5.3   Appropriately Displayed URL Links and Text for Computer Screen Viewing

A Summary of Three Important Pedagogical Works

Various pedagogical theories have been advanced in numerous scholarly works. Three of the most popular are ▪ Chickering and Gamson's *Seven Principles for Good Practice in Undergraduate Education,* ▪ Bloom's *Taxonomy of Intellectual Behavior,* and ▪Gagne's *Nine Events of Instruction.* The following is a summary of the major elements of each of these three works.

1. The Seven Principles for Good Practice in Undergraduate Education are:
   - Good practice encourages contact between students and faculty.
   - Good practice develops reciprocity and cooperation among students.
   - Good practice uses active learning techniques.
   - Good practice gives students prompt feedback.
   - Good practice emphasizes time on task.
   - Good practice communicates high expectations.
   - Good practice respects diverse talents and ways of learning.

2. Bloom's Taxonomy of Intellectual Behavior includes:
   - Knowledge
   - Comprehension
   - Application
   - Analysis
   - Synthesis
   - Evaluation

3. Gagne's Nine Events are:
   - Gain attention.
   - Inform students of the objectives.
   - Use recall.
   - Present the material.
   - Provide learning guidance.
   - Elicit performance.
   - Provide feedback.
   - Assess performance.
   - Enhance retention and transfer.

   - For additional information visit:
     Seven Principles: www.msu.edu/user/coddejos/seven.htm
     Bloom's Taxonomy: www.officeport.com/edu/blooms.htm
     Gagne's Nine Events: http://ide.ed.psu.edu/idde/9events.htm

provide students with an obvious means of returning to the overview screen after a jump to a document subsection has occurred.

Figure 5.4—which depicts the skeleton of an online course syllabus—provides an example of how to use text links in a document. The course syllabus is, of course, one of the most important elearning documents you will prepare, because in essence it is a course handbook. Figure 5.4 can be used as a checklist of information that you might include in your own

FIGURE 5.4   Online Syllabus Homepage

Syllabus Homepage

- **Course Information**
- **Instructor Information**
- **Staff Office Hours/Contact Information**
- **Technical Requirements**
- **Course Topics, Assignments, and Tests**

- **Course Calendar**
- **Grading Criteria**
- **Important Course How Tos**
- **Policies**
- **Student Conduct**

Course Information

Name of Course
Course Number
Term
Course Prerequisites
Revision Date—Last Revision of Course Syllabus
Course Description
Course Objectives
Required Texts and Other Materials

Home

Instructor Information

Instructor's welcome to the course
Instructor bio, picture, and résumé (consider a one-minute audio or video describing yourself)
Instructor contact information (office location, telephone and fax numbers, email address)
Instructor office hours (both virtual and face-to-face hours)

Home

Staff Office Hours and Contact Information

Teaching assistant contact information (location, telephone and fax numbers, email address)
Student assistant contact information (location, telephone and fax numbers, email address)
Help desk contact information (telephone and fax numbers, email address)
Library support contact information (telephone and fax numbers, email address)
Staff office hours and location (both virtual and face-to-face hours, including chat room hours)

Home

Technical Requirements

Technology Prerequisites
Technology Needed to Access Course

Home

Course Topics, Assignments, and Tests

Course Topics
Assignments
Tests

Home

(continued)

FIGURE 5.4 Continued

Course Calendar

> Due Dates—Specific Time-Zone Reference
> Week-by-Week Schedule

Home

Grading Criteria

> Assignments
> Participation in Discussions
> Peer Reviews
> Overall Grade

Home

Important Course How Tos

> Navigate in the LMS and find important course components.
> Take tests online.
> Submit assignments.
> Use the discussion tool.
> Get technical help.
> Express yourself using emoticons.

Home

Policies

> Mandatory Viewing Announcements and Checking Email
> Mandatory File Formats and Virus Free Files
> Copyright Compliance
> Intellectual Property Rights of Instructor
> Student Privacy Rights
> Email Policies and Procedures
> Attendance and Absenteeism
> Discussion Forum Policies
> Group Participation Policies
> Netiquette Policies
> Submitting Assignments
> Attachment Formats
> Getting Instructor Feedback
> Providing Instructor Feedback
> How to Get Technical Help
> How to Get Help with Course Components
> Academic Dishonesty: Cheating, Plagiarism
> Institutional Computer Policies and Computer Ethics
> What You Can Expect from Your Instructor

Home

Student Code of Conduct and Commitment

Home

course syllabus. If the syllabus were complete, some of the items in each subsection would themselves be links to separate documents. When the syllabus file opens on the screen, a top-level portion of the document—or document *homepage*—is visible. This homepage lists the major topics discussed in the syllabus, with a link to associated details for each topic. Note that the example syllabus uses white space appropriately and is consistent in its use of headings and fonts. Such formatting techniques help a student to determine quickly the organization of the syllabus and to navigate quickly to whatever specific information currently is being sought. Because you are viewing the syllabus skeleton in print, you cannot test the functionality of the hyperlinks, which are bolded and underlined while targets of the links are merely bolded. As an example of how the links work, if a student clicks on the words Course Calendar, at the top of the document, the subsection of the document named **Course Calendar** is immediately accessed. Clicking on **Home** in the Course Calendar subsection causes a jump back to the **Syllabus Homepage** target at the top of the syllabus.

Address User Viewing Preferences

A particular text *font* depicts the letters of the alphabet in characteristic shapes. In contrast, a text *attribute* is a property of text such as bolding, italics, underlining, or color. Of course, you choose which text fonts and attributes to use when you create an elearning document. A problem in designing such documents for screen viewing arises because students can customize their web viewing environments with preferred colors and fonts. Consequently, use colors and fonts with discretion to indicate organization in a document intended for screen viewing. It is quite possible they will appear differently on your computer screen than they do on your students' screens, depending on how your students have set their viewing preferences. Note, however, that this problem exists only when document files are saved in HTML format as opposed to a proprietary word processing format, for example, Microsoft Word's *.doc* format. When students view a word processing file on the web, they use the same software you used when you created the document, although embedding of the word processor window in a web browser window sometimes obscures this fact. In this case, font preferences and text attributes embedded in the word processing file override a student's default web viewing preferences. As indicated previously, these circumstances constitute yet another argument for using proprietary word processing software to produce elearning documents.

Require Standard File Formats

As explained in Chapter 4, you should adopt standard file formats to ensure that students will be able to open and view documents and other kinds of course resources. Although any web browser can read HTML files, we have seen that this file format is not as satisfactory for documents as a proprietary word processor format. A drawback of proprietary file formats is that students must have access to the software that handles such formats. However, assuming the cost of software continues to decrease, as it has in the past, this drawback will become less significant.

Summary of Document Design Techniques

Figure 5.5 provides a summary of useful practices for creating documents for web viewing. Some suggestions are more specific than the general information given here. The complex

FIGURE 5.5   Techniques for Designing Documents for Web Viewing

- To help the reader navigate through a lengthy document, include an overview page with text links to subsections.
- Divide lengthy textual information into small chunks.
- Leave ample white space.
- Limit the length of a document section to reduce vertical scrolling.
- Use bulleted lists instead of lengthy text to make important points.
- Use meaningful subheadings.
- Left-justify text.
- Use colors sparingly.
- Avoid using the color blue to emphasize words, because words so emphasized can be confused with hyperlinks.
- Be mindful of viewers with impaired vision:
  - Some color-blind viewers have difficulty distinguishing red from green. Avoid red characters on a green background, and vice versa.
  - Exaggerate color and shade contrast between foreground and background.
  - Avoid using noncontrasting colors adjacent to one another.
  - Use dark colors against light colors.
- Good fonts for web viewing of lengthy documents are Times New Roman and San Serif.
- Good fonts for viewing shorter text such as titles and subtitles are Verdana and Arial.
- Avoid the need for horizontal scrolling. Different screens support different line lengths. Design to the lowest common denominator, 75 to 80 characters.

- Use text attributes sparingly; avoid complex combinations of attributes. Bolding, large type, and italics can be used to emphasize words or phrases.
- Avoid using all capitals. IT CREATES A BLOCKED FORMAT THAT IS HARD TO READ.
- Italics are hard to read. Use italics only to stress single words, foreign phrases or clauses, or words requiring similar emphasis.
- When graphics are used in text, always provide a description so that a blind person using a reader will be able to know what the graphic depicts.
- Ensure copyright is not violated by any information you include in your documents. Seek permission to use anything you didn't author.
- Review URL links often to ensure currency.
- If possible, avoid placing URL links within important text. Instead, for easy reference organize them in a strategic position within the document such as at the end of a section.
- Provide instructions on how to return to the document from a URL or text link.
- Use colors sparingly. They display differently on different monitors and platforms.
- Some font sizes are readable on Windows but not on Macs. Test your documents on both platforms.
- Limit image file size to around 50K to minimize download time.
- Test downloading time on a 56K modem.
- Black text on a white background is the best for printing.
- Consider providing a web version of an HTML document with a link to a print copy.

subject of creating documents and coursesites is not completely addressable in a short discussion. Experience in creating and using documents will ultimately enhance your sense of design significantly. Also, feedback from colleagues and students about the usefulness of your web resources is an extremely important source of information.

DESIGNING PRESENTATION GRAPHICS SLIDE SHOWS

Many instructors rely on computer-generated slides when they conduct lectures and presentations. Several computer programs facilitate creating such slide shows. All fall into the general category of *presentation graphics* software. Because Microsoft PowerPoint is by far the most popular presentation graphics software currently in use, this discussion focuses on PowerPoint presentations.

As previously discussed, presentation graphics slide shows—including of course PowerPoint presentations—are intended to be viewed on a computer monitor or projected onto a display screen that reproduces the image on the monitor. Consequently, it is very important to follow good web-access design practices when creating a PowerPoint presentation. What follows discusses three basic slide show design techniques:

- Ensure brevity in the text appearing on an individual slide (the *six-by-six rule*).
- Use special effects and URL links sparingly.
- Minimize slide presentation file sizes.

Brevity: The Six-by-Six Rule

Many of the document design techniques discussed earlier apply equally well to the design of slide presentations. Slides should be brief and concise. Phrase, clause, or sentence length text should be very limited. Avoid paragraphs entirely. When the entire message will not fit on a single slide, reorganize your ideas to use several sequential slides or—alternately—create and post supplemental documents in the coursesite for students to reference. A good rule of thumb is summed up in the so-called *six-by-six rule:* Limit each slide to six lines of text with a maximum of six words to a line. Following the six-by-six rule ensures ample blank space on each slide to promote readability. Remember, when you are making a presentation, your audience will have to process and digest the information on a slide in real time, while at the same time trying to listen to what you are saying. Overly detailed slides encourage your audience to focus on the slides instead of listening to what you have to say in the presentation you make based on the slides.

An additional argument in favor of brevity is that PowerPoint files have a tendency to become very large in size very quickly. This presents a problem if you expect students to download and read the slides as opposed to viewing the presentation in a classroom where the instructor comments on each slide. Moreover, reading slides online is very different from hearing them explained face-to-face. If your students will view PowerPoint slides online, it is probably a good idea to limit the length of the presentation to however many slides can be read in about 10 to 15 minutes. Use a document and expect students to print it if the information you wish to convey requires treatment at more length than this restriction allows. This is especially important if you expect students to view a slide presentation while they are connected to the Internet with a dialup connection. Depending on the speed of their connection, downloading overly long PowerPoint slide shows can be very slow and frustrating. It is not uncommon for students to abandon entirely their effort to view a show requiring an excessive download time.

Use Special Effects and URL Links Sparingly

As stressed earlier, when presentation slides are crammed full with words and graphics, the resulting clutter distracts the audience from the important message of your presentation. Similarly, special effects such as placing words in motion, or adding sound when a slide changes, break the concentration of some viewers and likewise distract them from the presentation's message. More than a few viewers—the author is one—absolutely abhor the use of such techniques and believe they reflect the impulses of PowerPoint users more interested in the medium than the message. Such users tend to be either novices or naïve techies overly fascinated by technological capabilities devised mainly to sell software to people who like to listen to bells and whistles. In any event, PowerPoint presentations should use special effects with great discretion.

In a like fashion, URL links embedded in PowerPoint slides should be severely limited. As previously indicated in the discussion of documents, many students are unable to resist the temptation to follow a URL link immediately on encountering it. The interruption to their concentration is just as important in viewing a PowerPoint presentation as it is in reading a document. It may, therefore, be a good idea merely to *identify* relevant references in the slide, while putting actual URL *links* in a separate slide at the end of your presentation. Also, URL links should be checked and updated regularly. There are few things more frustrating to a student than following an instructor's recommended link only to find that the website it points to no longer exists.

Control File Sizes to Minimize Download Times

Chapter 4 discussed the problem created when large files download slowly over the Internet, particularly on dialup connections. We have noted that slide presentation files are often very large and hence download very slowly when accessed on the web. Consequently, you should take steps to limit PowerPoint file sizes and minimize download times, especially if you are planning to distribute your slide shows as email attachments. It is not uncommon for Power-Point files with numerous graphics to exceed the attachment size limit of many email programs. One method to reduce file size is to use Adobe software to convert a PowerPoint file to PDF format. Another is to save your presentation as an HTML file. The PowerPoint software directly supports this capability and creates a copy of the presentation that allows students to download and read slides one by one, rather than having to download an entire presentation before the first slide can be viewed. Another method is to use software specifically designed to reduce PowerPoint file sizes such as Presentation Pro PowerCONVERTER or Impatica, discussed in Chapter 4.

Summary of Slide Show Design Techniques

Figure 5.6 is a summary checklist of some of the major design techniques to ensure that students will be able to access and view PowerPoint presentations effectively. As in the summary of techniques for designing documents, the following list includes specific recommendations not necessarily addressed in the discussion of PowerPoint design just presented.

AN OVERVIEW OF MULTIMEDIA

Using multimedia resources in elearning can dramatically improve student responses to your course. As explained earlier, our definition of *multimedia* includes still pictures, moving pictures, and sound. Still pictures are images of various kinds—photographs, drawings, graphs, bar charts, pie charts, and so forth. Including images in elearning resources can improve stu-

FIGURE 5.6   Techniques for Designing PowerPoint Presentations

- Use bulleted lists instead of paragraphs.
- Avoid lengthy text. Instead, create separate supporting documents as necessary.
- Limit slide text to six lines with six words to a line (apply the six-by-six rule).
- Use ample blank space.
- Use colors appropriately.
- Use web links for emphasis, but ensure they do not distract audience concentration.
- Keep web links current.
- Use animations and special effects sparingly.
- Limit presentation lengths to 10 to 15 minutes when students must view them via the web.

- Use images and graphics sparingly.
- Keep graphics file sizes to less than 50K.
- Test the downloading time for the presentation on a 56K modem.
- Test the view of the presentation on different browsers.
- Consider posting PowerPoint files in HTML or PDF format to reduce download time.
- Consider using software specifically designed to reduce PowerPoint file size.

dents' understanding of information, especially for visual learners. Adding sound and video can make otherwise pedestrian information "come alive," particularly for auditory learners. Animations and simulations provide interactive learning opportunities that are especially important for tactile learners.

When you plan how you will integrate multimedia resources into your elearning environment, you must be aware of certain associated obstacles. Depending on the level of sophistication of the multimedia resources you want to use, creating them may require the assistance of trained multimedia personnel and the use of special technology. Also, students may need high-end computing equipment and browser plug-ins to view multimedia resources, and these needs must be addressed *before* students are expected to access the multimedia resources you use in your course. What follows provides a brief overview of multimedia resources and supplies tips on how to acquire them. It also defines common multimedia terms and processes. Chapter 7 contains additional information about multimedia and identifies a number of free web-based resources to help you integrate multimedia materials and activities into your elearning environment. Figure 4.12 in Chapter 4 identifies common multimedia file formats.

Images

As already explained, images—sometimes called *graphical images*—include elearning resources such as photographs, charts, graphs, drawings, and clipart. We will discuss various ways of obtaining images for use in elearning resources and explain the three common image file formats you are likely to encounter in preparing these resources.

Obtaining Images.   Images are easily obtained and integrated into elearning modules. For example, files of photographs taken with digital cameras can be inserted directly into course materials. The series of photographs in Figure 5.7 were produced with such a camera. Note that the photographs are displayed in a *thumbnail* configuration for easy access. A thumbnail photo loads quickly because its image size is small. Use of thumbnails represents a fast

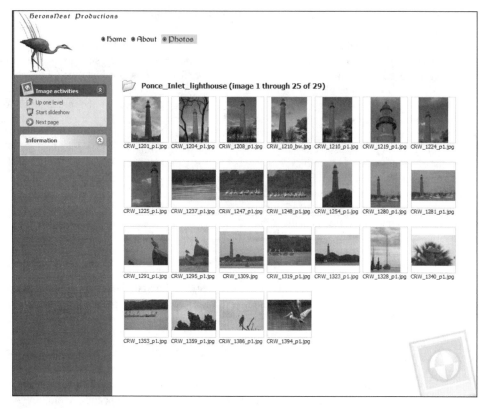

FIGURE 5.7 Thumbnail Display of Photographs Taken with a Digital Camera by Daryl LaBello

Used with permission.

way to display several related photos. Viewers then have the option of clicking on any specific thumbnail to display the same photograph in a larger image size.

In addition to digital cameras, there are many other ways to obtain images. Popular software programs such as Excel and PowerPoint can easily convert graphical data to charts and graphs. In addition, even if you are not artistically inclined, you can use any one of a number of drawing programs to create illustrations, for example, Adobe Elements. You can also obtain clipart by subscribing to a clipart service. Alternately, you may access one of the numerous free clipart services. The URL References at the end of this chapter provide additional information on accessing clipart.

Another way to obtain images is to copy them from existing websites, providing you do not violate the owner's copyright. The process is a simple one. When you find an image on the web that you want to save, place the cursor on the image and click the right mouse button. From the pop-up menu that appears, you can request to save a copy of the image on any one of your computer's mass storage devices, for example, on the hard disk, on a CD, a DVD, or on a zip disk. This works because to view the web image in the first place, it had to be resident in the main memory of your computer. If your course materials use an image copied from the web, you must determine whether the image is covered under fair use guidelines. If not, you must obtain permission to use it in order to avoid violating copyright laws. Also, as a courtesy, always include a credit line indicating the author of the work. Adhering to copyright laws is very important. Fair use guidelines and other copyright issues are addressed in more detail in Chapter 9.

Yet another popular way to obtain digital images is by *scanning* them from an existing image. For example, images currently displayed on paper, such as photographs, or pictures printed in a magazine or book, can be easily scanned. Scanners use a light-sensing device to turn analog images into digital format. Any object that can be placed on the bed of the scanner can be converted to digital format, but it certainly helps if the object is two-dimensional, that is, flat. Three-dimensional scanners do exist but are very expensive and are currently not available to most PC users. The *resolution* (dots per inch) you choose when you scan an image will profoundly affect the size of the image file you produce. High resolution means higher-quality images and correspondingly large file sizes. A scanned image is subject to the same copyright laws governing any other image. If it is not covered under fair use guidelines, you must obtain permission before you integrate it into your course materials, and of course, you should always identify the source of any image you use.

Image File Formats.   An understanding of common image file formats is very important when integrating multimedia resources into course materials. Three common graphics formats are JPEG, GIF, and TIFF. *JPEG* (pronounced *jay-peg*) is an acronym for Joint Photographic Expert Group. The JPEG format is commonly used for images with colors or gray tones. GIF (pronounced like *gift* without the *t*) is an acronym for Graphic-Interchange File Format. This format is often used for line drawings and similar black-and-white diagrams. Typically, saving an image in GIF format will result in a much smaller file than will saving it in JPEG files. However, the quality of a GIF image may not be as high as the quality of a corresponding JPEG image. When images of the highest quality are required—as, for example, in providing electronic images for print publications—the TIFF (rhymes with *GIF*) format is sometimes chosen. *TIFF* is an acronym for Tagged Image File Format. Whereas both JPEG and GIF use *image compression* to reduce file size, the TIFF format separately records the color and related attributes of every pixel (picture element) in the image. Image compression in general has the potential to compromise image quality slightly to obtain smaller image files. As a consequence, a TIFF image is generally of higher quality than a corresponding JPEG or GIF image. However, the very large file associated with a high image quality assures that most TIFF images are not suitable for downloading on the web, unless a very high-speed Internet connection is available.

Animations

Animations can be a very effective way to explain a concept, especially if the concept involves motion. Figure 5.8 depicts an individual frame from a simple animation explaining seasonal temperature variations in an introductory meteorology course. Successive frames in the animation were created using Macromedia Flash software, an easy-to-use animation program. One benefit of Flash is that it typically produces animations with small file sizes. Other ways to create animations include animated GIF files and Macromedia Shockwave animations.

In addition to creating animations, you can buy them from any one of a number of animation services. Moreover, sometimes you can use animations created by others free of

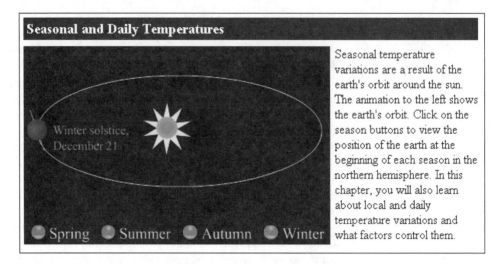

FIGURE 5.8   Seasonal Temperature Animation Frames Created Using Macromedia Flash

Compliments of the Educational Technology Department Embry-Riddle Aeronautical University, used with permission.

charge. Educational animations exist at many websites to which you can direct your students. An example is the website maintained by the ▪National Institute of Standards and Technology. This site provides numerous animations to illustrate the principles of physics and fluid dynamics, for example, those to predict the motion of fires, among other topics (Read, 2002a). Figure 5.9 depicts animations of a townhouse kitchen fire provided at the Institute's Building and Fire Research Laboratory website.

Audio and Video

Audio and video are perhaps the two most important features of multimedia. However, creating audio and video elearning resources is a very time-consuming effort. Thus one needs to weigh the benefits to students of such resources against the time and expense required to produce them. If you do create such resources, be aware of one complaint often reported by students watching a video in which only the speaker's head is shown. After a few minutes, students become extremely bored with the video. This phenomenon has become known as the "talking head" syndrome. Ultimately one must ask whether a talking head reciting text is a more effective approach to learning than simply recording the text in a well-made document and posting it to your course site or simply using an audio file.

Another disadvantage of multimedia audio and video is that file size for these resources is usually *very* large, so that download time becomes a significant problem. Consequently, many instructors prefer to use short audio and video clips. The following are examples of how short clips can be used effectively.

- Introduce the instructor of the course, a guest speaker, or key points in a new topic.
- Summarize key points.

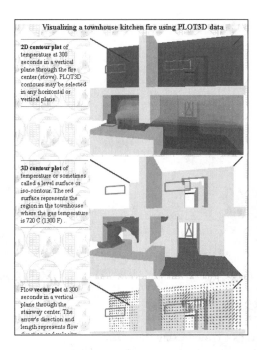

FIGURE 5.9 National Institute of Standards and Technology Website's Building and Fire Research Laboratory Animation of a Townhouse Fire

- Hear or see highlights of a guest speaker's presentation.
- Enhance course materials in music courses.
- Teach pronunciation in a foreign language course.
- Demonstrate hazardous processes and procedures, for example, firefighting methods and techniques.
- Capture activities that are physically inaccessible to students, for example, expeditions and field trips to remote locations.
- Re-create real-life situations, either through role playing or by capturing actual events.
- Hear from acknowledged experts who make brief comments or express opinions relevant to topics covered in the course.
- Clarify abstract concepts insensible to human perception, for example, the propagation of sound waves or the mechanics of nuclear fusion or fission.

Computer programs such as ▪RoboDemo, which can capture computer screen motion and sound, provide an easy means of creating video-like tutorials for online delivery. Figure 5.10 illustrates a tutorial created for the Embry-Riddle Aeronautical University (ERAU) faculty on how to use a feature of the Blackboard LMS. Note the associated narration that is indicated in the overlaid text box. These tutorials are posted on the web for convenient access by ERAU faculty.

Dealing with Large Audio and Video Files

In this subsection we identify two solutions to the problem of long download times associated with large multimedia audio and video files. One is to use *file streaming,* also referred to as *streaming media.* The other is to distribute large multimedia files on disk.

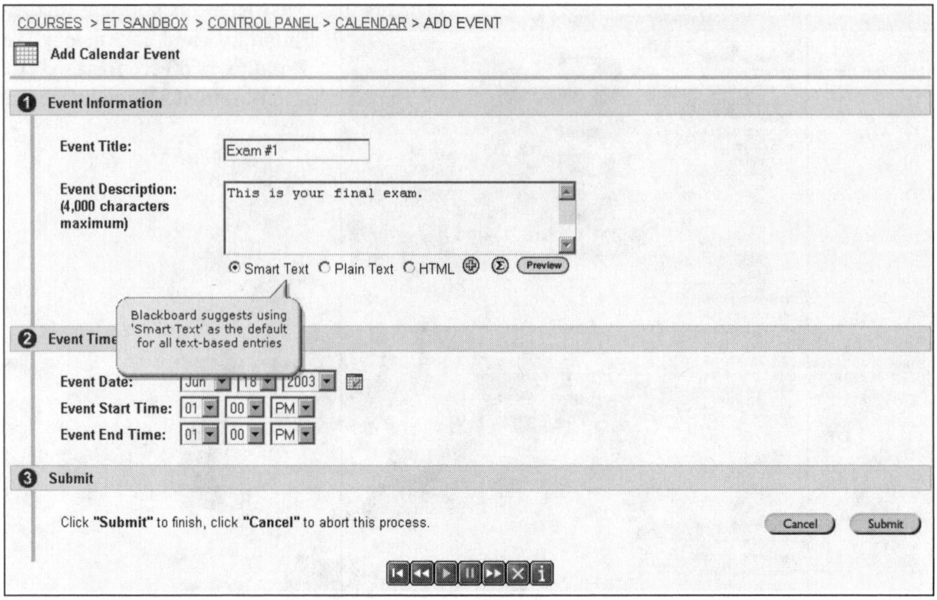

COURSES > ET SANDBOX > CONTROL PANEL > CALENDAR > ADD EVENT

Add Calendar Event

❶ Event Information

Event Title: [Exam #1]

Event Description: This is your final exam.
(4,000 characters
maximum)

○ Smart Text ○ Plain Text ○ HTML Preview

Blackboard suggests using 'Smart Text' as the default for all text-based entries

❷ Event Time

Event Date: Jun / 18 / 2003

Event Start Time: 01 : 00 PM

Event End Time: 01 : 00 PM

❸ Submit

Click **"Submit"** to finish, click **"Cancel"** to abort this process.   Cancel   Submit

FIGURE 5.10   Blackboard Tutorials Created Using RoboDemo

File Size verus Download Time.   File size is an especially important consideration when you use multimedia resources, because multimedia files tend to be very large files and—we have seen—are slow to download. *Bandwidth* is the speed at which information can be sent and received using the Internet. The bandwidth of students' Internet connections is what determines how quickly or slowly they can access elearning files. It is very important that you test downloading speeds of files that contain multimedia resources before requiring your students to view them. Even though some students will have high-speed Internet connections at home, many do not. Thus, it is best to test for the lowest speed Internet connections. As previously mentioned, download time as a function of file size is presented in Figure 4.13 in Chapter 4.

Streaming Media.   To alleviate the lengthy download time required for audio and video files, *streaming media* technology has been devised. The technology uses a process called *file streaming*. Streamed files are stored on a special streaming web server that enables a student to begin viewing or hearing a long video or audio file within a few seconds of requesting it. File data are sent to the requester in a continuous stream. As the first—or current—portion of the data is being played, the succeeding part is silently being accessed in the background. Only a small portion of the entire file—perhaps about 30 seconds' worth—actually resides on a student's computer at any one time. Once that segment of the data has been processed, it is discarded and replaced by more current data. A plug-in is needed to play streamed audio and video. Currently the RealOne Player, available free of charge from RealNetworks, seems to be the *de facto* standard software, although Microsoft might argue that the Microsoft Media Player is used equally often. On Internet connections with a modem, an audio or video stream is sometimes interrupted by slow data transmission. When this happens, the audio or video stops playing until the data stream's steady flow can be restored.

Popular applications of file streaming include the live broadcasting of institutional sporting events such as basketball games and football games. Live lectures and radio program broadcasts are other examples. One example of streaming media is a website illustrated in Figure 5.11 established by Bard College to broadcast the Slobodan Milosevic trials (Carlson, 2002a). Milosevic, of course, is the former Yugoslavian president who was accused of using torture and genocide in an attempt to create an ethnically pure Serbian nation. Through streaming media technology, this Bard College website was able to provide those interested in the trial the opportunity to watch its proceedings as they were being conducted (▪Bard College Slobodan Milosevic Trials). It also resulted in an archive of previous trial proceedings accessible through file streaming.

Incorporating streamed media into your course website requires special technology to create and stream audio and video files. You will probably need to invoke the assistance of technology specialists to achieve your goal. Check with your Information Technology Department, Media Services, Web Services, or other similar department to determine whether your institution supports streaming audio and video.

Distributing Files on CDs and DVDs.   Distributing multimedia files on CDs or DVDs is an alternative to posting them in a coursesite or placing them on a streaming server. For example, when sailors stationed aboard ship wanted to take an online biology course offered through the Navy College Program for Afloat College Education, their inability to access the web while underway had to be addressed. The course facilitator solved the problem by

FIGURE 5.11   Milosevic Trial Public Archive

Bard College/International Center for Transitional Justice, used with permission.

distributing the course web-based materials to students on a CD before the course began (Read, 2002c). A related example is the information available on the CD ▪*Electronic Beowulf.* This CD contains multimedia files that allow scholars to study manuscripts of the Old English alliterative epic *Beowulf,* the oldest known poem in the English language. The original manuscripts of *Beowulf* can be seen only at the British Library in London (Ludwig, 2001a). These manuscripts are over a thousand years old and far too valuable to allow the general public access to them.

REFERENCES

Bacro, T. R. (2002, September/October). Using a course management system and web-friendly multimedia to enhance an anatomy course. *The Technology Source.* Retrieved November 20, 2003, from http://ts.mivu.org/default.asp?show=article&id=977

Basden, J. C. (2001, November). Authentic tasks as the basis for multimedia design curriculum. *T.H.E. Journal, 29*(4), 16–21.

Carlson, S. (2002a, March 22). A Bard College web site streams and archives video of Milosevic trial. *The Chronicle of Higher Education.* Retrieved March 22, 2002, from http://chronicle.com/free/2002/03/200203220lt.htm

Carlson, S. (2002b, May 21). A professor finds that even statistics can be palatable via distance education. *The Chronicle of Higher Education.* Retrieved May 21, 2002, from http://chronicle.com/free/2002/05/20020521u.htm

Carmean, C., & Haefner, J. (2002, November/December). Mind over matter: Transforming course management systems into effective learning environments. *EDUCAUSE Review, 37*(6), 27–34.

Daugherty, H., Cohn, J., & Gorry, G. A. (2003). The EduPop: Improving streaming video for an electronic community. *EDUCAUSE Quarterly, 26*(4), 43–48.

Hanss, T. (2001, May/June). Digital video: Internet2 killer app or Dilbert's nightmare? *EDUCAUSE Review, 36*(3), 16–25.

Heid, J. (2000, April 10). How it works: Streaming audio. *PC World.* Retrieved September 23, 2002, from www.pcworld.com/howto/article/0,aid,16060,00.asp

Kiernan, V. (2002, April 10). Nebraska researchers measure the extent of "link rot" in distance education. *The Chronicle of Higher Education.* Retrieved April 10, 2002, from http://chronicle.com/free/2002/04/2002041001u.htm

Kovacs, P., Lincecum, L., & Rowell, R. (2001, December). Evolution of a digital production studio. *T.H.E. Journal, 29*(5), 31–34.

Ludwig, J. (2001a, January 11). A digitized "Beowulf" offers scholars new ways to study the manuscript. *The Chronicle of Higher Education.* Retrieved January 11, 2001, from http://chronicle.com/free/2001/01/2001011101.htm

Ludwig, J. (2001b, May 4). A geology class combines online demonstrations with field trips. *The Chronicle of Higher Education.* Retrieved May 4, 2001, from http://chronicle.com/free/2001/05/2001050401u.htm

Lynch, P. J., & Horton, S. (1999). *Web style guide.* New Haven, CT: Yale University Press.

Mangan, K. S. (2002, May 7). Online tool helps surgery residents find information and practice procedures. *The Chronicle of Higher Education.* Retrieved May 7, 2002, from http://chronicle.com/free/2002/05/2002050701t.htm

McKenzie, J. (2000, September). Scoring power points. *From Now On.* Retrieved July 17, 2003, from www.fno.org/sept00/powerpoints.html

Nielsen, J., & Tahir, M. (2002). *Homepage usability: 50 websites deconstructed.* Indianapolis, IN: New Riders Publishing.

Online hitchhiker's guide to American history [Editorial]. (2002, October). *Syllabus, 14*(3), 46.

Read, B. (2002a, March 13). In a TV studio and at a distance, students use computer models to study the dynamics of fire. *The Chronicle of Higher Education.* Retrieved March 13, 2002, from http://chronicle.com/free/2002/03/2002031301u.htm

Read, B. (2002b, April 22). A collection of virus images anchors an online guide to virology resources. *The Chronicle of Higher Education.* Retrieved April 22, 2002, from http://chronicle.com/free/2002/04/2002042201t.htm

Read, B. (2002c, May 13). Students in the U.S. Navy study general biology while at sea. *The Chronicle of Higher Education.* Retrieved May 13, 2002, from http://chronicle.com/free/2002/05/2002051301u.htm

Read, B. (2002d, May 31). An online course tracks Lewis and Clark's footsteps and their scientific contributions. *The Chronicle of Higher Education.* Retrieved May 31, 2002, from http://chronicle.com/free/2002/05/2002053101u.htm

Reed, R. (2003, February). Streaming technology improves student achievement. *T.H.E. Journal.* Retrieved May 1, 2003, from www.thejournal.com/magazine/vault/articleprintversion.cfm?aid=4320

Richards, S. L. F. (2003, July/August). The interactive syllabus: A resource-based, constructivist approach to learning. *Technology Source.* Retrieved July 17, 2003, from http://ts.mivu.org/default.asp?show=article&id=1017

Roberts, S. (2003, August). Campus communications & the wisdom of blogging. *Syllabus, 17*(1), 22–25.

William, R., & Tollett, J. (2000). *The non-designer's web book.* Berkeley, CA: Peachpit Press.

Winograd, K. (2002, June/July). For the love of art: Technology, trepidation and time. *Converge, 5*(3), 13–16.

URL REFERENCES

Animation Factory: www.animfactory.com

Artbeats: www.artbeats.com

Audio On Demand, the World Radio Network: www.wrn.org/ondemand

Bard College Slobodan Milosevic Trials: http://hague.bard.edu/video.html

Bellsnwhistles.com: www.bellsnwhistles.com

Boxes and Arrows—Information Architecture: www.boxesandarrows.com/about

Chin's Optimizing PowerPoint Presentations for the World Wide Web: www2.kumc.edu/ir/brownbag/PowerPoint

Clipart.com: www.clipart.com

Electronic Beowulf: www.uky.edu/AS/English/Beowulf/eBeowulf/main.htm

FlixDisc: www.flixdisc.com

Fulton's Scanning Tips: www.scantips.com

Guidelines on preparing documents for electronic distribution and printing: www.ust.hk/itsc/printing/preparing/GuidelinesOnPreparingDocs.html

Kodak Picture CD: www.kodak.com/global/en/consumer/products/pictureCD

Lifeart.com: www.lifeart.com

Lighthouse International: www.lighthouse.org/color_contrast.htm

Map Resources: www.mapresources.com

Media Tracks: www.media-tracks.com

The Music Bakery: www.musicbakery.com/Start01.htm

National Geographic Society—MapMachine: http://plasma.nationalgeographic.com/mapmachine

National Institute of Standards and Technology—Building and Fire Research Laboratory: http://fire.nist.gov/fds

National Transportation and Safety Board: www.ntsb.gov

Network Music: www.networkmusic.com/webaudio/pres_frames.html

Ofoto.com: www.ofoto.com

Punchstock: www.pubtool.com

Q-MUSIC: www.q-music.co.uk

RoboDemo: www.ehelp.com/products/robodemo

Royalty Free Music: www.royaltyfree.com

ScanDoc: www.scandoc.com

Scannability and Readability of Information on the Web: www.useit.com

Sercomm Download Calculator: www.sercomm.net/download.htm

Shockwave-Sound: http://shockwave-sound.com

Snapfish: www.snapfish.com

Web Style Guide: www.webstyleguide.com

What You Need to Know About Animation: http://animation.about.com

CHAPTER SIX

TWO-WAY COMMUNICATION: ELECTRONIC DISCUSSIONS

As defined in Chapter 4, in two-way communication students and instructors both send and receive messages. A *discussion* is the most common kind of two-way communication used in elearning. In the present context, a discussion occurs when students communicate with each other—and/or with their instructor—about a *specified* subject. Before the widespread use of desktop computers, such communications typically required a face-to-face meeting or some other synchronous activity such as a videoconference or a conference telephone call. In addition, asynchronous forms of discussion also exist, for example, the exchange of paper letters. However, before the advent of personal computers, discussions—synchronous or asynchronous—required expensive equipment and/or travel or alternately consumed much time in the exchange of paper documents. Today, by contrast, computers facilitate asynchronous as well as synchronous discussions with great ease and effect. In electronic discussions, students can engage each other in interactive learning without having to spend time traveling to and from meeting places in the physical world. Instead, they meet in the "timeless" virtual world of the Internet. In this chapter, we explain how to use the two common forms of electronic discussions supported by most LMSs: *forums* and *chats*. Elearning forums are ordinarily—although not necessarily—asynchronous, while chats are synchronous. Forums are useful for provoking critical thinking and creating a sense of community in groups of substantial size. Chats can also promote a sense of community but in large groups tend to dissolve into chaos. What follows on the subject of electronic discussions—discussions for short—is divided into three sections. The first provides an overview of discussions. The second explains how to plan and administer forums and chats. The third section gives some example topics for electronic discussions.

OVERVIEW OF ELECTRONIC DISCUSSIONS

Electronic discussions are one of the most powerful components of elearning, especially when they are designed to promote critical thinking, active learning, and the higher levels of Bloom's Taxonomy, as discussed in Chapter 2. Most instructors experienced in elearning would agree that online discussions are one of the easiest elearning activities to implement, yet produce one of the largest gains in critical thinking. An added bonus of electronic forums is that they improve a student's communication skills and ability to interact gracefully in a group. We first introduce and define terms relevant to discussions. Next, we describe advantages and then disadvantages of discussions. Finally, we discuss netiquette, emoticons, and acronyms used in electronic communication.

Types of Discussions

We will briefly describe two common forms of electronic discussions: forums and chats. Forums and chats are invariably supported by LMS software.

Forums.   A *forum* is an asynchronous electronic discussion on a specified topic. The term derives of course from the Latin word *forum,* which denotes the public square or marketplace of an ancient Roman city, where citizens often gathered to discuss topics of general interest. Because electronic forums are asynchronous, students—unlike the citizens of Rome—can participate at a time and location of their own choosing. A forum *topic* is the main topic of a discussion; in essence, it is the starting point of a forum. Forum *threads* are the online entries made by students, that is, student *responses* to the forum. Sometimes the term *thread* denotes an entry that introduces a new but related topic into a forum. A forum has a *facilitator*—sometimes referred to as a *moderator*—who reviews the threads and consults with the students who posted them as necessary to ensure that entries remain on topic. The facilitator is also responsible for ensuring that forum participants observe appropriate *netiquette,* as defined later, as well as course discussion policy.

In Chapter 4, Figure 4.7 illustrated a list of forum topics that had been set up in a coursesite. Note that when these topics were created, the LMS button selected to initiate a topic entry was labeled *Forum.* When students wish to contribute to a discussion forum, they need only click on the forum topic itself to activate a text box in which a response may be typed, as illustrated in Figure 6.1. This act is known as *posting* a thread in the discussion. Figure 6.2 depicts threads posted by several students. The verb *post* describes the act of posting—or entering—a thread. Threads can be posted in reply to the forum topic itself or as responses to existing threads entered by other participants in the forum.

Chats.   A *chat* is a synchronous electronic discussion. Like a forum, a chat has a *topic,* and as in a forum, students *post entries* in a chat. However, the entries in a chat are not called threads. All students must participate in a chat session at the same time, but not of course at the same location. Because it is synchronous, such an activity is also known as a *real-time chat.* As was illustrated in Chapter 4 in Figure 4.8, when students post chat entries—questions or comments—the text shows up next to their names. Every participant in a chat can see every other participant's entries. Like a forum, a real-time chat has a *facilitator,* sometimes called a *moderator.* One primary responsibility of the moderator is controlling who currently "has the floor," that is, who is authorized to post the next entry. Entries in chats ordinarily cannot be posted simultaneously; and even if your LMS software supports posting simultaneous entries, this practice can easily result in confusion. Unlike forum threads, chat entries do not endure beyond the end of a chat session, unless an archive procedure is invoked by the moderator before the chat session ends. As explained in Chapter 4, your LMS will likely provide a whiteboard that can dramatically increase a chat's communication power.

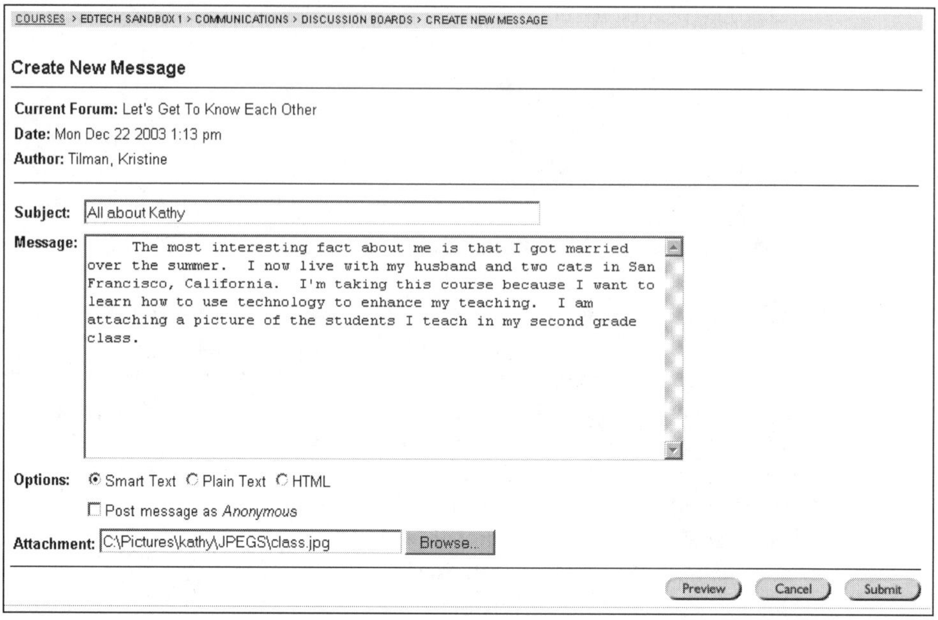

FIGURE 6.1   **A Discussion Reply Box in Blackboard**

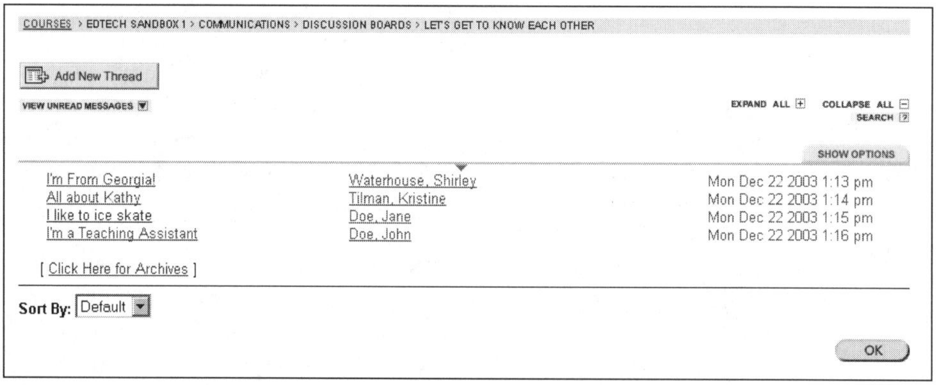

FIGURE 6.2   **Threads in a Discussion in Blackboard**

Benefits of Discussions

Electronic discussions create a student-centered, active learning environment where students frequently interact with their instructor and with each other. What follows identifies and discusses four distinct benefits of using discussions in an elearning course:

- Support convenient communication
- Encourage thoughtful responses

- Build community
- Create a permanent record of student responses

Support Convenient Communication.   One of the most important advantages of an electronic discussion is that it is conducted at the convenience of students. It allows distance learners to interact with their instructor and peers in a manner entirely impossible in a traditional educational environment. Adult learners with job and family responsibilities report that being able to engage in electronic discussions is extremely convenient, as compared to attending physical discussion groups. Students can participate in a forum by connecting to the Internet anytime anyplace. By contrast, a chat—which is synchronous—may be entered from any convenient location but does require time coordination.

A related phenomenon is that many students become more active course participants because of electronic discussions. Such students somehow feel freer and less inhibited in electronic discussions than they do in face-to-face discussions. Very reserved students, for example, will sometimes participate in an electronic discussion whereas in a conventional class discussion they would contribute little or nothing. This is truer of forums than chats, because a forum more than a chat allows participants to compose and edit their contributions before submitting them, thus negating the fear so common in conventional conversation that one will open his or her mouth and blurt out an inanity. Also, forums can be set up in a way that makes it possible for students to post responses anonymously for discussions of sensitive and controversial topics.

It is well documented that student interaction increases when electronic discussions are used. It follows that discussions enhance students' ability to learn from one another. Discussions also help students develop good communications skills, which are invaluable in the workplace.

Encourage Thoughtful Responses.   When participating in an electronic discussion, students often take more pride in their writing than they would when writing for a print environment. They exercise more initiative in word choice and in correcting grammar and punctuation (Lang, 2000). Electronic discussions also motivate students to think critically. Because replies in forums to the remarks of others do not have to be spontaneous, students can take as much time as they desire to phrase their contributions precisely, leading to more thoughtful responses. A related feature seems likewise to inspire students to write well in discussions: Their opinions become public *in writing* to their classmates and may also be archived and referenced by future students and instructors. Forums are usually archived automatically, whereas archiving chats requires special LMS-dependent procedures. If you reuse archives of electronic discussion responses, privacy right considerations mandate that you obtain your students' permission to do so. Student privacy rights are addressed in Chapter 9.

Build Community.   An electronic discussion helps an instructor overcome obstacles inherent in face-to-face discussions. We have already noted, for example, that reserved students may feel more comfortable speaking online than in class. Moreover, electronic discussions are gender, age, race, and disability neutral in the sense that such characteristics are not easily detected in an online environment. Another characteristic of online discussions is that they tend to be more detailed and involved than conversations in a classroom, which are always so severely time constrained. In fact, the limited time available in a conventional classroom environment often makes it difficult for students to get to know each other.

By contrast, students often report that electronic discussions facilitate their becoming acquainted with each other to a degree uncommon in a traditional educational environment. This fact—surprising at first—seems predictable, however, after considering how much easier it is to conduct a conversation at the time and/or place of one's choosing than to meet face-to-face. If you doubt this assertion, ask yourself how much time you spend on the telephone or using email with your friends, as opposed to actually meeting with them in person. In any event, students for whatever reason seem more willing to devote time to peer communications in an electronic environment than in a conventional educational environment. The result is that students participating in electronic discussion build a sense of community. In such online communities, they learn to collaborate and to work with each other. Through collaboration, they develop valuable interaction skills—for example, respecting each other's opinions and giving and receiving criticism—that will favorably affect their lifelong behavior in the workplace (Batane, 2002).

Create a Permanent Record of Student Responses. Electronic files on the Internet server hosting your elearning course preserve permanent records of forum responses contributed by your students. Such records of course are necessary to facilitate the asynchronous communication characterizing forums. However, they have two other important uses. First, a systematic review of student responses can help you detect course problems and take remedial action. For example, if you didn't get the type or quality of discussion responses you were expecting, it may be because the topic was not properly stated. Student comments allow you to determine how the discussion topic can be revised to help students address the topic more thoroughly the next time you use it. They can also reveal areas in which course materials supporting the electronic discussion need modification. A second and related use for response records is that they can be used to verify and substantiate a student's performances in discussions. This is especially important if you are grading discussion participation.

Disadvantages of Discussions

Though they provide many educational benefits, discussions are not without drawbacks. What follows identifies some disadvantages of forums and chats.

Lack of Human Contact. Students participating in electronic discussions must forego the pleasures of intimate face-to-face human contact. However, as we have seen, electronic discussions seem to increase students' motivation to participate in two-way communication with their peers.

Time Requirement. Discussions require both instructors and students to devote time to participating in them. This includes the time to prepare responses and the time to post them. In this respect, chats impose more taxing requirements than forums, because being synchronous they require students to be available to participate at a specified time. If students are geographically disbursed, time zones can be a problem in chats, especially if a student on the West Coast of the United States has to be available at 6:00 A.M. for a discussion that starts at 9:00 A.M. on the East Coast. Carefully think through the best time to conduct chats with the least amount of inconvenience to all. Of course, conversations of any kind—synchronous or asynchronous—are time-consuming, but if discussion topics are interesting, the perceived time requirement drawback is minimized.

Students with Poor Attitudes.   Students occasionally exhibit dominating and controlling behaviors in electronic discussions, behaviors they would hesitate to display in face-to face meetings. Negative comments made by students with poor attitudes can dampen the enthusiasm of other students. Establish course policies that clearly state acceptable and unacceptable behavior and the penalties for violations. Be prepared to eject students who violate discussion policy from the discussions. Chapters 9 and 10 have more information on this subject.

Students with Poor Writing, Spelling, and/or Typing Skills.   Students with poor writing and spelling skills are often very uncomfortable in discussions. For example, international students may have difficulty expressing themselves in a second language. This problem is more pronounced in chats than in forums, because responses in chats must be made in real time. In addition, discussion participants with poor typing skills are at a disadvantage in chats, not to mention the frustration of chat participants waiting and watching while comments are slowly typed. Acronyms—to be discussed later in this chapter—can be used to expedite comment entry in discussions.

Fear of Public Writing.   There exist students who exhibit a significant fear of "public writing." Some of these students lack good written communications skills, but there are many other reasons for their lack of confidence in their written expression. Whatever the cause of their fear, students who shy away from discussions tend to prefer oral to written communication, because people generally find awkward or lack of clarity in expression far more acceptable in speech than in writing. When presented with an electronic discussion assignment, some shy students may become embarrassed and frustrated, and may even refuse to participate. Chats are especially problematic for such students, because they must enter their comments in a live setting. Often they perform better in a forum, because they have time to think about their responses before making them. Posting chat topics ahead of time and allowing students to bring electronic notes to the chat session is especially helpful for shy students.

Number of Participants.   Discussions of any kind become troublesome as the number of participants increases. Chats are particularly difficult to manage when many people become involved. If feasible, the number of participants in a chat should not exceed three to seven. This ensures that the discussion is more likely to stay focused and coherent. If more than seven participants need to discuss a topic, use a forum instead of chat.

Facilitator Frustration.   Facilitators are required for both forums and chats, and the responsibilities of the facilitator can lead to frustration. Chats are particularly difficult to facilitate, because coordinating chats involves rapidly scanning the many comments, keeping up with fast typists, overcoming obstacles created by slow typists, and staying alert to provide the floor to students or to eject students when necessary. The best way to overcome this frustration is to practice using the technology as often as is necessary to become comfortable.

Technical Difficulties.   Technical difficulties cause problems when students can't enter a discussion or when technical problems require that a discussion be canceled. Test out the technology well ahead of chat time, and create backup plans well ahead of discussion time, just in case the technology malfunctions.

Netiquette, Emoticons, and Acronyms

Netiquette—a term commonly associated with two-way computer communications—is simply etiquette for the Net. Just as etiquette provides guidelines for acceptable behavior in our face-to-face interactions with others, netiquette provides guidelines about what is acceptable behavior in electronic discussions and similar communication transactions, for example, email. Figure 6.3 provides a few example netiquette guidelines. The URL References at the end of the chapter provide additional references on netiquette.

Emoticons are symbols used to convey emotions in online communications. Some of the most common emoticons express sadness, humor, smiles, frowns, winks, and other common expressions of emotion. Of course, it would be better if students learned to write well enough to express their emotions verbally in online communications, but because it is so difficult to relay body language and visual cues when students are not in face-to-face discussions, the use of appropriate emoticons has some merit. Also, brevity is sometimes called for in electronic communications, and emoticons do in fact provide shortcuts for communicating emotions. Give careful thought to the emoticons that are appropriate for your course, and be sure to show your students how to use them to avoid creating unintended negative reactions (Liu & Ginther, 2001). Figure 6.4 depicts some of the most common emoticons and their meanings.

Related to emoticons are the *acronyms* used in online communication. Of course, an acronym is simply an abbreviation for a phrase or clause. A famous example is POSH, an acronym that has become a standard English word. It is believed that POSH stands for "port-outbound-starboard-homebound." In Victorian England, ocean travel between Britain and India was common. Cabins on the left (port) side of the ship were shady during the outbound voyage, whereas cabins on the right (starboard) side were shady during the journey back to England. These more desirable and hence more expensive cabins were available to those passengers with the financial resources to pay for them. Thus the current meaning of *posh:* "smart, fashionable, exclusive." Figure 6.5 gives some of the more common acronyms used in electronic communications.

FIGURE 6.3   Netiquette Guidelines

- Follow the same standards of behavior in electronic communications that you would follow in real life.
- Respect other people's time by keeping replies short and to the point and attachments small in file size.
- Avoid writing messages that are in ALL CAPS. This is the equivalent of shouting online.
- Check the spelling in your electronic communications.
- Use appropriate punctuation and grammar.
- Keep the focus of your responses in forums and chats on topic.
- Use caution when using sarcasm and humor. Emotion is very difficult to convey without face-to-face communications, and jokes may be viewed as criticism. Instead, use emoticons to express humor and other emotions.

FIGURE 6.4   Appropriate Emoticons

:)	Happiness, sarcasm, or joke	^^^	Giggles
: (	Unhappiness	<:-)	Dunce hat on and innocently asking dumb question
:-\	Undecided or skeptical	%-(	Confused
:O	Surprise or realization of an error	:- X	My lips are sealed

FIGURE 6.5   Acronyms Used in Electronic Communications

AAMOF—as a matter of fact
ASAP—as soon as possible
BRB—be right back
BTW—by the way
CMIIW—correct me if I'm wrong
FAQ—frequently asked question
FITB—fill in the blank
FWIW—for what it's worth
FYI—for your information
F2F—face to face
HTH—hope this helps

IAE—in any event
IDK—I don't know
IMO—in my opinion
IOW—in other words
LOL—laughing out loud
LP—last post
OIC—oh, I see
OTOH—on the other hand
RSN—real soon now
TIA—thanks in advance
WYSIWYG—what you see is what you get

PLANNING AND ADMINISTERING DISCUSSIONS

This section explains how to set up and conduct electronic forums and chats. It is divided into three subsections. The first subsection describes planning considerations that apply to both types of discussions. The second considers student participation in discussions, and the third subsection explains how to facilitate forums and chats.

Generic Planning Considerations

Electronic discussions will not succeed as learning experiences unless students are motivated to participate in them. They are also more likely to participate, of course, if they perceive the experience will be enjoyable and result in their learning something of value. This will more likely be the case if you follow the suggestions identified in this bulleted list and explained next.

- Phrase topics to encourage critical thought.
- Explain response techniques and provide practice sessions.
- Establish and enforce discussion policies.
- Know how to deal with difficult and/or nonparticipating students.
- Provide clear instructions for each discussion assignment.
- Consider workloads.
- Identify facilitators/leaders for discussions.
- Have a plan for rewarding students who participate in discussions.

Phrase Topics to Encourage Critical Thought.   Discussion topics should be phrased to stimulate students intellectually and require them to think critically. A well-formulated topic explicitly or implicitly poses interesting questions. The following list contains six recommended practices for creating thought-provoking topics that stimulate critical thinking. When this happens, students' interest in a discussion peaks, increasing the likelihood that they will participate.

- Ask open-ended questions that require students to explain "why" or "how." Questions that can be answered yes or no, or in a few words, are unchallenging and should be few in number, but are far more appropriate in chats than in forums.
- Ask questions designed to get students excited, such as questions about controversial topics that are based on real-life situations or current events.
- Pose questions that are relevant to course content.
- Inform students about the number of responses they should make in a forum and deadlines for posting these responses. This helps ensure that students will participate in a forum.
- In forums—but not so much in chats—pose questions that require students to debate or to analyze topics.
- Ask questions that require answers based on knowledge recently acquired in the course.

Figure 6.6 provides an example discussion question on intellectual property rights of faculty designed to encourage critical thought and analysis.

Explain Response Techniques and Provide Practice Sessions.   Before students new to elearning participate in electronic discussions, they need time to learn how to use the technology. Such learning is best accomplished through practice. You can help them succeed by providing practice discussion sessions. Early on in your course, you might initiate an ungraded discussion on a nonthreatening topic. A forum is probably preferable to a chat, especially if your class has more than just a few students. A "water fountain" forum, as described later, would be one good choice. Chapter 10 suggests that students be introduced to discussions and to each other using a get-acquainted forum. Be sure to provide very specific instructions on how to access the practice forum, how to respond initially, and how to respond to another student's response. It is best to include these instructions in a "how to" tutorial that students can refer to until they are comfortable with the process. Posting an online self-assessment test on the how tos of electronic forums can further reinforce students' learning about how to participate. It also provides students valuable practice in taking online tests.

Responses posted in practice discussions can alert you to students who have difficulty writing in English or who have other special needs. When you do notice students with writ-

FIGURE 6.6   Example Discussion Question—Intellectual Property Rights

Please defend your position on whether faculty should own the rights to the elearning materials they create. Also, attach a file that contains a description of the example intellectual property policy you found as a result of your research in Assignment 5.

ing difficulties, contact them privately to discuss their needs and differences and to make recommendations on how they can improve. If your LMS does not have spelling and grammar checkers—and some currently don't—one tip worth mentioning to students concerned about their spelling and grammar skills is as follows. Suggest that they write their discussion responses using a word processor, for example, Microsoft Word, so that they can use the spelling and grammar checkers in that software to remedy difficulties in their writing. When they are satisfied with the correctness of what they have written, they can then copy the word processor text into the text box area of the discussion.

You should consider giving students specific suggestions about how and when to compose discussion responses. One of the best ways to get the types of responses you want is to provide students with examples of good responses to emulate. Examples of poor responses are probably as important to student learning as examples of good ones. Also, realize that your own conduct in electronic discussions will be an example for your students to follow. As a consequence, your behavior should always reflect the behavior you expect of your students.

Establish and Enforce Course Discussion Policies. One of the most important considerations in promoting students' success in discussions is to establish discussion policies. Policies must be stated clearly and completely, and students must be briefed on them *before* they are expected to participate in a forum. The policies should be stated in a document prominently placed on the coursesite where students can access it easily. The policies themselves, of course, address what is considered acceptable behavior in discussions and what is not. In addition, penalties for violations must be articulated. As previously explained, if forums require a minimum level of participation with respect to number and length of responses, this requirement should also be stated in your discussion policies if it is the same for all discussions. Otherwise, the number and length of responses should be clearly stated in discussion assignment instructions as explained shortly. Chapter 9 provides specific information on discussion policies.

Know How to Deal with Difficult and/or Nonparticipating Students. For a variety of reasons, some students will be reluctant to participate in electronic discussions or will participate in an unacceptable way. While the proportion of such students in your class is likely to be small, you need to be prepared to deal with them when they appear. This topic is addressed further later. In addition, Chapter 10 includes a section on managing students that addresses this subject in some detail.

Provide Clear Instructions for Each Discussion Assignment. Each discussion assignment must include specific instructions to ensure students know exactly what you expect of them. For example, if you want students to respond to threads posted by other students as well as to the forum topic itself, this expectation must be stated clearly. Inform students about the desired length of their responses, as well as about how many responses you expect them to make. Provide examples of the types of responses you expect. Be specific about the time and date that responses are due, including the time zone of the due time. This is especially important when students are in geographically dispersed areas. Figure 6.7 illustrates instructions for the students participating in a forum on intellectual property rights illustrated in Figure 6.6. Chapter 9 on policies provides additional information on this subject.

FIGURE 6.7   Instructions for Intellectual Property Rights Discussion

---

Assignment Topic: Intellectual Property

Points: 5

Description: In this assignment, you will explore the controversial topic of intellectual property. You will conduct research on the issue to review valid points on both sides of the issue. Your research should result in your forming an opinion about your position on whether faculty should own the rights to the elearning materials they create for their courses. In this assignment, you will also conduct research to identify examples of intellectual property rights policies and examples of formal faculty intellectual property rights contracts.

Assignment Objectives: On completion of this assignment, students will be able to:

1. State an opinion on whether faculty should own rights to the elearning materials they create.
2. Describe example intellectual property rights policies.

Specific Instructions:

1. Perform a web search on the issue of intellectual property rights of faculty. In your search find websites, articles, or reports on the issue.
2. Based on your research, summarize the pros and cons of this issue in a one-page, double-spaced Word document. Document your references in a bibliographic list as a second page of this report. Please use APA style to compose your reference list. Email the document to your instructor by midnight EST, February 2.
3. Perform a web search to find examples of intellectual property policies established at educational institutions. Select the example that you consider to be the best example and one that could serve as a model for other institutions. Include the actual policies in a Word document. Be sure to identify the name of the institution and the URL to the website where the policies can be located. Email the document to your instructor by midnight EST, February 6.
4. Share your views with your classmates by participating in the intellectual property discussion posted in the Discussion section of the coursesite. State your position in one brief paragraph. Attach the file that describes the intellectual policies you selected as the best example. Post your comments by midnight EST, February 8.
5. Review all the comments posted to the discussion by your classmates. Engage in further discussion with at least one other student with whom you either agree or disagree. State your position in one brief paragraph. Complete this further discussion by midnight EST, February 12.

Consider Workloads.   Students become "burned out" on electronic discussions when too many of them are required. Thus, you must choose your discussion assignments with discretion. Be mindful of the time it will take students to prepare to contribute, as well as the time it will take them to compose and post their responses and monitor responses posted by other students. Consider your students' overall work commitments as well as your own when planning discussion dates. Make sure that a cutoff date for posting discussion responses does not coincide with course tests or the due dates of other major course projects.

Identify Facilitators/Leaders for Discussions.   Both forums and chats require leaders who are known as facilitators. You should be sure to identify a discussion leader before the discussion begins and ensure that the leader is aware of and can discharge the responsibilities of the position. You will quickly find that it pays to use student or teaching assistants to facilitate discussions. Otherwise you will spend a good deal of your time bogged down in the mechanics of two-way elearning communication.

Have a Plan for Rewarding Students Who Participate in Discussions.   Incentives are an acknowledged method for motivating people. Students participate in discussions more willingly, and with greater ardor, when they know their participation will influence their grade in the course. There are as well other kinds of incentives for participation. Recognition in class or on a coursesite and exemption from other course requirements for exemplary performance are two that come readily to mind. In any event, it is important that you have a well-conceived plan for motivating students to participate in discussions. Chapter 11 contains information on grading discussions.

Guidelines for Student Participation in Discussions

Students must be given very specific instructions about how to participate in discussions. What follows are suggested student guidelines for engaging in forums and chats. You might consider posting some version of these guidelines on your website so that students can access them.

Guidelines for Participating in Forums

- Distribute responses evenly throughout the discussion period. For example, if you are to respond to your classmates' posts and the discussion period extends over several days, do not post all your responses on the same day. Waiting until the last day to post responses implies disinterest.
- Use complete sentences instead of only "yes" or "no" answers, which will not suffice to answer most questions.
- Provide evidence of your critical thinking on the subject. For example, support your responses with examples of your prior knowledge and/or use quotes from articles, websites, books, or other sources that will give your posting credibility.
- Find ways to relate your response to course content by referring to textbook readings, lectures, or other relevant course components.
- Fully explain your viewpoints, but be as brief as you can. In most cases, limit your response to no more than four sentences per paragraph and no more than two paragraphs. If a challenging topic requires a longer, more sophisticated response, prepare it using a word processor, and attach the resultant file to the response you type in the forum text box. The more powerful formatting capabilities of the word processor will make your long response more readable.
- Do not introduce new topics of discussion; stay focused on ideas related to the topic.
- Compose your responses using a word processor and paste them in the discussion text box after you have checked spelling and grammar.
- Give careful thought to the title of your posting. Keep it brief and make it as interesting as possible.
- To encourage dialogue from classmates, end your post with an open-ended, challenging question. Make sure the question is relevant to the forum topic.

Guidelines for Participating in Chats

- On entering a chat, announce yourself and greet everyone.
- If entering a chat after it has started, read through the last 10 or 15 posts to review the discussion before entering a comment.
- Do not block capitalize words. It will give the impression of SHOUTING.
- Be as brief as possible. Very rarely should a comment exceed three sentences.
- Use the individual's name when responding to someone in particular. This ensures that everyone will know to whom you are responding.
- Indicate your last post by entering "LP" either before or after your last comments.
- Say good-bye before you leave the chat, that is, in your last post.

Facilitating Discussions

The *planning and development* stage of an electronic discussion ends when the topic is posted and students commence using the discussion. Our discussion of this stage revealed that both forums and chats require a facilitator. This subsection explains how to administer a discussion once it has actually begun, that is, how to be an effective discussion *facilitator.* Facilitators for forums and chats have responsibilities in common. However, as we have seen, facilitating a chat involves real-time actions, whereas facilitating a forum does not. What follows is divided into two subsections. The first provides general guidelines for facilitating discussions—both forums and chats, with perhaps an emphasis on forums. The second discusses additional considerations for facilitators of chats.

General Guidelines for Discussion Facilitators.   The role of discussion facilitator is quite complex. As a facilitator, you must coach and question students, provide them feedback on their responses, and perhaps post addenda to the discussion topic, all to the end of ensuring that forums become more meaningful to students than classroom discussions (MacKnight, 2000). Early on, your students must be informed of your role as a facilitator and the level of participation they can expect from you in discussions.

For a discussion facilitator, balancing workload against the proper amount of attention students need is a challenging undertaking. Unless you discharge your responsibilities efficiently, the workload you allow a discussion to impose on you can quickly become overwhelming. First of all, you must strive to create an environment where students feel comfortable engaging in discussions without close supervision from you. Second, you will need efficient methods to keep discussions on target, to encourage students, and to monitor students who may be disrespectful or disruptive. Of paramount importance is that these methods must ensure an acceptable level of your own participation in a forum. Otherwise, your students may assume that you are not very interested in their comments, and their learning experience will suffer accordingly. Experience is an excellent teacher for discussion facilitators. Don't be alarmed if initially you are spending more time on discussions than you would wish. With practice, you will become more facile in facilitating them efficiently.

Several facilitation methods allow you to oversee discussions and provide appropriate feedback without responding to all comments. One is to come into the discussion only after students have completed posting their comments and then make summary comments about the overall discussion. Another method involves responding to only a few selected responses. For instance, you might respond to some of the most excellent responses. You can publicly commend authors of such responses by sending email to the entire class or by posting an announcement.

Dealing with problematic responses is another matter entirely. Obviously, they must be dealt with privately. Individual email to students having difficulty should contain specific suggestions for improvement. For example, you might suggest they review the relevant course materials and try posting additional responses. Note that this strategy involves responding individually to *every* underachiever. Presumably there will be relatively few such students. Otherwise, you might want to reexamine your forum statement for imprecision and/or review the effectiveness of your elearning modules related to the forum. Also, when underachieving results from lack of effort, you must detect this fact quickly and—at some early point—stop trying to encourage a student who is unreceptive to your advice.

Another method for limiting the amount of time you spend replying to discussion is to create multiple discussion groups of five or six students, with teaching assistants or student group leaders serving as group monitors. If group monitors deem it necessary, they can contact you for help in getting the group discussion back on track or for any other assistance they might need. This approach also suggests a time-saving way to deal with students displaying unacceptable behavior in discussions. It is highly desirable to minimize the possibility that abusive comments will actually reach a public discussion. If you anticipate problems on a particular forum, you can ask the small group discussion monitor to screen responses before they are posted. Once responses are approved, students can be cleared to post them. Email is a suitable vehicle for implementing this effective but time-consuming strategy. If the monitor is an unpaid student group leader, you must compensate him or her in some other appropriate manner, perhaps by awarding credit toward the course final grade.

Additional Considerations for Facilitating Chats.   We have already seen that chat and forum facilitators share a number of common responsibilities. Facilitating a chat, however, can be more challenging than facilitating a forum because chats occur in real time. The following additional considerations apply to facilitating chats.

- Limit chat size as experience dictates. Large chats are essentially unmanageable.
- Assure topics can be discussed with short responses. Use a forum for topics that require more detailed consideration.
- Keep students focused by reminding them as necessary to stick to the topic. When chats begin to lose focus, participants are encouraged to digress, and chaos results.
- Ensure that you are well prepared. Chat participants exhibit "rapid-fire" behavior. You must have a thorough grasp of the chat subject and the technology. Quick responses are crucial, for example, to give the floor to a student whose hand has been raised or to respond to a student's question. Consider preparing pretyped questions, answers, and comments that you can cut and paste from a word processor document to the chat dialogue.
- Enforce discussion policies rigorously. Promptly eject any student displaying inappropriate behavior. An initial offensive comment, if ignored, makes it more likely that others will follow. Chat comments—unlike forum comments—cannot be screened.
- Personalize chats. Use students' names as often as possible when you "address" them.
- Provide preview information. Announce the chat topic ahead of time and encourage students to make electronic notes to help them participate.

- Start with an *ice breaker.* Spend the first five minutes discussing a topic of general interest, for example, a current event. This allows students briefly to socialize with one another, much as they would do before a face-to-face meeting is called to order.
- Set a time limit. About 45 minutes seems to be appropriate, and shorter is better than longer assuming the limit is adequate to accomplish the goal of the chat.
- Archive chat dialog. If your LMS does not support doing so, copy the chat session and paste it into a file posted on the coursesite. This method allows nonparticipants to review the chat. When several chat groups address the same topic, posting archives lets everybody see everybody else's comments. Reviewing chat archives helps reinforce the material and provides students an excellent study tool.
- Ensure the technology is working before a chat starts. When people "gather" for a chat and the server is down, it's like a World Series game or a favorite concert has been rained out.
- Know how to deal with legitimate nonparticipants. Students in widely separated time zones or adult learners with job and home responsibilities may have legitimate reasons for not participating in a chat. Occasionally students will lose their Internet connections during a chat. A backup plan would be to have such students respond to the chat archive.

CATEGORIES OF DISCUSSION TOPICS

Electronic discussions can be used to pursue an almost infinite variety of educational goals, for example, promoting critical thinking about course content, brainstorming an idea, fostering team collaboration, encouraging students to socialize with each other, and topic clarification, among many others. To promote a better understanding of how discussions can be devised, this section identifies common categories of discussion topics. These categories are informal, suggestive rather than exhaustive, and not always mutually exclusive. In most cases, the discussion categories are appropriate for both forums and chat, although forums are much more commonly used than chats in elearning. When a topic category is not particularly suitable for a chat, we indicate this fact.

Discussions to Promote Critical Thinking

Almost any learning activity—a lecture or a textbook reading assignment, for example—lends itself to treatment as well in an electronic discussion, and the topic can almost always be formulated so as to engage students in critical thinking. Figure 6.6 exhibits a discussion topic encouraging students who are studying elearning to think critically about the intellectual property rights of instructors who spend considerable effort creating course resources. Critical thinking discussions are more suitable for forums than for chats.

Brainstorming Discussions

A brainstorming discussion encourages students to share their more or less unstructured ideas on any appropriate topic. For example, suppose you wish to foster a constructivist learning environment where student input influences course goals and how they are pursued.

You might ask students to participate in an electronic discussion in which you describe the types of projects you have in mind for the course, and ask them to comment on which of the projects would best serve their needs. In such a situation, students could be encouraged to comment on each other's responses as well. Brainstorming discussions work well as either forums or chats. Figure 6.8 is an example of such a brainstorming forum topic.

Discussions to Summarize and Clarify

Electronic discussions can be used to summarize or clarify ideas treated elsewhere in your course. For example, after a lecture or a reading assignment, you could post a forum requiring students to apply the knowledge gained in the lecture. Alternatively, you might ask them to pose questions to the forum that—when answered by other students—will enhance their understanding of the information covered in the lecture or reading.

New Topics Discussions

A new topics discussion can be used to introduce upcoming subjects treated elsewhere in your course. For example, you could post questions to get students thinking about issues that will be treated in upcoming class activities.

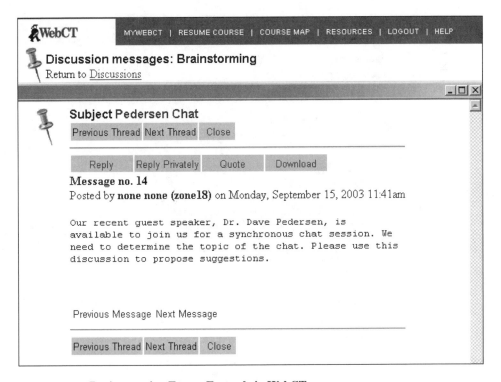

FIGURE 6.8   Brainstorming Forum Example in WebCT

Water Fountain Discussions

A "water fountain" discussion provides students with an electronic gathering place where they can meet to socialize. Water fountain discussions allow students to express their ideas about nonacademic subjects such as sports, hobbies, current events, and other topics of interest to them. Students should be encouraged to make a water fountain discussion informal and pleasant. This type of discussion builds community among students and encourages interpersonal relationships. For small groups, water fountain discussions work well as chats. Figure 6.9 presents an example of a water fountain discussion.

Get Help/Online Tutoring Discussions

An online tutoring discussion allows students to request help and assistance in understanding the materials of your course. Students can post questions about course content and receive timely answers. You need not answer all the questions yourself. Rather, it is advisable to have tutors serve as discussion facilitators and to post responses to student questions. Tutors can be advanced students in the course, student assistants, or teaching assistants. Of course the best tutor is presumably the course instructor, but any extensive online tutoring that you personally conduct can quickly make demands on your time that are difficult or impossible to meet. For one-on-one tutoring, this type of discussion is better as a chat than as a forum.

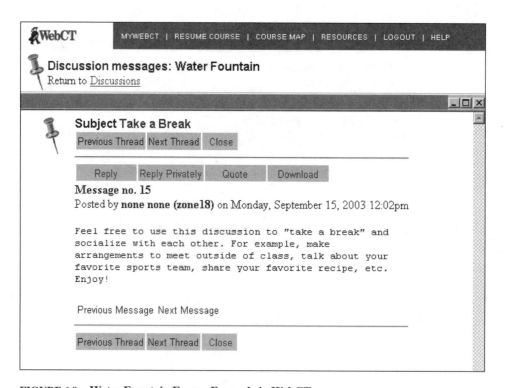

FIGURE 6.9   Water Fountain Forum Example in WebCT

Private Consultation Discussions

A private consultation discussion can facilitate your communication with a single student. This kind of discussion—conducted as a chat—allows you to establish virtual office hours, by which you communicate privately with students just as you would in face-to-face office hours. Email is a potential but less suitable alternative to private consultation discussion. Figure 6.10 depicts an example of virtual office hours conducted in the WebCT LMS. Here a student and an instructor are discussing a math problem.

Frequently Asked Questions (FAQ) Discussions

We use the term *FAQ* in a somewhat unconventional sense. Here it means the kind of straightforward questions that typically arise among students when an academic course is in progress. A good example is "When is the next exam?" Often, but not always, the answer to such a question is available in your online course materials, but the student asking it does not know how to find it or is unwilling to take the effort to search for the answer. Ordinarily, better-informed students in the same class can answer such questions. In any event, in the present context an FAQ is a simple question about your course that one student asks and another student answers.

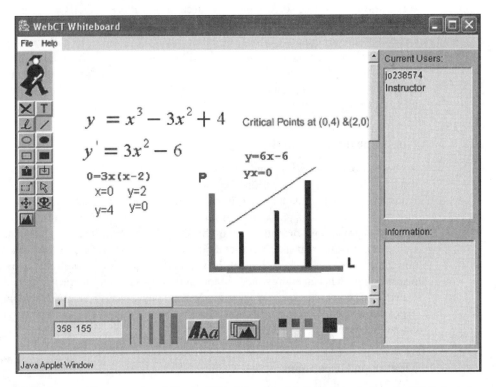

FIGURE 6.10   Instructor and Student Working on a Math Problem using the Whiteboard in a WebCT Coursesite

An FAQ discussion can be used to help you control your workload by encouraging students to answer each other's straightforward questions. For example, students can post questions in an FAQ forum about assignment due dates, test dates, and other subjects pertaining to course information. Student assistants or any student in the class with the answer would be expected to respond. You yourself review an FAQ forum only occasionally, at which time you provide answers that students themselves were unable to supply.

You can motivate students to participate in an FAQ forum by giving them academic credit for questions they answer correctly. Be sure to devise a method that requires students to submit proof—for example, a screen printout—that demonstrates they deserve academic credit for participating in an FAQ discussion. Note the potential here for pairs of students to engage in grade manipulation by alternately posing and answering rhetorical questions for each other. Perhaps a better solution is to award extra grade credit to select capable students who volunteer to oversee FAQ forums.

Homework Discussions

A homework discussion allows students to share solutions to homework problems or assignments. The instructor can review the responses and post comments on the best solutions proposed by students. As with an FAQ forum, students will be motivated to participate in a homework forum if they are given academic credit—or perhaps some kind of in-class recognition—for doing so. A homework discussion works especially well for certain kinds of technical and scientific subjects—for example, math and physics—in which problems have short answers that are either correct or incorrect. If the LMS software does not provide access to a sophisticated equation editor often required in scientific writing, Microsoft's relatively powerful equation editor available in Word and PowerPoint provides a solution to this difficulty. Students can create a document containing the required equations and post the document to a discussion.

Guest Speakers Discussions

A guest speaker discussion can introduce a guest speaker or summarize the speaker's presentation. This kind of discussion is known to be an excellent means of involving students with a speaker and extending their interactions with him or her (Downes, 2002). One approach to constituting a guest speaker forum is to ask the speaker to pose questions to the class, thus provoking students to begin thinking about the forthcoming presentation. As a follow-up to a guest speaker's presentation, a discussion might allow students to present questions asking for clarifications of the speaker's ideas. Note as well that a guest speaker discussion presents an entirely new opportunity for students to interact with subject matter experts in a course. The guest speaker need never appear face-to-face with students. Instead, his or her entire interaction with your class—should you prefer—can be conducted in an electronic discussion.

Mentoring Discussions

The mentoring discussion is a variation of a guest speaker discussion. In this discussion, mentors or other experts working in a designated field of interest can collaborate electronically with students on current issues, topics of interest, or projects designed to share experiences and knowledge (Raths, 2001).

Field Experience Discussions

As some point in their education, many students become involved in field experiences such as student teaching, student nursing, or a cooperative education job. Electronic discussions can facilitate up-to-the minute reporting on such experiences and help students engaged in them stay connected with their instructors and classmates. Field experience discussions provide students working or studying off-campus with a means of sorting out their thinking and reactions to their off-campus experiences. They also enable such students to seek advice and obtain guidance when needed (DeBourgh, 2002). Note the potential for students who have already completed an off-campus field period to interact with and advise students currently involved in a similar experience.

Small Group Meeting Discussions

Discussions can greatly facilitate small group work because they are more convenient than face-to-face meetings. This type of discussion is typically conducted as a chat involving from three to seven members. Such chats are especially beneficial at the outset of a small group project, when brainstorming sessions are needed to determine meeting times, how the work will be divided, and other essential getting-started activities. Also, chats are useful when groups need to touch base to clarify points or to follow up on face-to-face meetings. Chapter 10 provides details about small group management in elearning courses.

Discussions to Reinforce Foreign Language Skills

Discussions can facilitate language courses wherein students are asked to write sentences in the language they are studying. Chatting in the foreign language helps improve students' verbal and written skills. Also, student comments can be analyzed for correctness of grammar and spelling, and appropriateness of vocabulary.

Discussions to Quiz Students

You can use discussions to explore the depth and breadth of your students' subject matter knowledge. By having students meet individually in a chat, you can ask questions and know within a few minutes whether they know the course material. If you are concerned that a student did not actually author an assignment that he or she submitted, you could conduct a chat with the student to ask questions about the paper. The feedback you obtain can help you determine whether the student was capable of writing the paper submitted.

Role-Playing Discussions

Students seem to enjoy discussions in which they are asked to create a scenario by playing roles. As an example, consider a real-world situation in which a university wants to redesign a large-enrollment freshman course in computer literacy to make it more student centered.

The university believes a constructivist elearning environment—rather than the objectivist approach currently in use—will better suit entering freshmen who have widely diverse skills in using computer application software. Four students are briefed about how to play the roles of the computer department chair, the educational technology director, the faculty member heading the departmental course redesign committee, and an undergraduate who has previously taken the course as it currently exists. These four students then enter the discussion in their assigned roles—perhaps with prepared scripts—to represent the points of view of their respective characters in the course redesign project. Other discussion participants respond to and evaluate the positions taken by the four role players.

It is easy to imagine variations of this role-playing scenario that could make the discussion even more immediate and realistic for students. For example, when the scenario is nearing completion, students in the course redesign discussion might be informed that academic budgets are going to be reduced by 10 percent for the next year's budgeting cycle. They would then be asked how to modify the redesign project to accommodate this budget cut.

An interesting use of real-world role playing in an online discussion is reflected in an approach to the study of child behavior used at Lesley College in Cambridge. Students from Lesley interacted with teams of students from Angola, Norway, and Japan in this online project. Designated members from each team played the roles of children with various behavior problems in order to make learning about these behaviors more realistic (Read, 2002).

REFERENCES

Batane, T. (2002, October). Technology and student collaboration: A research project in one Botswana secondary school. *T.H.E. Journal, 30*(3), 16, 20–22.

Bender, W. (2002, September/October). Twenty years of personalization: All about the "daily me." *EDUCAUSE Review, 37*(5), 21–22, 24–26, 28–29.

Brown, D. G. (2002a, January). Interactive teaching. *Syllabus, 15*(6), 23.

Brown, D. G. (2002b, December). The role you play in online discussions. *Syllabus*. Retrieved May 1, 2003, from www.syllabus.com/article.asp?id=6988

Cooper, L. (2003, April). Interdisciplinary, intercultural online courses provide a global education experience. *T.H.E. Journal, 30*(9), 24.

DeBourgh, G. A. (2002, May/June). Simple elegance: Course management systems as pedagogical infrastructure to enhance science learning. *The Technology Source*. Retrieved June 10, 2002, from http://ts.mivu.org/default.asp?show=article&id=925

Ditto, R. (2004, April). Teaching and learning through online collaboration. *Syllabus, 17*(9), 31.

Dong, F. H. (2001, September). Succeeding as a cyber student. *e-learning, 2*(9), 12.

Downes, S. (2002, September/October). LearnScope virtual learning community. *The Technology Source*.

Retrieved October 31, 2003, from http://ts.mivu.org/default.asp?show=article&id=1035

Foreman, J. (2003, July/August). Distance learning and synchronous interaction. *The Technology Source*. Retrieved July 17, 2003, from http://ts.mivu.org/default.asp?show=article&id=1042

Hofmann, J. (2001, May). Synchronous exercises from scratch. *Learning Circuits*. Retrieved June 10, 2002, from www.learningcircuits.org/2001/may2001/hofmann.html

Klemm, W. R. (2002, September/October). Extending the pedagogy of threaded-topic discussions. *The Technology Source*. Retrieved September 3, 2002, from http://ts.mivu.org/default.asp?show=article&id=1015

Lang, D. (2000, September). Critical thinking in web courses: An oxymoron? *Syllabus, 14*(2), 20–21, 23–24.

Liu, Y., & Ginther, D. (2001). Managing impression formation in computer-mediated communication. *EDUCAUSE Quarterly, 24*(3), 50–54.

MacKnight, C. B. (2000). Teaching critical thinking through online discussions. *EDUCAUSE Quarterly, 23*(4), 38–41.

Morgenstern, D., Plasencia, A., & Selz, R. (2003, November). Students as designers and content creators: An online multimedia exchange between the U.S. and Spain. *Syllabus, 17*(4), 32–33.

Raths, D. (2001, January). Make me a match: With online mentoring programs, experienced employees can share their knowledge with newcomers. *Online-Learning, 5*(1), 36–38, 40, 42.

Read, B. (2002, March 26). Teaching children with behavior problems is the topic of an online course from Lesley College. *The Chronicle of Higher Education.* Retrieved June 10, 2002, from http://chronicle.com/free/2002/03/2002032601u.htm

Williams, C. B., & Murphy, T. (2002). Electronic discussion groups: How initial parameters influence classroom performance. *EDUCAUSE Quarterly, 25*(4), 21–29.

Young, J. R. (2003, May 30). Haute cyber: Fashion and computer students collaborate to create a virtual runway. *The Chronicle of Higher Education.* Retrieved July 17, 2003, from http://chronicle.com/weekly/v49/i38/38a03101.htm

URL REFERENCES

About.com: Learn the Net: www.learnthenet.com/english/html/09netiqt.htm

Colorado State University: Example emoticons and acronyms: http://writing.colostate.edu/references/documents/email/com2g2.cfm

Computer User High-Tech Dictionary: www.computeruser.com/resources/dictionary/emoticons.html

Euforic: Electronic Discussions—Guidelines for Moderators: www.euforic.org/inter/en/moderation.htm

Group Size in Electronic Discussions: www.dsv.su.se/jpalme/e-mail-book/group-size.html

The Net: User Guidelines and Netiquette: www.fau.edu/netiquette/net

Purdue University Online Writing Lab: http://owl.english.purdue.edu/lab/owl/tutoring

Tutor.com: www.tutor.com

CHAPTER SEVEN

EXTERNAL RESOURCES

There is an immense body of external elearning resources, available either online or in CD/DVD format. Many of these resources are free of charge. In fact, one can envision creating the bulk of an elearning course using only external materials. The goal of this chapter is to make you aware of the richness and variety of such resources.

The chapter is organized into four sections. The first identifies and discusses six categories of specialized online educational resources: virtual experiments, online expeditions, online museums, online periodicals, textbook supplements, and miscellaneous liberal arts learning resources. The second section describes and discusses four categories of digital library resources including general-purpose digital libraries, specialized digital libraries, online periodical collections, and ebook collections. The third section is on web research. One of the most important skills you and your students will ever develop is the ability to find high-quality web-based resources quickly. This section examines the role of librarians in web research, identifies web search engines, and discusses how to evaluate the quality of the web resources you discover. The fourth and final section of the chapter explains how to devise effective and meaningful web-based research assignments. You must ensure that information students glean from browsing the web contributes to accomplishing well-defined course learning goals.

EXAMPLES OF SPECIALIZED ONLINE EDUCATIONAL RESOURCES

Web-based resources available for use in elearning are multiplying rapidly. So varied and numerous are these resources that categorizing them presents a significant challenge. Six of the most important categories are identified in this list. A brief discussion of each category follows the list.

- Virtual experiments
- Online expeditions
- Online museums
- Online periodicals
- Textbook supplements
- Miscellaneous liberal arts learning resources

Virtual Experiments

A *virtual experiment* is an experiment simulated on a computer. One of the major advantages of performing virtual experiments is the convenience of working "anytime anyplace." Another is that experimental activities that might be dangerous in the real world can be performed with complete safety in a virtual environment. A third is that the equipment needed for conducting experiments is often cost prohibitive. Textbook publishers, online learning providers, and many educational institutions offer a variety of virtual experiments. In addition, many technically savvy instructors create their own virtual experiments through easy-to-use software such as Macromedia Flash. The following is a description of five websites that feature virtual experiments.

- Figure 7.1 illustrates the ▪Virtual Mass Spectrometry Laboratory (VMSL) website. A mass spectrometer is an expensive device used for analyzing chemical compounds that is available only at the most advanced technical universities. Professors at Carnegie Mellon University and the University of Pittsburgh developed the VMSL. At the VMSL website students can operate a virtual mass spectrometer and read a molecule's "fingerprint" (Carnevale, 2003b).
- Figure 7.2 illustrates the ▪Online Meteorology Guides at the Weather World 2010 Project website, a collection of web-based meteorology instructional modules developed by the Department of Atmospheric Sciences at the University of Illinois at Urbana-Champaign.
- Figure 7.3 depicts ▪Open College's E-Learning Content Library in physics, astronomy, mathematics, chemistry, economics, and biology.

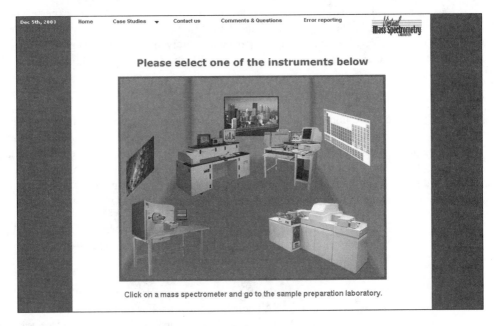

FIGURE 7.1   Virtual Mass Spectrometry Laboratory

Carnegie Mellon University and the University of Pittsburgh, used with permission.

FIGURE 7.2   Online Meteorology Guides, Weather World 2010 Project

Department of Atmospheric Sciences, University of Illinois at Urbana-Champaign, used with permission.

- The ▪Learn Anytime Anywhere Physics website at the University of North Carolina at Greensboro is a virtual lab that promotes active learning and discovery. The environment includes virtual lab instruments and associated curriculum models (Meisner & Hoffman, 2003).
- Figure 7.4 illustrates the ▪Virtual ChemLab website at Brigham Young University. This virtual lab provides students with a hands-on chemistry experience without requiring them to actually handle dangerous chemicals. This virtual lab allows students to conduct imaginative experiments safely, instead of having to follow rigid procedures, as they would in a conventional lab (Carnevale, 2003a).

Online Expeditions

Online expeditions and field trips provide exciting web-based learning experiences whereby students can follow the adventures of real-world travelers and explorers. Typically, expedition leaders and explorers post daily reports to the website. These reports may include pictures, narratives, and videos that illustrate the day's activities. To promote active learning, many online expedition websites provide suggested assignments and related learning activities. The following are two examples of online expeditions.

- The ▪NOVA/PBS website has allowed online adventurers to follow scientists and explorers into the field to visit places such as Denali, Madagascar, Mt. Everest, the Nile River, and Easter Island, among many other locations. Each NOVA/PBS expedition provides numerous resources on the area being explored.
- Figure 7.5 depicts the ▪NASA Quest website. NASA Quest allows the public to share the excitement of NASA's scientific pursuits. For example, one may take a simulated flight in the Space Shuttle to the International Space Station, explore distant planets, and learn about the construction of aircraft of the future. NASA Quest also provides

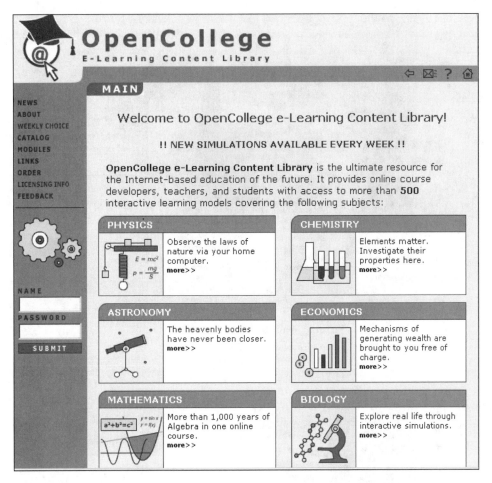

FIGURE 7.3   Open College E-Learning Content Library

OpenTeach Group, used with permission.

opportunities for electronic discussions with NASA experts, as well as opportunities to work on educational projects related to the site's online expeditions.

Online Museums

Online museums make it possible for students to view museum collections via the web. The following are three examples.

- The ▪Vatican Museums provide visitors with the opportunity to take a virtual tour of some of the dozens of museums and galleries that make up the Vatican collection. One of the online museums features Michaelangelo's Sistine Chapel. Visitors to the site can also view a three-dimensional video of the Sistine Chapel.

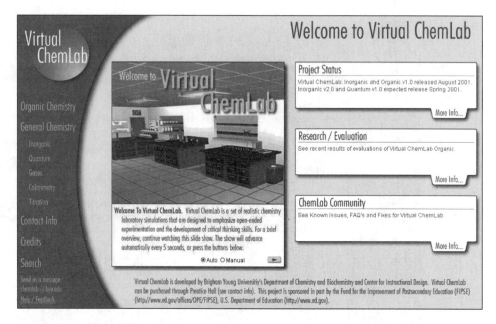

FIGURE 7.4   Virtual ChemLab

Brigham Young University, used with permission.

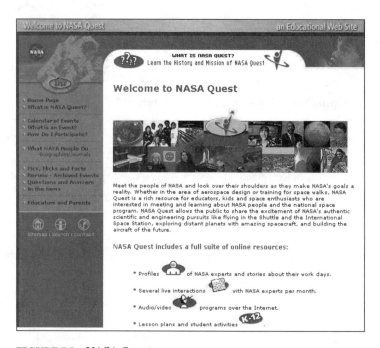

FIGURE 7.5   NASA Quest

- ▪Einstein Archives Online, produced through the collaborative efforts of the California Institute of Technology and Hebrew University of Jerusalem provides a glimpse into one of the twentieth century's greatest minds. Scholars and students can view the physicist's manuscripts—in his own handwriting—on a website that contains a searchable database with 43,000 items written by or about Einstein (Read, 2003c).
- Cornell University's online museum entitled the ▪Making of America is one of the several excellent digitized collections available from the university. This Making of America collection contains over 100,000 historical items reflecting life in late nineteenth-century America, including manuscripts, photographs, and newspaper and journal articles.

Online Periodicals

In the present context, the term *periodical* denotes a periodic publication such as a newspaper, magazine, or scholarly journal. An *ejournal* is a periodical delivered entirely online as opposed to in print. ▪*The Technology Source* illustrated in Figure 7.6 is an example. This peer-reviewed bimonthly ejournal, published by the Michigan Virtual University, is devoted to the subject of elearning. Many of the references in this book are from *The Technology Source.*

Many periodicals that are not ejournals nevertheless have substantial online components, for example, the *Wall Street Journal.* For an additional charge, Wall Street Journal subscribers can access resources and services not found in the printed edition of the newspaper (Green, 2002). Services such as ▪NewspaperDirect provide the digital delivery of newspapers from around the world. A subscription to a digital newspaper service typically allows users the capability of viewing numerous newspapers online or the capability of

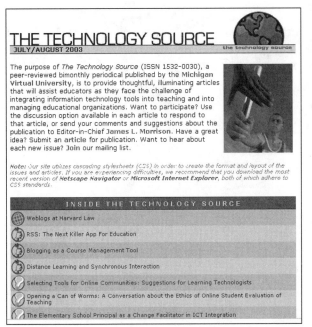

FIGURE 7.6   The Technology Source
Michigan Virtual University, used with permission.

printing a newspaper on demand. At least 90 percent of the bibliographic references in this book are accessible online in periodicals such as ▪*The Chronicle of Higher Education,* ▪*Syllabus,* ▪*T.H.E. Journal,* ▪*EDUCAUSE Review,* ▪*EDUCAUSE Quarterly,* and *The Technology Source.*

Textbook Supplements

Many publishers provide an assortment of external resources to supplement their printed textbooks. These resources include learning materials on reference CDs, companion coursesites, URLs to websites that contain information related to the subject of the textbook; and banks of test questions relevant to courses based on the textbook; among other materials. Such supplemental textbook resources can provide excellent material on which to base learning activities. When you review a textbook for possible use in an elearning course, you should be sure to evaluate companion web-based resources available from the textbook's publisher.

An example of a publisher that makes good use of elearning is Pearson Publishers. This company has created elearning resources available online or on CD to support their textbooks. In addition, it has created a companion coursesite for several hundred Pearson textbooks. The CourseCompass program, illustrated in Figure 7.7, provides access to these companion coursesites. If you adopt a Pearson text with a companion coursesite, you can download material from the companion coursesite to your own coursesite. Alternately, if your institution does not provide LMS support, you may request Pearson to create a personalized instance of its companion coursesite on Pearson's web server for you to use in

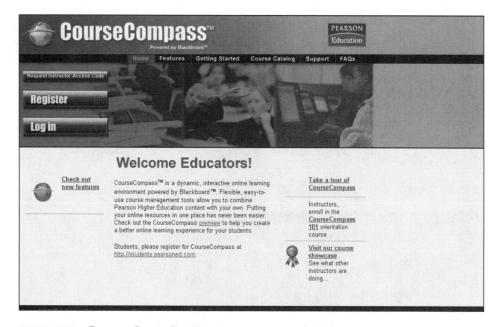

FIGURE 7.7   Pearson CourseCompass

your own course. You can tailor this coursesite to your needs by adding your materials to it. Students visiting the coursesite have access to all LMS functionality, including forums and online testing.

Like Pearson, McGraw-Hill Publishers exemplifies good elearning practices. The company has developed ▪McGraw-Hill Digital Solutions, a website that provides elearning resources to supplement its textbooks. These resources include lecture materials, quizzes, PowerPoint presentations, and a number of interactive learning exercises. The ▪Houghton Mifflin Company provides similar elearning resources such as instructor websites with teaching guides, lecture outlines, exercises, test banks, and videos relating to specific texts, among many other resources. For students, study materials, chapter summaries, chapter links, definitions, practice texts, and other supplements are available. Houghton Mifflin also features *A Cyber Evaluation (ACE),* a series of free online self-testing programs allowing students to assess their mastery of a subject they are studying with the assistance of a Houghton Mifflin textbook and related elearning resources.

Miscellaneous Liberal Arts Learning Resources

Other websites provide students a variety of opportunities to interact with elearning re-sources in the liberal arts—language, history, philosophy, the humanities, abstract sciences such as math, and so on. They are indicative of the rapid advancements in the use of the web for learning. Many of these sites include sound and video, and allow students to test their knowledge about a specific subject. Some of them include games. Others illustrate ways for students to select, explore, and control the learning path they take at the website, practices which allow students constructivist opportunities for learning. Some examples of such sites follow.

- The ▪Hotmath site, illustrated in Figure 7.8, helps students solve math homework problems. This site provides step-by-step explanations for many of the actual home-work problems in popular math textbooks from middle school math through algebra, geometry, precalculus, and calculus.
- ▪The Imagination Station website provides research-based resources to help pre-kindergarten through third-grade children learn to read. The interactive reading mate-rials meet the requirements of the Reading First portion of the federal No Child Left Behind Act. The fee-based website also provides an assessment feature to collect per-formance data on a child's reading progress and provides continuous assessment ser-vices to schools or individuals who enroll students in the reading program.
- The ▪Shakespeare: Subject to Change site, illustrated in Figure 7.9, is a multimedia online exploration of textual variations in Shakespearean plays and poems. The site features multisensory experiences that learners can read, listen to, and interact with, and they can create their own variations of Shakespeare's classics. The site includes video clips of actors reciting different versions of the famous "To Be or Not to Be" so-liloquy from *Hamlet.* It also contains rarely seen early printed versions of Shake-speare's work, among other items, many of which are interactive.
- Instructors can use the ▪Online Conservatory sponsored by the Boston Symphony Or-chestra to supplement a course in classical music. Composers featured on the web-site are described through documentary film, musical excerpts, and narrations. The

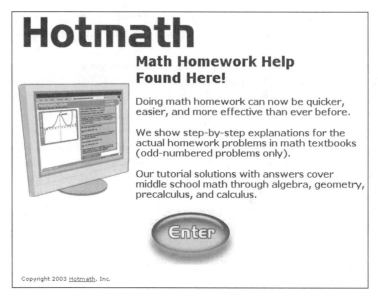

FIGURE 7.8   Hotmath, Inc.

Used with permission.

FIGURE 7.9   Shakespeare: Subject to Change

Cable in the Classroom, used with permission.

information on a composer culminates in a brief listening guide followed by a quiz. Anchoring the site is a series of interactive games used to demonstrate key concepts in modern classical music (Read, 2003b).

■ Figure 7.10 illustrates a University of Virginia website—■The Valley of the Shadow—that allows students to learn about the American Civil War. Visitors are able to draw their own conclusions about reasons advanced by the Northern and Southern sides to support their entries into the war. The site is a hypermedia archive of thousands of resources including newspapers, letters, diaries, photographs, maps, church records, population and agricultural census statistics, and military records. These resources explore the eve of the war, the war years, and the aftermath of the war. Students can examine every dimension of the conflict and write their own histories, reconstructing the life stories of women, African Americans, farmers, politicians, soldiers, and families.

■ ■Beetle Science on Explore Cornell, illustrated in Figure 7.11, is a site containing information of interest to students of entomology, including unusual and absorbing resources such as a video of a beetle laying eggs (Read, 2003d).

■ Next-generation online learning contexts—called multi-user virtual environments—will combine online museums, virtual experiments, and online collaborations to provide total immersion into the subject of the environment. An example is the ■Multi-User

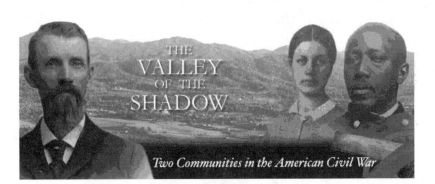

The Valley Project details life in two American communities, one Northern and one Southern, from the time of John Brown's Raid through the era of Reconstruction. In this digital archive you may explore thousands of original letters and diaries, newspapers and speeches, census and church records, left by men and women in Augusta County, Virginia, and Franklin County, Pennsylvania. Giving voice to hundreds of individual people, the Valley Project tells forgotten stories of life during the era of the Civil War.

Enter the Valley Archive

FIGURE 7.10   The Valley of the Shadow

Virginia Center for Digital History, University of Virginia, used with permission.

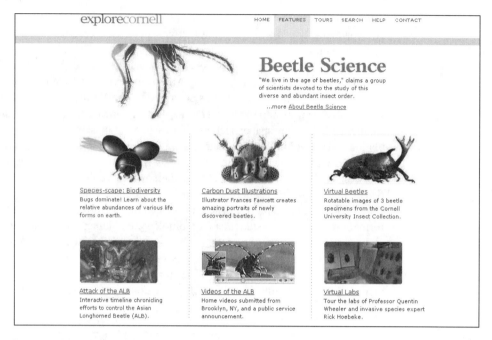

FIGURE 7.11   **Explore Cornell's Beetle Science**

Cornell University, used with permission.

Virtual Environment Experiential Simulator (MUVEES) illustrated in Figure 7.12. The learning environment—funded by a National Science Foundation grant—is designed to motivate middle school students to learn about science and its impact on society. Students participating in the environment represent themselves as graphical figures known as *avatars*. The students—through their avatars—populate a fictitious metropolitan area known as River City, where multiple simultaneous participants access virtual architectures configured for learning, interact with digital artifacts, and communicate both with other participants and with computer-based agents in collaborative learning activities. A number of digital objects from the Smithsonian's collection are used to create the River City environment, including "data collection stations" that provide detailed information about water samples at various spots in the world (Dede, 2003).

EXAMPLES OF DIGITAL LIBRARY RESOURCES

The traditional library is an essential component of learning and is often a campus focal point for students and faculty. The digital age has brought many changes to such libraries. One major change is in the way libraries' holdings are cataloged and accessed by users. The paper card catalog is being replaced with a catalog accessed via a computer and the Internet. Also, libraries are now equipped with wireless Internet connectivity, so that students and faculty can move freely around the library and use their laptops or handheld computing devices to connect to the Internet from anywhere in the library. Another major change is in the atmosphere of libraries. Many have added cafés where students and faculty can socialize and work

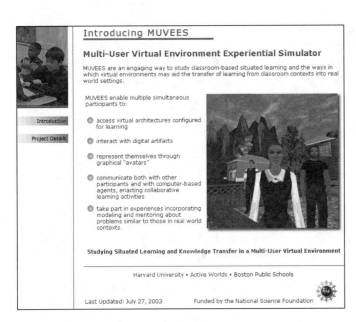

FIGURE 7.12   Multi-User Virtual Environment Experiential Simulator (MUVEES)

Harvard Graduate School of Education, used with permission.

collaboratively in a casual environment. Many are reconfiguring student study spaces to more easily accommodate teamwork.

Perhaps the most profound change in traditional libraries over the past few years has been the addition of digital library resources. Digital library resources are those items that can be accessed in digital format such as articles, specialized databases, learning objects, and digitized photographs. Such resources provide a foundation for a variety of elearning activities. Of growing importance to instructors, instructional technologists, and librarians is the integration of library materials into elearning coursesites (Carlson, 2003b). One way to accomplish this integration is to use the coursesite as a portal to the library by incorporating direct links to library resources.

In addition to changes in traditional libraries that accommodate elearning, websites are emerging that essentially offer library resources in an online environment. These websites are numerous, varied, and evolving rapidly, making it difficult to categorize them definitively. In what follows, we organize online library websites into four categories:

- General-purpose digital libraries
- Specialized digital libraries
- Online periodical collections
- Ebook collections

General-Purpose Digital Libraries

A *general-purpose digital library* is a full-service library "without walls" whose holdings are accessed via a computer. Like a traditional library, its holdings include books, articles, specialized databases, and other collections in digital format. Digital libraries are especially advantageous for learners who are studying in a totally online environment and for individuals with disabilities who are physically unable to make use of a traditional library.

One example of a general-purpose digital library is the ▪Electronic Text Center at the University of Virginia, which features 51,000 digital texts and 350,000 digital images. Thousands of the books and images are available to the public via the Internet. Disciplines represented include history, literature, philosophy, religion, and history of science. The collection also has resources in a number of different languages.

Specialized Digital Libraries

We use the term *specialized digital libraries* to refer to collections of digitized resources that pertain to a specific topic. Five examples of specialized digital libraries follow.

- The ▪Perseus Digital Library, sponsored by Tufts University, provides resources for the study of the ancient classical world and other early civilizations.
- The ▪Visible Human Project from the National Library of Medicine provides complete, anatomically detailed, three-dimensional representations of the male and female human body.
- The ▪National Geographic MapMachine is a free digital library collection from which visitors can create customized snapshots of the world as seen from Earth orbit. Users can zoom in on a geographic area of interest and obtain details about the region's vegetation, mineral resources, earthquakes, and agriculture, among other interesting information.
- Columbia University's ▪Bartelby.com is a website that archives the works of more than 50 fiction writers and dozens of poets and nonfiction writers. This site also presents a word of the day with audio pronunciation, a quote of the day, and information about featured authors.
- (ARTstor, created by The Andrew W. Mellow Foundation, is a digital library collection of approximately 300,000 art images covering art, architecture and archeology. The library also includes extensive descriptive information about the images as well as tools to facilitate pedagogical and research activities. Users can view and analyze images through features such as zooming and panning, saving groups of images online for personal or shared uses, and creating and delivering presentations both online and offline.

Online Periodical Collections

Online periodical collections are the digital archives of conventional library periodicals: journals, newspapers, magazines, and the like. Four examples of online periodical collections follow.

- ▪JSTOR (Journal Storage) is an archive of the back issues of significant scholarly journals published before 1990, some dating back to the nineteenth century. Like ARTstor, it was previously sponsored by the Mellon Foundation. Instructors can use the JSTOR archive to establish journal article reserves in eformat for use in course research (Bazillion & Braun, 2001).
- The ▪NASA Astrophysics Data System is a digital library and abstract service on the subjects of astronomy and astrophysics, instrumentation, and physics and geophysics. This site is the largest free full-text science archive in the world.

- Stanford University's •HighWire is a science archive with links to more than 216 journals and 180,000 articles in the life sciences, medicine, physical sciences, and the social sciences. In addition to archives of journal articles, this site also provides access to the *Oxford English Dictionary*.
- The •Accessible Archives is a website that is the digitized full text of nineteenth-century newspapers.

Ebook Collections

*Ebook collection*s are websites that provide the full text of books in digital format. Some ebook websites also provide the text of journal articles. The number of ebook websites is growing rapidly. Some are accessible free of charge; others charge an access fee. Five examples of ebook collections follow.

- The •International Children's Digital Library (ICDL), illustrated in Figure 7.13, is supported by a team of interdisciplinary researchers from computer science, library studies, education, art, and psychology. Focusing on the needs of child readers, the ICDL website contains over 260 ebooks in 15 languages representing 27 cultures. With help from participants from around the world, ICDL is building an international collection that reflects the diversity and excellence of children's literature.
- •Project Gutenberg is a website that in 2003 had over 6,267 full-text electronic books available for free distribution. Begun by Michael Hart through a grant he received at the University of Illinois in 1971, Project Gutenberg reflects Hart's belief that the

FIGURE 7.13   An Example Screen from the International Children's Digital Library Website

University of Maryland and the Internet Archives, used with permission.

greatest value created by computers will not be computing but the storage, retrieval, and searching of material that before the advent of electronic computing was stored in printed format in the world's libraries (Epstein, 2003).

- The creators of ■netLibrary, which has more than 35,000 titles in its collection, have established relationships with 210 publishers of trade, academic, reference, and scholarly books. Students and faculty in institutions that subscribe to netLibrary can electronically check out a volume in the collection.

- ■Questia provides an assortment of ebooks and journal articles. The Questia database contains about 40,000 full-text books and journal articles intended primarily for undergraduates studying the humanities and social sciences. A subscription to Questia provides access to the collection 24 hours a day, 7 days a week, a convenience that suits many students' habits of working on reports and projects at all hours of the day or night. As an added attraction, Questia has an automatic reference citation feature that will create footnotes and bibliographic information in proper format.

- Users may access the ebook collection at ■ebrary without a fee, but are charged for any pages that are stored to disk or printed.

WEB RESEARCH

As illustrated in this chapter, the web provides an enormous number and variety of resources to enhance and supplement learning. It is very likely that your library contains numerous web-based resources. However, when your institutional library does not have the resources you need, with good web searching skills, you are likely to find relevant information by searching the Internet. The key to using these resources effectively is knowing how to find them, whether they reside in your library or externally on the Internet. It is also very important to be able to evaluate the quality of the resources. These are invaluable skills for both you and your students. What follows consists of suggestions to help you to find and evaluate digital library resources. First we discuss the role of librarians in helping you and your students locate quality digital library resources. Next we provide an overview of search engines. Finally, we propose a rubric for evaluating websites.

The Role of Librarians in Web Research

The role of librarians in elearning is an important one, and the library staff at your institution is most likely an excellent source of information. Library staff are familiar with the electronic holdings of the library and also know how to locate and evaluate resources on the Internet. They can be especially valuable in helping you integrate digital library resources into your course. As discussed earlier, you should integrate library services and the services of librarians into your coursesite whenever possible. For example, with the permission of a designated librarian, you could establish a policy by which students are instructed to contact the librarian directly with relevant "library reference" questions. Contact could be by email as well as via electronic discussions monitored by librarians (Shank & Dewald, 2003).

Forming a liaison with a knowledgeable librarian at your institution may be one of the most important acts you perform as an elearning instructor. In fact, with the development of instructional materials, it is becoming more commonplace for librarians, instructional designers, educational technologists, and others to work more closely than in the past and to engage in collaborations. The following is a list of services librarians potentially can provide you and your students:

- Identify internal library resources pertinent to your course or discipline.
- Identify external resources pertinent to your course or discipline.
- Organize resources on a specific subject that constitute "packets" of information to support a learning activity.
- Provide training and tutorials on methods of locating information within the library's holdings.
- Provide training and tutorials on methods of locating information in external digital library resources.
- Provide guidance on how to evaluate digital resources.
- Provide guidance on copyright policies.
- Provide guidance on how to formulate bibliographic references.

Search Engines

With the growing number of web resources available, it is extremely important that you and your students develop the skills needed to find and evaluate them. The basic tools needed for effective web research are readily available. An Internet connection, a web browser such as Netscape or Explorer, and a search engine are all you will require. A *search engine* is software that enables you to request that a web search be conducted for resources relevant to the *keywords* you specify. The search engine examines databases of website content and compiles lists of websites that are relevant to the keywords of your search request. These databases are compiled by *spiders*—also referred to as *crawlers,* software robots regularly sent out by search engine software to find and categorize new information as it continually appears on the web. If you create a course website and a few weeks later search for information on the subjects your coursesite treats, you may be surprised to find your own website appearing in the list of relevant resources the search engine compiles.

Many different search engines are available for your use free of charge. *Google* is one of the most popular and best known. To use a search engine, you need only specify its URL address, enter your *keywords* in a text box when the search website appears, and select the button that begins the search. For example, to find websites that pertain to the Wright Brothers, open your browser and type in the URL of your preferred search engine. (You should consider bookmarking your favorite search engines for easy access.) Once the search engine screen appears, enter the words "Wright Brothers" as the keywords you are searching for. This is known as a *search query.* When entering a search query, the rules of the search engine must be followed. Because each may have unique rules, it is best to review the guidelines of the search engine to establish the most efficient way to enter a search query. Placing the words in quotations typically instructs the search engine to find website references that contain both the words "Wright" *and* "Brothers." When a search for "Wright Brothers" is conducted at Google, for example, thousands of websites will be revealed.

Conducting a search on the same keywords with different search engines is likely to return different results. A search at a *subject search engine* may return fewer results that are more specific because these search guides have been compiled by human beings. For example, ▪Education Planet is a website that catalogs online educational materials and provides access to quality, teacher-approved educational resources. When "Wright Brothers" is entered as the search query at Education Planet, the search reveals numerous references to Wright Brothers as well as references to materials such as lesson plans and supplemental materials to teach students about the Wright Brothers. Search engines also exist that will search through the databases of other search engines. Such a search is known as a *metasearch*. An engine performing this kind of search is called a *metasearch engine.*

Neither Google nor any other search engine can index all the information on the Internet. Web content that is most likely not indexed by conventional search engines is referred to collectively as the *invisible web* (Vidmar, 2003). Other terms for the invisible web are the *deep web* and the *opaque web.* The majority of the information comprising the invisible web is made up of information contained in databases that can be accessed via the web, but that search engines cannot find. Why? In order to gain access to information in databases, you must be able to interact with the database to tell it exactly what information you want. One way to search the invisible web is to use a specialized search engine.

Software and search engines are now emerging that aid in analyzing and organizing the results of searches. One such search engine is ▪Vivisimo. A search conducted through Vivisimo would return results that are automatically sorted and listed by clickable categories. Another emerging category of metasearch engines is *federated search engines.* One of the major functions of a federated search engine is to perform a search on the specific electronic content licensed by an organization such as a university library, a school district, and others.

Figure 7.14 summarizes the names of a few popular search engines in the categories of keyword searches, subject searches, metasearches, and specialized searches (for invisible web searching).

Evaluating the Quality of Websites

Anyone with web access potentially can post a website. No governing body exists to ensure or evaluate the accuracy of information posted on the web or the quality of its presentation. Also, even when you carefully compose search queries, your searches are likely to reveal many more websites than you have time to peruse. Consequently, a method for evaluating websites is needed. Perhaps the first thing to consider in assessing website quality is the reputation of the site author or sponsor. However, individuals totally unknown to the world except for their web presence author many good websites—as well as even more bad ones. The

FIGURE 7.14   Search Engines

KEYWORD	SUBJECT	METASEARCH	SPECIALIZED
▪AltaVista	▪Education Planet	▪Dogpile	▪CompletePlanet
▪Google	▪Encyclopedia Britannica	▪Excite	▪Direct Search
▪Hotbot	▪LookSmart	▪MetaCrawler	▪Infomine
▪Lycos	▪Yahoo!	▪WebCrawler	▪Internet Public Library

currency of a site is another very important indicator of quality. It can be deduced by noting when the site was last updated, as well as when it was first established, information that should be clearly posted on the site.

A site's popularity is also a measure of its quality, and determining what kind of websites reference the site you are evaluating can provide information about that site's users. Such information can be obtained using a *link-to* query. At the AltaVista website, for instance, entering "link:www.educationplanet.com" in the URL text window of your browser will return a list of websites with links to Education Planet. The types of sites listed by the link-to query may help you evaluate the quality of the Education Planet website.

The purpose of a website is also an indicator of its quality. For example, if the site is designed to market or sell something, the contents may be biased. Try to determine whether the site is intended to provide information, to explain something, to persuade an audience, to market products or ideas, or for some other purpose. Also, try to ascertain sources of information on the site. Design quality such as grammatical correctness of the text is another indicator, as are whether colors and graphics are used appropriately and whether site navigation is easy to use. In short, look for signs of the intent, web savviness, and intellectual prowess of a website's author.

Figure 7.15 is an evaluation checklist intended to help you and your students evaluate the quality of websites. The 25-item checklist is organized into four main evaluation categories. To appraise overall site quality, the form addresses general information about the site's author or sponsor, site purpose, currency and accuracy of site information, and site design. Note, however, that no checklist is a substitute for professional knowledge and good judgment when you are assessing a website's quality. Just remember that a website—unlike the peer-reviewed journals or published books you may be used to referencing—has not undergone evaluation by a third party before it becomes available for your use. URL references at the end of this chapter provide further information on digital library resources, information literacy skills, and website evaluation.

DESIGNING WEB RESEARCH ASSIGNMENTS

Computers and the Internet afford students the opportunity to find and use a wide variety of resources when they perform research. Such research is one of the most important aspects of a student-centered learning environment. Besides accruing knowledge specific to course content, students performing web research are also learning how to learn in a medium that seems likely in the near future to equal or exceed the importance of the print medium in education. Yet while web research assignments can be very enriching when they are properly formulated, they can also be very frustrating if they are improperly focused. Much of the learning potential of web-based research is lost when research assignments are not coordinated with course content or when students have difficulty understanding the relevancy and value of the assignment. For example, requesting that students conduct web searches just to locate sites does little to enhance learning. What is needed is a focused, thought-provoking assignment that directs students to use the information they find in meaningful ways. The web research assignments illustrated in Figures 2.2 and 6.7 provide examples.

FIGURE 7.15 Website Evaluation Checklist

I. General Information

Name of Website: _____ Date Last Updated: _____

URL: _____ Date Reviewed: _____

Author or Sponsor: _____ Type of Website (Commercial, Scholarly,

Contact Information: _____ Informational, Political, or Religious): _____

Date First Established: _____ Purpose of the Website: _____

II. Website Credibility *Indicate answers by checking yes or no.*	Yes	No	Comments
1. Does an author or sponsor search indicate additional relevant works?	☐	☐	
2. Can the author or site sponsor be contacted for clarification?	☐	☐	
3. Is there a link to more information about the author or sponsor?	☐	☐	
4. Is the site one that many other credible sites link to?	☐	☐	
5. Does the information at the site appear to be accurate?	☐	☐	

Overall Credibility Rating: *In the last column, rate the overall credibility of the site.* _____
Please use the following scale: 0—Very Poor; 1—Poor; 2—Average; 3—Good; 4—Excellent.
(Please use this scale to rate overall website design and overall quality also.)

Comments on Credibility: *Include any comments you have on the credibility of this site:*

III. Website Design *Indicate answers by checking yes or no.*	Yes	No	Comments
6. Does the site utilize graphics appropriately?	☐	☐	
7. Is the site easy to navigate?	☐	☐	
8. Is the site easy to read?	☐	☐	
9. Is the number of clicks needed to get to further information limited to 2 or 3?	☐	☐	
10. Are links to other sites current and well maintained?	☐	☐	
11. Does the site have a text-only viewing option?	☐	☐	
12. Is it possible to search the site?	☐	☐	
13. Is the site designed for fast scanning and readability?	☐	☐	
14. Are colors used appropriately?	☐	☐	
15. Have flashing, scrolling, or otherwise distracting graphics been avoided?	☐	☐	
16. Are alt tags included for text readers?	☐	☐	
17. Is a site map included?	☐	☐	
18. Does every page include a way to get back to the homepage?	☐	☐	
19. Is the site generally available with few downtime periods?	☐	☐	
20. Do site pages load quickly?	☐	☐	

Overall Design Quality Rating: _____

Comments on Design Quality: *Include any comments on design quality:*

FIGURE 7.15   Continued

IV. Quality of Content *Indicate answers by checking yes or no.*	Yes	No	Comments
21. Does the message of the information avoid biases?	☐	☐	
22. Does the information appear to be original?	☐	☐	
23. Does the site provide substantial information? (The site can stand alone and does not rely totally on links to other sites.)	☐	☐	
24. Are external sources identified and clearly documented?	☐	☐	
25. Would you visit the site again for further information?	☐	☐	

Overall Quality of Content Rating: ⎯⎯⎯⎯⎯

Overall Rating (Total Score from Credibility, Design, and Quality) ⎯⎯⎯⎯⎯

This list identifies four techniques that can help you devise effective web research assignments. A discussion of each technique follows the list.

- Coordinate assignments with learning content.
- Design thought-provoking assignments.
- Provide specific assignment instructions.
- Address student workloads.

Coordinate Assignments with Learning Content

Coordinating web research assignments with course content promotes active learning and helps students better understand the value of such assignments. Consider associating web-based research assignments with textbook readings, lectures, guest speakers, case studies, and other learning activities. For example, teams working on case studies can be asked to include in their research the information discovered at relevant websites that supports various points of view on a controversial or multifaceted issue. As another example, when a guest speaker will be joining the class, prior to the speaker's visit you can ask your students to gather web information about the speaker or the speaker's presentation topic.

Design Thought-Provoking Assignments

Web-based research assignments should be designed to provoke and reinforce critical thinking. For example, in a meteorology-related web research assignment, having students search the web for facts about unspecified weather catastrophes may be mundane. Perhaps a more interesting research assignment would require that they look for information about the devastation caused by hurricanes, tornadoes, and other high-wind catastrophes, and to adduce facts about specific storms causing such devastation. Having students discuss their findings in an electronic forum could further enrich this assignment. Another method to encourage critical thinking is to prepare a list of specific questions you would like students to answer, either by searching the web in general or by perusing specific predetermined websites.

Provide Specific Assignment Instructions

Before students begin a web research assignment, they will want to know exactly what is expected of them and exactly how they will be graded. Consequently, your assignment must include specific instructions about these issues. The instructions must clearly inform your students about what you expect them to do with the information they obtain from a web search or website visit, and how you will determine the degree to which they have met your expectations.

Address Student Workloads

Contemporary students may well be the busiest generation ever. Many college students work outside the learning environment to support their education. Other students are full-time workers and part-time learners. Thus you must be mindful of your students' workloads when you make an assignment. Do not underestimate the amount of time it will take them to complete a web research assignment. Looking for information on the web can be very time-consuming, and much time can be wasted sorting through volumes of irrelevant information on the web. One way to reduce the amount of time required for web research is to preview the results of a web search and provide students with a list of high-quality sites to use in their research. Another approach is to provide students with a starting point for their research by directing them to a portal where they will find information about other relevant sites to visit. Still another method is to maintain a list of websites found by previous students and to provide current students with this list as a starting point. If you do this, bear in mind that websites become obsolete. Thus, it is important to check your list of recommended sites often to ensure the currency of each entry. The professionalism and hence the effectiveness of your course is diminished when you recommend students visit out-of-date or nonexistent websites.

REFERENCES

Arms, W. Y. (2000). *Digital libraries.* Cambridge, MA: MIT Press.

Bazillion, R. J. (2001). Academic libraries in the digital revolution. *EDUCAUSE Quarterly, 24*(1), 51–55.

Bazillion, R. J., & Braun, C. L. (2001, January). History on reserve: Using online journal collections. *Syllabus, 14*(6), 44–46.

Beard, R. (2000, May/June). Faculty initiative in expanding classroom web usage. *The Technology Source.* Retrieved September 23, 2002, from http://horizon. unc.edu/TS/development/2000–05.asp

Branigan, C. (2002, April 3). Microsoft explores new game-based learning environment. *eSchool News.* Retrieved June 10, 2002, from www.eschoolnews. com/news/showStory.cfm?ArticleID=3642

Carlson, S. (2003a, February 6). Web-loving students can be prodded to cite peer-reviewed works in term papers, study suggests. Retrieved December 1, 2003 from http://chronicle.com/free/2003/02/2003020601t.htm

Carlson, S. (2003b, March 21). New allies in the fight against research by Googling: Faculty members and librarians slowly start to work together on courseware. *The Chronicle of Higher Education,* p. A33.

Carnevale, D. (2002a, December 10). Online-lab software simulates chemical interactions and explosions. *The Chronicle of Higher Education.* Retrieved December 13, 2002, from http://chronicle.com/free/2002/12/2002121001t.htm

Carnevale, D. (2002b, December 16). A virtual laboratory simulates physics experiments. *The Chronicle of Higher Education.* Retrieved December 17, 2002, from http://chronicle.com/free/2002/12/2002121601t.htm

Carnevale, D. (2003a, January 31). The virtual lab experiment: Some colleges use computer simulations to expand science offerings online. *The Chronicle of Higher Education,* p. A30.

Carnevale, D. (2003b, April 29). Online spectrometry lab will let undergraduates try out costly equipment. *The Chronicle of Higher Education.* Retrieved April 29, 2003, from http://chronicle.com/free/2003/04/2003042901t.htm

Cline, N. M. (2000, May/June). Virtual continuity: The challenge for research libraries today. *EDUCAUSE Review, 35*(3), 22–28.

Cudiner, S., & Harmon, O. (2000, December). An active learning approach to teaching effective online search strategies. *T.H.E. Journal, 28*(5), 52–58.

Dede, C. (2003, May/June). Multi-user virtual environments. *EDUCAUSE Review, 38*(3), 60–61.

Epstein, S. L. (2003, April). Where did all the books go? *Syllabus, 16*(9), 12–16.

Foreman, J. (2003, July/August). Next-generation educational technology versus the lecture. *EDUCAUSE Review, 38*(4), 12–22.

Foster, A. L. (2003, January 10). Scientists plan 2 online journals to make articles available freely and universally. *The Chronicle of Higher Education,* p. A29.

Gandel, P. B., Katz, R. N., & Metros, S. E. (2004, March/April). The "weariness of the flesh:" Reflections on the life of the mind in an era of abundance. *EDUCAUSE Review, 39*(2), 40–42, 44–46, 48, 50–51.

Gaunt, M. (2002, March). A bridge to the future: Observations on building a digital library. *Syllabus, 15*(8), 12–16.

Green, K. C. (2002, April/May). The new king. *Converge, 5*(2), 46–48.

Kiernan, V. (2004, April). Professors are unhappy with limitations of online resources, survey finds. *The Chronicle of Higher Education.* Retrieved May 10, 2004, from http://chronicle.com/prm/weekly/v50/i34/34a03401.htm

Killmer, K. A., & Koppel, N. B. (2002, August). So much information, so little time: Evaluating web resources with search engines. *T.H.E. Journal, 30*(1), 21–29.

Laverty, C., Leger, A., Stockley, D., McCollam, M., Sinclair, S., Hamilton, D., & Knapper, C. (2003). Enhancing the classroom experience with learning technology teams. *EDUCAUSE Quarterly, 26*(3), 19–25.

Long, P. D. (2002, March). Can libraries find a new home in courseware? *Syllabus, 15*(8) 8–10.

Lynch, C. (2000, January/February). From automation to transformation: Forty years of libraries and information technology in higher education. *EDUCAUSE Review, 35*(1), 60–68.

Meisner, G. W., & Hoffman, H. (2003, June). Leading the way to virtual learning: The LAAPhysics laboratory. *Syllabus, 16*(11), 26–28.

Miller, F. (2004). Disposable scholarship? *EDUCAUSE Quarterly, 27*(1), 8–9.

Overholtzer, J., & Tombarge, J. (2003). Promoting information fluency. *EDUCAUSE Quarterly, 26*(1), 55–58.

Pitt, S. P., Updike, C. B., & Guthrie, M. E. (2002). Integrating digital images into the art and art history curriculum. *EDUCAUSE Quarterly, 25*(2), 38–44.

Read, B. (2002a, April 1). A professor puts future ethnographers in the field with a CD-ROM simulation. *The Chronicle of Higher Education.* Retrieved April 1, 2002, from http://chronicle.com/free/2002/04/2002040101t.htm

Read, B. (2002b, September 18). University of Pittsburgh digitizes decades of astronomy data to aid today's researchers. *The Chronicle of Higher Education.* Retrieved September 18, 2002, from http://chronicle.com/free/2002/09/200209180lt.htm

Read, B. (2002c, November 21). Online library for children aims for 10,000 titles and child-friendly design, with professors' help. *The Chronicle of Higher Education.* Retrieved December 13, 2002, from http://chronicle.com/free/2002/11/2002112101t.htm

Read, B. (2003a, February 28). An interactive web site offers students a whimsical introduction to psychology. *The Chronicle of Higher Education.* Retrieved February 28, 2003, from http://chronicle.com/free/2003/02/2003022801t.htm

Read, B. (2003b, April 3). An online conservatory lets visitors try remaking classical standards. *The Chronicle of Higher Education.* Retrieved April 3, 2003, from http://chronicle.com/free/2003/04/2003040301t.htm

Read, B. (2003c, May 20). New web site opens 3,000 pages of Einstein's notes to scholars and students. *The Chronicle of Higher Education.* Retrieved May 20, 2003, from http://chronicle.com/free/2003/05/2003052002t.htm

Read, B. (2003d, May 29). A web site offers the latest buzz about bugs. *The Chronicle of Higher Education.* Retrieved May 29, 2003, from http://chronicle.com/free/2003/05/2003052901t.htm

Shank, J. D., & Dewald, N. H. (2003). Establishing our presence in courseware: Adding library services to the virtual classroom. *Information Technology and Libraries.* Retrieved August 8, 2003, from www.lita.org/Content/NavigationMenu/LITA/LITA_Publications4/ITAL_Information

Suber, P. (2002, March). Noesis: Is it a library with built-in searching or a search engine with a built-in library? *Syllabus, 15*(8), 18–22.

Vidmar, D. (2003, April). Getting in deep: After Google, the invisible web. *Syllabus, 16*(9), 25–27.

Waters, D. (2001, September/October). New horizons: Developing digital libraries: Four principles for higher education. *EDUCAUSE Review, 36*(5), 58–59.

Young, J. R. (2002, July 5). "Superarchives" could hold all scholarly output: Online collections by institutions may challenge the role of journal publishers. *The Chronicle of Higher Education.* Retrieved July 5, 2002, from http://chronicle.com/free/v48/i43/43a02901.htm

URL REFERENCES

Accessible Archives: www.accessible.com
The Alberta Library: www.thealbertalibrary.ab.ca
AltaVista: www.altavista.com
ARTstor: www.artstor.org/index.html
Bartelby.com: http://bartleby.com
Beetle Science: www.explore.cornell.edu/scene.cfm?scene=Beetle%20Science
BUBL LINK (Libraries of Networked Knowledge) Center for Digital Library Research, Strathclyde University, Scotland: http://bubl.ac.uk/link/
Canadian University Reciprocal Borrowing Agreement: www.coppul.ca/rb/rbindex.html
The Chronicle of Higher Education: http://chronicle.com
CompletePlanet: www.completeplanet.com
CORE (Comprehensive Online Research Education): http://core.lib.purdue.edu/index.html
CourseCompass: www.coursecompass.com/ccindex.html
Creative Commons: http://creativecommons.org/
Direct Search: www.freepint.com/gary/direct.htm
DOAJ (Directory of Open Access Journals): www.doaj.org/
Dogpile: http://dogpile.com
ebrary: www.ebrary.com
Education Planet: www.educationplanet.com
EDUCAUSE Quarterly: www.educause.edu/pub/eq
EDUCAUSE Review: www.educause.edu/pub/er
Einstein Archives Online: www.alberteinstein.info
Electronic Text Center at the University of Virginia: http://etext.lib.virginia.edu
Encyclopedia Britannica: www.britannica.com
Evaluating Web Pages: Techniques to Apply & Questions to Ask: www.lib.berkeley.edu/TeachingLib/Guides/Internet/Evaluate.html
Excite: http://search.excite.com
Fathom: The Source for Online Learning: www.fathom.com/
Google: www.google.com
HighWire: http://highwire.stanford.edu
Hotbot: www.hotbot.com
Hotmath: www.hotmath.org
Houghton Mifflin Company: www.hmco.com
The Imagination Station: www.istation.com/en/corpsite
Infomine: http://infomine.ucr.edu

Information Literacy Tutorial: www.stjohns.edu/images/sjuimages/libraries/ilt_home.htm
International Children's Digital Library: www.icdlbooks.org
The Internet Public Library: www.ipl.org/
JSTOR: www.jstor.org
Learn Anytime Anywhere Physics: http://laap.uncg.edu
Librarians' Index to the Internet: http://lii.org/
LiveRef: A Registry of Real-Time Digital Reference Services: www.public.iastate.edu/~CYBERSTACKS/Academic
LookSmart: www.looksmart.com
Lycos: http://search.lycos.com
Making of America at Cornell University Library Digital Collections: http://library8.library.cornell.edu/moa
McGraw-Hill Digital Solutions: www.mhhe.com/catalogs/solutions/olc.mhtml
MetaCrawler: www.metacrawler.com
Multi-User Virtual Environment Experiential Simulator (MUVEES): www.gse.harvard.edu/~dedech/muvees
NASA Astrophysics Data System: http://adswww.harvard.edu
NASA Quest: www.quest.arc.nasa.gov
National Geographic MapMachine: http://plasma.nationalgeographic.com/mapmachine
netLibrary: www.netlibrary.com
Net Links, State Library of Queensland: http://netlinks.slq.qld.gov.au/
NewspaperDirect: http://newspaperdirect.com
NOVA/PBS Online Adventures: www.pbs.org/wgbh/nova/adventures
OASIS (Online Advancement of Student Information Skills): http://oasis.sfsu.edu/index.html
Online Conservatory, Boston Symphony: www.bso.org/itemB/detail.jhtml?id=12300008&area=bso
Online Expeditions: www.ctcexpeditions.org
Online Meteorology Guide: WW2010: http://ww2010.atmos.uiuc.edu
Open College e-Learning Content Library: www.opencollege.com
Perseus Digital Library: www.perseus.tufts.edu
Princeton University Press Ebooks: http://pup.princeton.edu/ebooks.html

Project Gutenberg: www.gutenberg.net

Project SAILS (Standardized Assessment of Information Literacy Skills): http://sails.lms.kent.edu/plans/sample.html

Questia: http://questia.com

Refdesk.com: www.refdesk.com/

RIO (Research Instruction Online): http://dizzy.library.arizona.edu/rio/index.html

Shakespeare: Subject to Change: www.ciconline.org/bdp1

Syllabus: www.syllabus.com

TAFE (Technical and Further Education): http://library.chisholm.vic.edu.au/nationalReciprocal.htm

The Technology Source: http://ts.mivu.org

T.H.E. Journal: www.thejournal.com

TILT (Texas Information Literacy Tutorial): http://tilt.lib.utsystem.edu

The Valley of the Shadow: http://valley.vcdh.virginia.edu

Vatican Museums: www.vatican.va

Virtual ChemLab: http://vchemlab.byu.edu/home/index.htm

Virtual Mass Spectometry Laboratory: http://mass-spec.chem.cmu.edu

Virtual Reference Desk: www.vrd.org

Visible Human Project: www.nlm.nih.gov/research/visible/visible_human.html

Vivisimo: http://vivisimo.com

WebCrawler: www.webcrawler.com

The WWW Virtual Library: http://vlib.org

University of Canterbury American Studies Portal: http://library.canterbury.ac.nz/art/amst/amst_portal.shtml

Yahoo!: http://search.yahoo.com

CHAPTER EIGHT

COURSESITE DESIGN AND MAINTENANCE

Your coursesite is where students seek out elearning resources, stay abreast of course announcements, and communicate with each other and with you. As such, it is a focal point of your elearning course. If it is not easy to use and readily available, the result will be frustration for you and your students, and a diminishment of elearning effectiveness. This chapter—organized in four sections—explains how to design and maintain your coursesite. The first section discusses various ways to organize resources on a coursesite. The second addresses the very timely and important subject of how to provide for coursesite access by students with disabilities. The third section offers a rubric for evaluating the usability of your coursesite. The fourth explains how to back up your elearning resources and related files to protect against failures of the file server that supports your LMS.

COURSESITE ARCHITECTURE

The term *coursesite architecture* describes the organization of elearning resources in a coursesite. As we saw in Chapter 4, this organization is hierarchical, with resource files residing in top-level folders and related subfolders that should be appropriately named. When you use an LMS to design your coursesite, navigation functionality is created automatically, allowing you to concentrate on hierarchical design. This section advances some ideas about how you might begin thinking about coursesite design. Of course, you should plan your coursesite just as carefully as you plan the resources you will post to it. The VPODD planning model described in Chapter 3 works for planning a coursesite as well as for planning a course and its elearning resources. If you will be developing coursesites for more than one course, creating a *template* for a standard coursesite organization will probably save you time in the long run.

What follows consists of three subsections. The first discusses two important characteristics of an effective coursesite architecture—consistency and ease of navigation. The second section discusses two common ways of organizing coursesite information—by course topics or by resource types. The third explains how decisions about coursesite architecture are related to creating an objectivist and/or a constructivist elearning environment.

Characteristics of an Effective Architecture

A straightforward coursesite architecture increases the likelihood that students will be able to find and access course resources easily and quickly. An uncluttered opening screen should clearly indicate to students what information is contained in the coursesite. Subfolders must be accessible without having to click too many times. Consider establishing a course architecture that limits top-level folders on the opening page to a dozen or fewer, with the underlying resource files never more than three clicks away. Figures 8.1 and 8.2 depict opening screens for the same web-enhanced Introduction to Elearning course implemented using two different LMSs, Blackboard and WebCT, respectively. While the top-level folders in both courses are conceptually identical, as are the underlying course architectures, the two opening screens differ significantly in look and feel, owing to design constraints imposed by the LMSs used to create the courses.

Your major concern in designing your coursesite architecture is how you will organize your course resources. Will you group them by course topics, by units or weeks, by chapters in a textbook, by resource categories, or by some other method? Once you have determined the organizational method, adhere to it rigorously. An effective coursesite design is invariably consistent. For example, if you organize by course topics and the first topic has a set of objectives, assignments, self-tests, discussion questions, and external links, each subsequent unit ordinarily should reflect the same organization. We will refer to this practice as *orthogonal* design. Consistency in coursesite organization allows students—once they become familiar with your organizational method—to anticipate what to expect when they navigate your coursesite.

Two Alternative Architectures

Diagramming your coursesite architecture can help you ensure that the hierarchical organization of your resources is complete and consistent. Such a diagram can be created using either a tree structure or an outline structure, because the two approaches are logically

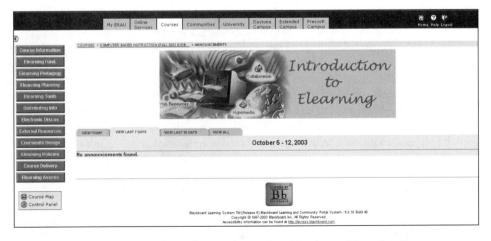

FIGURE 8.1   Blackboard Opening Screen for an Introduction to Elearning Course

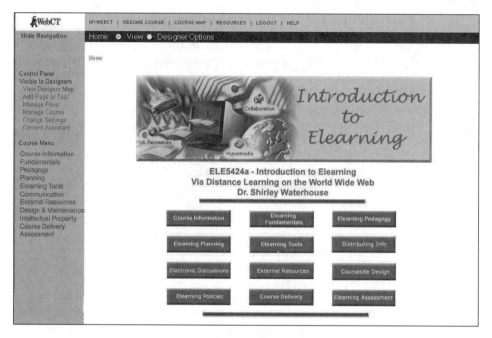

FIGURE 8.2   WebCT Opening Screen for the Same Introduction to Elearning Course

equivalent. In this subsection, we discuss two different approaches to organizing elearning course resources:

- Organization by topics
- Organization by resource types

Organization by Topics.   Figure 8.3 provides a tree-structure diagram for the architecture of the Introduction to Elearning course organized by topics and depicted in Figures 8.1 and 8.2. Figure 8.4 shows the same architecture diagrammed in outline form. As all four figures reveal, the course organizes its resources by course topics—*Elearning Fundamentals, Elearning Pedagogy, Elearning Planning,* and so forth—which in fact reflect the organization of this book into chapters. Under each top-level folder shown in Figure 8.3, except the folder called *Course Information,* there are consistently organized resources for that course topic—a Power-Point presentation the instructor will use to deliver a lecture; an assignment, which in some cases is an electronic discussion; an online quiz; and relevant external links. Three of the course topics additionally include a major test resource. The similar substructure of each topic folder reflects the orthogonal design of the architecture. The first topic, Course Information, is one that differs structurally from the other topics. Its resources are files containing staff information, a course syllabus, course policies, and related information. From the architecture as depicted, it seems likely that the instructor intends that the first course meeting provide students with an overview of the entire course, and that there will be no quiz or assignment related to this topic. It also seems likely that in total, students in the course would meet the instructor

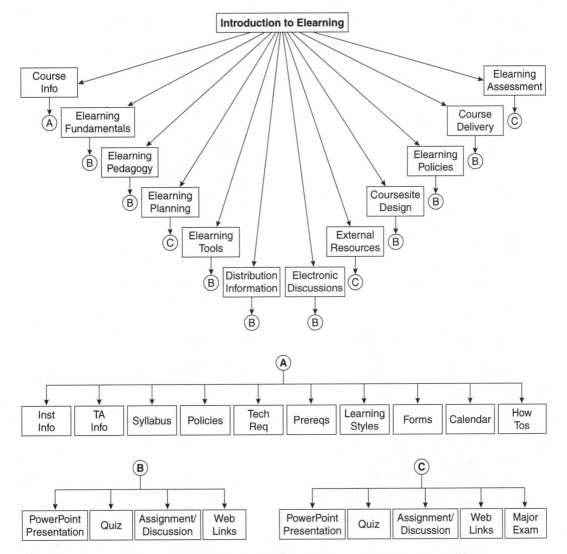

FIGURE 8.3   Tree-Structure Organization by Topic for the Introduction to Elearning Course

face-to-face at least 12 times. The initial meeting is a course introduction, with each of the 11 subsequent meetings focusing on 1 of the 11 subject topics identified in the course architecture.

Organization by topic is a good choice if you wish to combine resources into "packets" of information that will be accessed as single units. Organizing resources by weeks or by sessions of an elearning course exemplifies organization by topic. Because this architecture groups different kinds of resources, it encourages students to use the contents of an individual folder together. The organization does have the very slight drawback of duplicating folder substructures at different places in the architecture. For example, note how many times the subhierarchies labeled B and C in Figure 8.3 recur in the course organization.

FIGURE 8.4   Outline Organization by Topic for the Introduction to Elearning Course

1. Course Information
   a. Instructor Information
   b. Teaching Assistants Information
   c. Course Syllabus
   d. Policies
   e. Technical Requirements
   f. Course Prerequisites
   g. Learning Styles Inventory
   h. Forms
   i. Calendar
   j. How Tos
2. Elearning Fundamentals
   a. PowerPoint Presentation 1
   b. Quiz 1
   c. Assignment 1
3. Elearning Pedagogy
   a. PowerPoint Presentation 2
   b. Quiz 2
   c. Discussion 1
4. Elearning Planning
   a. PowerPoint Presentation
   b. Quiz 3
   c. Assignment 2
   d. Major Exam 1
5. Elearning Tools
   a. PowerPoint Presentation 4
   b. Quiz 4
   c. Discussion 2
6. Distributing Information
   a. PowerPoint Presentation 5
   b. Quiz 5
   c. Assignment 3

7. Electronic Discussions
   a. PowerPoint Presentation 6
   b. Quiz 6
   c. Assignment 4
8. External Resources
   a. PowerPoint Presentation 7
   b. Quiz 7
   c. Assignment 5
   d. Major Exam 2
9. Coursesite Design
   a. PowerPoint Presentation 8
   b. Quiz 8
   c. Assignment 6
10. Elearning Policies
    a. PowerPoint Presentation 9
    b. Quiz 9
    c. Discussion 3
11. Course Delivery
    a. PowerPoint Presentation 10
    b. Quiz 10
    c. Assignment 7
12. Elearning Assessment
    a. PowerPoint Presentation 11
    b. Quiz 11
    c. Assignment 8
    d. Major Exam 3

Organization by Resource Types.   The Introduction to Elearning course could also be organized by resource type, as depicted in the course architecture of Figure 8.5. In Figure 8.5, the top-level folders—except for the first, Course Information—now contain resources of the same type—PowerPoint presentations for lectures, discussions, assignments other than discussions, and quizzes and exams. When resources are grouped by type rather than by topic, students may have less immediate information about the order in which they will use the resources as they progress through your elearning course. However, when you use organization by resource types to create your course architecture, it is not difficult—as discussed later—to imply an ordering of elearning resources in each resource folder.

Objectivist versus Constructivist Architectures

Recall from Chapter 2 the distinction between objectivist and constructivist learning environments. In the former environment, you encourage students to process course information

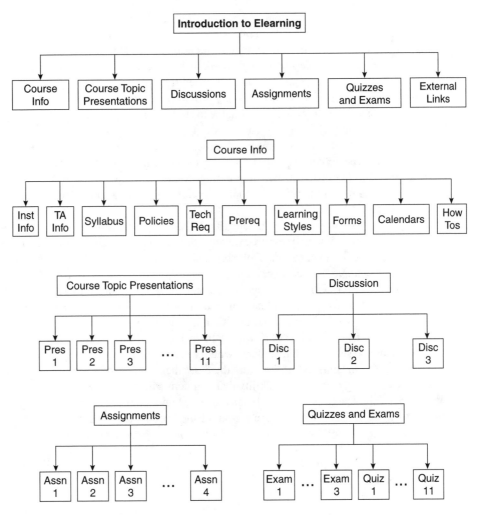

FIGURE 8.5   The Introduction to eLearning Course Organized by Learning Resource Types

in a prescribed order, whereas in the latter they are freer to choose the order in which they learn the information your course presents.

If you wish to create an objectivist elearning environment, your course architecture should reflect the sequence in which you want your students to use the elearning resources on your coursesite. Organization by topics works well in this case. In Figures 8.1 and 8.2, the top to bottom and/or left to right ordering of the top-level folders implies a sequence in which the information they contain will be processed. Relabeling the top-level folders numerically—*Unit 1: Elearning Fundamentals; Unit 2: Elearning Pedagogy; Unit 3: Elearning Planning,* and so forth—would further cue students that the information the folders contain is to be processed in the order indicated. Of course, organization by topics can also support a constructivist approach to learning if you explicitly avoid implying an ordering of the topic folders you create.

Organization by resource types may be slightly preferable to organization by topics for instructors who want to create a constructivist elearning environment. When the resources in each folder are arranged "randomly," students are encouraged to "browse" through your course resources in no particular order. If you want to constrain such browsing to a limited extent, so that within a specified time period only a certain subset of your resources are accessible, your LMS may provide an option that allows you to specify the inclusive dates a resource will be available to students. Organization by resource type can also support an objectivist approach to learning. This is the case in Figure 8.5, in which the ordering of lectures, assignments, discussions, and quizzes and exams in their respective resource-type folders is implied by the fact that they are numbered consecutively and arranged in the order of their numbering. Many instructors, however, will probably feel that an architecture arranged by topic is preferable to one arranged by resource for the predominately objectivist course.

Another way to create a constructionist environment is to use a *hybrid* architecture that combines topic and resource organization. Figure 8.6 depicts such an organization for the Introduction to Elearning Course. As shown in Figure 8.6, the top-level folders are organized by topic. Students are required to digest the information in Units I, II, and III in that order. However, within individual units, the course is organized by resource types. The intention is that within individual course units students will choose the order in which they view unit PowerPoint presentations, complete unit assignments, participate in unit discussions, and take unit quizzes and tests. In such circumstances, the quizzes and tests would probably be self-tests that students would retake until the results suggest that subject mastery has been achieved. If this were the case, there should be several versions of each quiz and test, to preclude the possibility that a student will learn a quiz or test rather than the material a single assessment instrument covers. Although the architecture of Figure 8.6 might not be the most desirable organization for the Introduction to Elearning course under consideration, it is offered here as an example of how a hybrid architecture is constructed.

COURSESITE ACCESS FOR STUDENTS WITH DISABILITIES

When planning your coursesite, you may want to ensure that your resources are available to students with special needs. Before you categorize this subject as being of minor importance, you might like to consider that the number of individuals in the general population with disabilities may be larger than you imagine. One in five individuals has a vision, hearing, or physical limitation (Kiser, 2001). Twenty-nine percent of families in the United States have at least one family member with a disability (Amador, 2003). It is estimated that up to 7.2 percent of students entering higher education have visual, hearing, cognitive, or motor impairment (Lamar, 2003). Among these are individuals with

- Visual disabilities such as blindness, low vision, and color blindness
- Hearing disabilities such as deafness and hard of hearing
- Mobility disabilities such as the inability to use hands, hand tremors, and slow muscular movement
- Learning disabilities, reading disorders, and attention deficit disorders

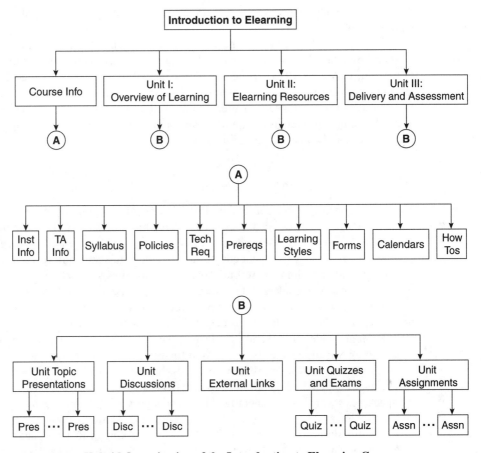

FIGURE 8.6   Hybrid Organization of the Introduction to Elearning Course

It should be quite obvious that students in some of these categories will be unable to use your elearning resources if you do not make special provisions for obliging them when you design your course.

Voluntary Compliance with Federal Law

This subsection discusses laws current in the United States. However, because most developed countries follow similar laws and guidelines, the information we present is relevant worldwide. Depending on the relationship existing between your organization and the federal government, you may or may not be required to design your coursesite to accommodate students with disabilities. For example, state-controlled colleges and universities are required to make their websites accessible to students with disabilities, whereas private institutions are not. However, there are at least two reasons why you should be aware of federal guidelines about web access for individuals with disabilities. First, it is desirable to follow these guidelines because they reflect compassion for all web users including elearning students. Second, the guidelines embody requirements that in the future may apply in general to individuals who author websites.

In 1990, the U.S. government passed the Americans with Disabilities Act (ADA). ADA makes it illegal for organizations to discriminate against people with disabilities. Eight years later, in August 1998, President Clinton signed into law the so-called Section 508 amendment to the 1973 Rehabilitation Act. Section 508 requires that information technology and websites developed, procured, maintained, or used by the federal government be accessible to people with disabilities. Many people in the elearning community believe that instructors should voluntarily abide by Section 508, even if they are not required to do so.

How to Accommodate Special Needs

The accommodations your coursesite provides for students with disabilities will vary according to the nature of a student's special need. For blind students, *screen readers* exist that can read text aloud to them. However, these students will still experience difficulty in processing the images shown on your coursesite. To remedy this problem, you can attach an *alt tag* to an image or multimedia resource. An alt tag contains text that describes a visual resource, so that screen readers can read a description of the resource to a visually impaired coursesite user. Color-blind students have difficulty discriminating certain color combinations. Avoiding these combinations can easily remedy this difficulty. The end-of-chapter URL References identify several excellent websites with detailed information on this subject. Hearing-impaired students may have difficulty with video clips or audio resources in your coursesite. As an example of how to address this difficulty, if you post a video of a guest speaker, you could include captions to go with the video and provide a text transcript of what the speaker is saying. More generally, it is a good idea, when posting media in your coursesite, to provide as many alternative "views" as possible (Horton, 2000). Students with impaired motor skills may run into difficulty when working with web pages that can be navigated only by mouse clicks instead of keystrokes. Such students can use one of a number of hardware alternatives to a traditional mouse. Such an alternative is an example of an *assistive technology,* as addressed in the next subsection.

It is worth noting that accommodating the special needs of individuals with disabilities is part of a larger movement emphasizing that web materials must be flexible enough to serve learners with differing needs not necessarily based on disabilities. Called *universal design,* the movement—as described on the ▪WebAIM (Web Accessibility in Mind) website—emphasizes the need to make web content available to larger, more diverse audiences. Web users currently use a wide variety of devices to access the web—traditional browsers, handheld devices, cell phones, and hands-free devices. A tenet of universal design is that web designers must accommodate all varieties of users:

> Web developers who ignore the emerging trend toward multiple-environment Internet access will be left to lament their inability to reach important segments of the population. . . . Web developers who design with accessibility in mind are often able to improve their Web site for all users, and not just for those users with disabilities. . . . Improving a site's accessibility for individuals who are blind also improves its accessibility for individuals who access the Web in environments that prohibit visual web surfing, such as in the car. (Bohman, 2000)

A similar idea is expressed on the ▪CAST (Center for Applied Special Technology) website: "The central practical premise of UDL [universal design learning] is that a curriculum should include alternatives to make it accessible and appropriate for individuals with different backgrounds, learning styles, abilities, and disabilities in widely varied learning contexts" (CAST, 2003).

Assistive Technologies

In the present context, *assistive technologies* is a term used to describe hardware devices and/or related software intended to help individuals with disabilities overcome problems they may encounter when attempting to view web pages. For example, individuals with hand immobility may be unable to use a traditional mouse. For such individuals, existing alternatives include a switch that can be actuated using one's mouth, a voice activated mouse, voice recognition software, or perhaps an alternative keyboard. General interest in assistive technologies for the web is increasing rapidly, and there is a growing need for instructors who understand the importance of assistive technologies in education. Some universities are leaders in addressing this need and have already begun to offer degrees in assistive technology. Included among these universities are the California State University system, the University of Kentucky, and the North Carolina State University (White, Wepner, & Wetzel, 2003). Also, the ▪Alliance for Technology Access (ATA) is an organization that focuses on helping individuals gain information about assistive technologies.

We close this subsection with the observation that the term *assistive technologies*—in a broader sense than used here—refers to any device that assists persons with disabilities in overcoming difficulties they may encounter in functioning in society at large.

Checking Websites for Disabilities Access Compliance

A number of excellent websites exist to help you gain insight into whether the websites you recommend that your students visit are "disabilities friendly" (Thombs, 2003). At the ▪Vischeck website, you can view examples of how things appear on a web page to someone who is color-blind. The ▪WebAIM site provides simulations that allow a user to see how individuals with little or no vision, and those with color blindness, experience a website. WebAIM also provides a number of online tutorials that will help you develop accessibility-compliant elearning resources.

A number of tools exist that allow you to evaluate an existing website for disabilities access compliance. One is ▪Bobby, an online evaluation tool developed by the Center for Applied Special Technology. When you visit Bobby, you may invoke software that will accept a website's URL and produce a report that rates the site's compliance with disability access standards. The report provides specific information about problems with a website. Pages that pass Bobby's compliance test are entitled to use the "Bobby Approved" logo. The World Wide Web Consortium (W3C) Web Accessibility Initiative (WAI), or W3C-WAI, maintains another website providing disabilities access compliance information. The ▪W3C-WAI website contains detailed information about 508 compliance. W3C-WAI permits the use of its logo on web pages it has verified to be 508 compliant.

Louis is an online database whereby instructors or students can find elearning resources appropriate for use by the blind. Visually impaired individuals who visit this website—using a screen reader—can identify and then rent or purchase these resources. Hosted by the ■American Printing House for the Blind in Louisville, Kentucky, Louis contains information about learning materials contributed by the 200 members of the Louis consortium. The database cites titles of more than 152,000 educational resources suitable for use by blind individuals, including works in large print Braille, sound recordings, computer files, and similar products.

The end-of-chapter References and URL References provide additional information on the Section 508 guidelines, tutorials on how to ensure compliance with 508, and resources and services for checking the compliance of coursesites.

Summary

The scope of this book is too broad to allow addressing in detail the very important topic of website disability access compliance. At a minimum, the following is a list of coursesite design techniques that may aid students with disabilities.

- Use clear, distinct images.
- Avoid the flamboyant use of color or color contrasts, or color combinations that color-blind individuals cannot discriminate. This caveat applies equally to fonts, images, and backgrounds.
- Set up text so that users can increase the size of fonts if they need to do so.
- On visual resource, attach alt tags readable by the screen readers used by blind students. Describe the image in the context of its importance to the lesson, to ensure that users who hear the description receive the same information as those who actually see the image.
- Include captions to describe audio and video clips to hearing-impaired students.
- Some existing images or videos include signing for the hearing impaired. Be aware that deaf students find it difficult to view such a resource and "listen" to it via signing at the same time. Use a text file to preview such a resource before you actually display it.
- Write in a clear and simple style. Avoid pop-up windows that may confuse students.
- Use simple navigation.
- Label navigation buttons with text, not icons, because screen readers can read text but not icons.

EVALUATING COURSESITE USABILITY

When you have designed and developed your coursesite, you should consider asking student evaluators to test its usability before you deliver your course the first time. This precaution will enable you to discover design shortcomings before they cause trouble for an entire class of students. Time and effort spent thinking through the usability process help to avoid significant design mistakes that could compromise the success of your course (Gale, 2001).

The goal of a coursesite usability evaluation should be to determine whether students find your coursesite effective and easy to use. In addition to using student evaluators, you might also ask a colleague to observe student evaluators and report on the evaluators' experiences when working with coursesite components. Figure 8.7 provides a model coursesite usability checklist that you might be able to modify to suit the architecture of your own coursesite. Major coursesite categories addressed by the form as written include navigation, accessing course materials, and coursesite resources. You will probably be able to think of other evaluation categories you might wish to include in the checklist.

FIGURE 8.7   Coursesite Usability Checklist

Students and Observers Complete the Following

Architecture/Navigation	Yes	No	Comments
Easy to navigate?	☐	☐	
Announcements easy to view?	☐	☐	
Easy to find what you want?	☐	☐	
Easy to return to start?	☐	☐	
Consistent coursesite design?	☐	☐	

Accessing Course Materials	Yes	No	Comments
Files download quickly?	☐	☐	
Effective web design?	☐	☐	
Documents print OK?	☐	☐	
Easy to find how to get help?	☐	☐	

Coursesite Resources	Yes	No	Comments
Forum features easy to use?	☐	☐	
Chat features easy to use?	☐	☐	
Easy to respond to forum topic?	☐	☐	
Easy to respond to chat topic?	☐	☐	
Whiteboard easy to use?	☐	☐	
Calendar easy to use?	☐	☐	
Tutorials easy to use?	☐	☐	
Gradebook easy to use?	☐	☐	
Online tests easy to take?	☐	☐	

Observers Only Complete the Following

Time Required to Find Each of the Following

Feature	*Time*	*Feature*	*Time*	*Feature*	*Time*
Grading Policy	_____	Quiz 3	_____	Exam 2	_____
Get Technical Help	_____	Forum 2	_____	Assignment 4	_____
Contact Instructor	_____	PowerPoint Pres. 5	_____	Gradebook	_____

Describe Coursesite Problem Areas Below

FILE MAINTENANCE

Whether your institution contracts with an outside provider for LMS services or manages the LMS itself, the course resources you create will be hosted on an Internet file server over which you personally have little or no control. Although computer administrators routinely perform file backups on the systems they oversee, catastrophic hardware failures and/or operator errors do sometimes occur. Moreover, fire has been known to destroy entire computer installations, including all offline file backups. In short, a small but finite possibility exists that some or all of the information you store on your LMS server will be irretrievably lost. Such an eventuality rarely occurs, but when it does, the results can be devastating. We know, because we have seen it happen, and what we observed was *not* pretty: The elearning courses for an entire university summer school term were lost and had to be re-created by individual faculty members. Perhaps the saddest part of such computer system failures is that the horrible consequences they can occasion for elearning instructors need never occur. Because you put a lot of work into developing your course resources and coursesite structure, it behooves you to assure that the learning materials you have created are protected against loss. This brief section makes suggestions about how you can do this.

System Administrator Policies

The first step toward protecting your work against loss is determining what backup and archiving policies your LMS system administrator follows. Having this information is important because it enables you to determine what measure of responsibility you have in maintaining your coursesite and its resource files. The following are some of the relevant questions to which answers you should seek. How often are the files on the server backed up? Are the backups stored in the same room as the server, so that they might also be destroyed if some catastrophe destroyed the server? What happens to your coursesite and its resource when the course it over? Are the course files kept active on the server or archived for use in the future? If courses are archived, are items such as discussion postings saved or discarded? What is the process for activating your course the next time you teach it? If your course will be archived, how can you arrange to view it if the need to do so arises? What is the process for preserving a record of course grades for your course? How will your coursesite be affected by releases of new versions of the LMS software?

If the answers to these questions suggest that your system administrator's policies make it unlikely that your work will be irretrievably lost—and they probably will—you can rest easier, but only a *little* easier. There are still a number of precautions you should take to assure the safety of your elearning files.

Course Resource File Backups

Even if your system administrator backs up your course and/or archives it, we feel very strongly that you should maintain for every elearning course you create a personal backup of its elearning resources. This backup should exist *in at least two different places.* One backup should reside on your personal computer and the other should be stored to an external disk.

To this end, you should create a directory structure on your hard drive that mimics the organization of your coursesite architecture. Keep a copy of each course resource file in the appropriate directory of this structure. For resources that cannot be backed up directly—for example, forums, chats, and announcements—keep a file that contains the information required to re-create the resource such as the wording of announcements and discussion forums.

Using a directory structure that replicates the coursesite organization makes it easy to locate a resource file when you need to revise it and also facilitates faster re-creation of your coursesite architecture in the unlikely event the server disk drive fails and there exists no current server backup of the files that were stored on it. If you follow this procedure each time you create or modify a resource file and post it to your coursesite, the directory structure you have created on your hard drive will contain an image of the current version of each of your coursesites. In essence, the directory structure constitutes a backup of your coursesite. This backup directory structure should be stored to some kind of offline storage—a CD, a DVD, or a zip disk. The offline storage is of course the *second* backup of your coursesite. You should copy the course files on your hard drive to offline storage on a regular basis. We recommend doing this religiously every time you create a new or modify an existing course resource file and store it in your hard drive course directory structure. If you fail to keep your secondary backup current and your hard drive fails, you risk losing work if the LMS server crashes simultaneously. As is the case with LMS server failure, PC hard drive failure is not a matter of small concern. It happens.

Figure 8.8 illustrates three distinct directory structures to support backing up the three different Introduction to Elearning architectures illustrated in Figures 8.3, 8.5, and 8.6. It is unlikely that you yourself would create three different versions of the same elearning course. However, if you teach more than one elearning course, you would of course create a multiple-directory structure similar to that of Figure 8.8 to back up your various coursesites. Note that each backup directory structure in Figure 8.8 precisely reflects the organization of the corresponding architecture in Figures 8.3, 8.5, and 8.6. Of course, if you were teaching the Introduction to Elearning course, you would use only one of the three directory structures shown in Figure 8.8—the one reflecting the course architecture you actually chose for the course.

The directory structures shown in Figure 8.8 were created on the hard drive of a personal computer, then copied with all their contents to a CD. A single drag and drop will copy everything in the directory you drag to offline storage, including all subdirectories and their contents. You may wonder why numbers are used in the directory and subdirectory names in Figure 8.8. Using leading numbers in subdirectory names assures that directories in the backup file structure appear in the same order as resource directories in the corresponding course architectures. For the three top-level directories, numbers in a directory name refer to corresponding text figures. For example, the directory name *Fig8.3-IntroElearnTopicOrg* refers to the topic organization diagram of the Introduction to Elearning course shown in Figure 8.3.

Backing Up Other Files

In addition to course resource files, certain other kinds of elearning files—although they do not persevere on your coursesite through successive iterations of your elearning course—need to be backed up. These are files created by or about individual students and stored on your coursesite or submitted to you personally in the process of satisfying the requirements of your course. For example, you may wish to archive and then erase forum postings periodically throughout the course, especially if electronic discussions are an important component of your

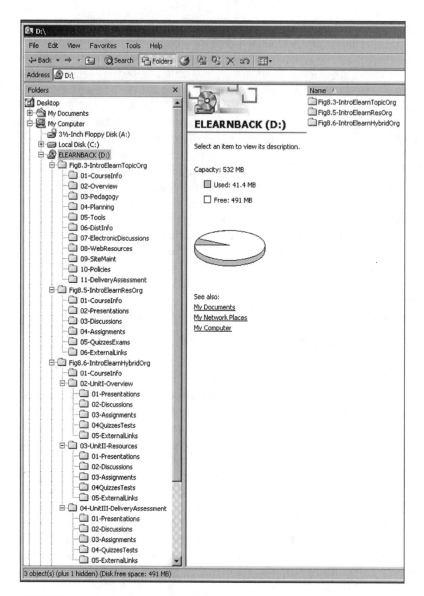

FIGURE 8.8   Example Directory Structures for Backing Up Coursesite Files for Various Architectures of Introduction to Elearning Course

course and large volumes of postings are accumulating. More generally, any kind of assignment a student submits needs to be archived in case questions arise—either during the course or after it is over—about how an assignment was submitted or graded.

Student Grades.   It is critically important to maintain backup copies of online gradebooks. Plan in advance how you will re-create grades if a technology failure erases gradebook entries. Doing so may require you to refer to saved copies of student assignments. If you fail to keep grade and assignment backups, only one gradebook failure and the subsequent embarrassment or outright disaster it occasions will strongly motivate you to perform backups in the future. We have already pointed out that you should keep two distinct backup copies of course resource files. This requirement applies with even greater urgency to backing up student grades.

Because capabilities of different LMSs vary with respect to copying online gradebooks, it is difficult to make specific recommendations about how you should back up student grades. If you can copy the gradebook file to your hard drive, include an appropriate directory in your backup file structure and update your personal copy of the gradebook without fail every time it changes. If your LMS does not support copying a gradebook file, it may allow you to copy the data it contains into a spreadsheet file on your personal computer, providing an alternative approach to backing up grades. Finally, as discussed in Chapter 4, you may decide to forego use of the online gradebook and use a spreadsheet gradebook instead. When you do this and post a copy of the spreadsheet gradebook to your coursesite, the problem of backing up grades is already half solved. You simply need to be sure you save a copy of your gradebook to secondary storage each time its content changes.

Regardless of what means you use to back up grades, be aware that failure to do so is highly unprofessional and places you at great peril if student complaints ever arise because of your inaction.

Student Assignments

Chapter 9 discusses how to formulate a policy for submission of student assignments. Depending on what policy you adopt, you will receive the files either by email or through a common LMS storage area. In the former case, the original files will reside on your personal computer; in the latter, they will be stored initially on the LMS server. Chapter 10 explains alternatives for organizing assignment files when you receive them. One alternative is to store the files by individual students. Another is to store them by assignment number. In either case, assignment files ultimately should be stored on your own computer's hard drive rather than on the LMS server. Otherwise, you may not be able to make personal backup copies of the files.

Regardless of how you decide to receive and organize student assignments, remember that the assignment files stored on your hard drive must also be saved regularly to secondary storage, even as course resource files are saved in two distinct storage locations. If you receive assignment files by attachments to email, you may choose to save them using directories created in your email program. In that case, you can back up the directories using the email utility that allows you to archive directories and their contents to an offline storage medium such as a CD or zip disk. Otherwise, you will organize the files by creating directories on your hard drive using your file management system and periodically write the directories to secondary storage. We think the latter method is superior to the former, because saving assignment files using an email program requires that an email message be saved along with the assignment file attached to it. Also, the contents of directories archived using an email program can be retrieved and accessed only by using the email program itself. This takes longer to accomplish than when files are backed up and retrieved using your computer's file management system.

REFERENCES

Alley, L. R. (2001, November). What makes a good online course? *Converge, 4*(11), 50–53.

Amador, O. (2003, February/March). Techtidbits. *Converge: Visions & Trends for Higher Education, 6*(1), 20–21.

Barone, C. A. (2002, March/April). WINWINI and the next killer app: An interview with Carl F. Berger. *EDUCAUSE Review, 37*(2), 20–22, 24, 26.

Bohman, P. (2000). Universal design and disability access to the web. *WebAIM.* Retrieved December 28, 2003, from http://webaim.org/coordination/articles/universal

Carnevale, D. (2003, November 28). Congress may boost online programs that aid students who have disabilities. *The Chronicle of Higher Education.* Retrieved May 10, 2004, from http://chronicle.com/prm/weekly/v50/i14/14a03401.htm

CAST. (2003). Summary of universal design for learning concepts. *Center for Applied Special Technology.* Retrieved December 28, 2003, from www.cast.org/udl/index.cfm?i=7

Coombs, N. (2002). Electronic ramp to success: Designing campus web pages for users with disabilities. *EDUCAUSE Quarterly, 25*(2), 45–51.

Coombs, N. (2003, August). Building an access ramp to information technology. *Syllabus, 17*(1), 26–29.

Cunningham, C. (2001, February). Breaking the barriers to math and science for students with disabilities. *Syllabus, 14*(7), 41–42.

Gale, S. F. (2001, July/August). Use it or lose it: Ten ways to improve your WBT with usability testing. *Online-Learning, 5*(7), 34–36.

Horton, S. (2000, October). User-centered design for media-rich web sites. *Syllabus, 14*(3), 22, 24, 26.

Kiser, K. (2001, June). Web-enabled? Web-based training's promise of learning anytime, anyplace may not hold true for people with disabilities. *Online-Learning, 5*(6), 29–30, 32–33.

Lamar, C. (2003, July). Creating accessible online math courses. *Syllabus, 16*(12), 42–43.

Natalicio, D. (2000, September/October). Information technology: Focusing on improved teaching and learning. *EDUCAUSE Review, 35*(5), 10–11.

Otto, J. C. (2002, February). Building a great web site. *T.H.E. Journal, 29*(7), 40–41.

Paoletti, J. (2003, November/December). Wanted: Course revision without pain. *The Technology Source.* Retrieved December 1, 2003, from http://ts.mivu.org/default.asp?show=article&id=1034

Robertson, J. S., & Harris, J. W. (2003, January/February). Making online information accessible to students with disabilities, part II. *The Technology Source.* Retrieved April 7, 2003, from http://ts.mivu.org/default.asp?show=article&id=1008

Ruffini, M. F. (2001, March). Blueprint to develop a great web site. *T.H.E. Journal, 28*(8), 64, 66, 68, 70, 72–73.

Thombs, M. M. (2003, January). Accessible web pages: Advice for educators. *Syllabus, 16*(6), 26.

White, E. A., Wepner, S. B., & Wetzel, D. C. (2003, February). Accessible education through assistive technology. *T.H.E. Journal, 30*(7), 24–26, 30, 32.

Young, J. R. (2002, January 21). Designer of free course-management software asks, what makes a good web site? *The Chronicle of Higher Education.* Retrieved June 10, 2002, from http://chronicle.com/free/2002/01/2002012101u.htm

URL REFERENCES

Access Board: www.access-board.gov/indexes/accessindex.htm

Accessible Webpage Design: Resources (University of Wisconsin in Stevens Point): http://library.uwsp.edu/aschmetz/accessible/pub_resources.htm

Alliance for Technology Access (ATA): www.ataccess.org/

American Printing House for the Blind (Louis): http://www.aph.org/louis.htm

A-Prompt Web Accessibility Verifier (University of Toronto): http://aprompt.snow.utoronto.ca

Bobby: http://bobby.watchfire.com

CAST (Center for Applied Special Technology)—Universal Design for Learning: www.cast.org/udl/index.cfm?i=7

Diamond Tool on 508 Compliance: www.508compliant.com/tools.htm

EASI (Equal Access to Software and Information): http://easi.cc/workshop.htm

Guide to Providing Equal Access in University Computer Labs, University of Washington in Seattle: www.washington.edu/doit/Brochures/Technology/comp.access.html

Macromedia Accessibility Website: www.macromedia.com/macromedia/accessibility

Microsoft Accessibility Technology for Everyone: www.microsoft.com/enable

North Carolina State University—ISTE Judges' Rubric: Multimedia Mania 2000: www.ncsu.edu/midlink/rubric.judge2000.htm

Self-Evaluation Questionnaire for Web Sites and 508
    Compliance (U.S. Department of Justice): www.
    usdoj.gov/crt/508/web2.htm
TechDis Web Accessibility & Usability Resource: www.
    techdis.ac.uk/seven/precepts.html
Trace Center: http://trace.wisc.edu
U.S. Government 508 website: www.section508.gov
VisiBone on Color Deficient Vision: www.visibone.com/
    colorblind

Vischeck: www.vischeck.com
WebAIM: http://webaim.org
West Loogootee: Evaluation Rubrics for Web Sites:
    www.siec.k12.in.us/~west/online/eval.htm
World Wide Web Consortium (W3C) Web Accessibility
    Initiative (WAI): www.w3.org/WAI

PART III

COURSE MANAGEMENT

CHAPTER NINE

INTELLECTUAL PROPERTY RIGHTS AND COURSE POLICIES

This is a chapter about rules. Drive your car through a stop sign and you may end up paying a traffic fine. Download an MP3 music file illegally and you may face a lawsuit from the Recording Industry Association of America (Seabrook, 2003). Just as there are laws and rules in the greater world that one must obey, there are rules in elearning that instructors and students must abide by. For instructors, we are concerned here with rules that protect intellectual property rights—of individuals whose work instructors use to construct elearning resources and of the instructors themselves. For students, the rules of interest are found in policies that govern their behavior in an elearning course. What follows is divided into two sections. The first treats intellectual property rights including copyright law and the need for elearning instructors to be aware of implicit or explicit intellectual property rights agreements between themselves and their institutions. The second explains how to construct course policies that will help make each course delivery a fair and rewarding learning experience for students and a relatively trouble-free undertaking for you as instructor.

INTELLECTUAL PROPERTY RIGHTS

This section is about rules you need to be aware of when you create elearning resources. It is organized in three subsections. The first—a prelude to the second and third—briefly discusses copyright law and intellectual property rights. When a person has a copyright on something he or she has created—a poem, a song, a photograph, an article in a periodical, a book, a video—that person possesses what is sometimes called *intellectual property rights* to that artifact. The second subsection addresses the question of how to respect the intellectual property rights of individuals whose work you use when you create elearning resources. The third subsection addresses the related question of whether you or the institution that employs you owns intellectual property rights to the elearning resources you create. As we shall see, this question—though it is of paramount importance to everyone concerned—currently remains unanswered at many if not most institutions of higher learning.

We stress at the outset that the information in this section is presented from a layman's point of view. Moreover, our remarks provide merely an overview of an important subject far too broad to be treated here in detail. Legal insight is required for those seeking a thorough understanding of copyright law and intellectual property rights. What follows has been researched with care. In addition, the end-of-chapter references reveal how to locate some of the voluminous existing information about the subject of this section. Nevertheless, the author of this book is not a lawyer, nor has she obtained the advice of lawyers about the subjects discussed here.

eLearning Implications of Copyright Law

Copyright is legal exclusive right of a creator of a work to control the copying of all or a portion of that work. The creator need take no action to be granted this right. As soon as the work is placed in a medium that can be distributed or copied, copyright is granted to the author automatically. Moreover, the work doesn't even need to have a copyright notice attached to it. A copyright is implied by the existence of the work. Copyright law—by providing a basis for lawsuits to compensate for financial or emotional loss resulting when someone else uses our work without authorization—attempts to assure that we can profit fairly from what we create.

Copyright law has an obvious application for you as an elearning instructor. *Anything* you want to use in your course resources or in your coursesite design that you didn't author is subject to copyright violation. The Internet makes it very easy to obtain and use work created by others, hence very easy to violate their copyrights on this work. Moreover, depending on who has access to your coursesite, the Internet probably makes it easier for you to be detected if you unfairly post copyrighted material.

Copyrights are not eternal. When an artifact becomes old enough to be out of copyright, you may use it as you wish. Such material is said to be in the *public domain.* For example, editions of Charles Dickens's novels published in the nineteenth century are long out of copyright, hence are in the public domain. You are free to quote from any of these old editions or indeed to post such a book in its entirety to your website, in the unlikely event you might wish to do so. Except under the fair use guidelines explained next, however, you would *not* be free to post, for example, photocopied pages from a contemporary edition of one of Dickens's novels. This remains true even though the copyrighted contemporary edition was itself produced from an edition of the novel in the public domain.

Many web authors, but certainly not all, consider their websites to be in the public domain and are willing to share freely the information they contain. To be on the safe side, however, you should assume that material created by others—electronic or otherwise—is not available free of charge. This includes everything you obtain from the web—text, images, audio, or video—as well as anything you use or scan from a picture, book, magazine, or other source. This doesn't mean, however, that you can't use materials from the web and other sources to create your elearning resources. It simply means that you must follow the "rules" when you use such materials. The next subsection explains what these rules are.

Respecting Copyright Law: Fair Use Guidelines

Fair use is a legal principle that defines the limitations on the exclusive rights of copyright holders. Fair use permits you as an instructor—*within the confines of your classroom*—to legally use information you did not create without obtaining the permission of the creator of the information. There are stringent guidelines that govern what is considered to be fair use. The following discussion is intended only to provide you with an awareness of fair use. Ask your institution to help you obtain legal advice when you cannot decide for yourself whether information you contemplate using violates copyright law. That said, we believe most instructors will not feel the need to resort to this extreme sort of action to make a prudent decision about using someone else's information to create web resources.

Fair use guidelines about citing the copyrighted work of others fall into four categories in this list (Besek, 2003). Each is briefly described in the form of questions and answers following the list.

- Purpose
- Nature
- Amount
- Effect

What Is Your Purpose and Intent in Using the Information?   Fair use allows you to use information you did not create as long as you do not intend to profit financially from it. In addition, nonprofit educational use is favored over commercial use, although the latter is not automatically disqualifying. Uses that transform original work creatively weigh in favor of fair use. Examples are parody and sequels. As an instructor, it is likely that your use of the information will not be for profit. If the information you use is posted on a coursesite that requires password access—and LMSs invariably do require passwords—then the information is not available to the public.

What Is the Nature of the Work You Take the Information From?   Fair use is more likely if the work you copy is fact based, for example, history or biography, rather than imaginative, such as a novel. Fair use is more likely if the source is published as opposed to unpublished.

How Much Information Will You Take from the Work?   The amount of information fair use allows is based on the full length of the work you take the information from. The longer the original work is, the more information you may appropriate from it, up to a certain maximum limit. One source advocates using a 10 percent rule (Ko & Rossen, 2004). This rule specifies that you may use the smaller of

- One thousand words or 10 percent of a prose work
- Thirty seconds of music or 10 percent of the length of the complete composition
- Three minutes or 10 percent of a video
- Two hundred fifty words or 10 percent of a poem

What Effect Will Your Use of the Information Have on the Work You Take the Information From?   Citations that significantly diminish the market for the original are unlikely to constitute fair use. For example, if you use large amounts of information from a textbook, and if as a consequence your students do not have to buy the book they might otherwise be required to purchase, this might decrease the author's royalties.

Additional Fair Use Considerations.   Copyright and fair use are rather complicated issues. Always err on the side of safety. If you become subject to litigation because of a copyright violation, your institution will almost surely have more financial liability than you do, because its pockets are ordinarily deeper than yours. The following suggestions may help you avoid inadvertently engaging in copyright infringement.

- Find out whether your institution has promulgated specific guidelines for posting copyrighted material on the web. If so, obey them to the letter.
- When in any doubt, obtain written permission to use copyrighted information.
- Use links to works instead of placing the work directly in your materials. As a courtesy, notify the source that you are planning to link to the website.
- Create elearning resources without using copyrighted information.
- Take materials from the public domain.
- Always credit the source of work you place on your coursesite under fair use.

Figure 9.1 includes a checklist—taken from the ▪Copyright Management Center at Indiana University–Purdue University–Indianapolis—that you might consider using to determine whether information you contemplate using in an elearning course meets fair use guidelines. To obtain further information on fair use, visit the Copyright Management Center website, the ▪University of Texas System's Crash Course in Copyright, and the ▪Stanford Copyright & Fair Use Center.

The DMCA and the TEACH Act.   In addition to fair use guidelines, two pieces of U.S. federal legislation are relevant to intellectual property rights. One is the ▪Digital Millennium Copyright Act (DMCA), enacted in 1998. The other is the Technology, Education, and Copyright Harmonization Act (TEACH) signed into law in 2002. These two acts—too broad to address in detail in this book—are summarized here. To determine your institution's guidelines for compliance with DCMA and TEACH, consult your institution's legal department or a knowledgeable reference librarian at your institution.

DMCA is a significant comprehensive reform of United States copyright law focusing on copyright for the digital age. The act was designed in part to implement a copyright protection treaty signed in 1996 by member countries of the ▪World Intellectual Property Organization (WIPO), an agency of the United Nations. It specifies the terms according to which instructors, librarians, students, and staff may use email, websites, and other technology at their institutions. One major aspect of this act for instructors is that if your coursesite allows students to download text, graphics, or other web content, you could be liable for any copyright infringement if you have not taken the precautions prescribed in the DMCA.

The TEACH Act of 2002 updated U.S. copyright law in the area of online education (Carnevale, 2003). It was specifically motivated by the development of distance education elearning courses that use the Internet to distribute information. The act specifies conditions under which an accredited, nonprofit educational institution in the United States may digitally transmit—without permission or license fees—a copyrighted work (or a portion thereof) to a legitimate student audience. For further information on TEACH, an excellent website to consult is ▪The TEACH Toolkit maintained by North Carolina State University.

Protecting Your Intellectual Property

The preceding subsection focuses on protecting the intellectual property rights of others. In this subsection, we focus on protecting your own intellectual property rights. You will put a

FIGURE 9.1   Copyright Management Center Checklist for Fair Use

PURPOSE

Favoring Fair Use

- ☐ Teaching (including multiple copies for classroom use)
- ☐ Research
- ☐ Scholarship
- ☐ Nonprofit educational institution
- ☐ Criticism
- ☐ Comment
- ☐ News reporting
- ☐ Transformative or productive use (changes the work for new utility)
- ☐ Restricted access (to students or other appropriate group)
- ☐ Parody

Opposing Fair Use

- ☐ Commercial activity
- ☐ Profiting from the use
- ☐ Entertainment
- ☐ Bad-faith behavior
- ☐ Denying credit to original author

NATURE

Favoring Fair Use

- ☐ Published work
- ☐ Factual or nonfiction based
- ☐ Important to favored educational objectives

Opposing Fair Use

- ☐ Unpublished work
- ☐ Highly creative work (art, music, novels, films, plays)
- ☐ Fiction

AMOUNT

Favoring Fair Use

- ☐ Small quantity
- ☐ Portion used is not central or significant to entire work
- ☐ Amount is appropriate for favored educational purpose

Opposing Fair Use

- ☐ Large portion or whole work used
- ☐ Portion used is central to work or "heart of the work"

EFFECT

Favoring Fair Use

- ☐ User owns lawfully acquired or purchased copy of original work
- ☐ One or few copies made
- ☐ No significant effect on the market or potential market for copyrighted works
- ☐ No similar product marketed by the copyright holder
- ☐ Lack of licensing mechanism

Opposing Fair Use

- ☐ Could replace sale of copyrighted work
- ☐ Significantly impairs market or potential market for copyrighted work or derivative
- ☐ Reasonably available licensing mechanism for use of copyrighted work
- ☐ Affordable permission available for using work
- ☐ Numerous copies made
- ☐ You made it accessible on Web or in other public forum
- ☐ Repeated or long-term use

lot of effort into creating an elearning course, and both you and your institution may have an interest in seeing that the course resources are not used in an unauthorized or inappropriate manner. What follows is divided into two subsections. The first applies to all instructors. It discusses the need to assure that students understand and respect the fact that resources they access on your coursesite, as well as the coursesite itself, are copyrighted. The second subsection is specific to instructors who work in higher education. It discusses how to deal with your institution to ensure that you can benefit fairly from any instructional materials you create. It may surprise you to learn that some administrators believe that not you but the institution owns the elearning resources you create.

Students and Copyright Issues.   It is important to alert students to the fact that the elearning resources they use are copyrighted. Post a formal statement that your course resources—together with announcements you post and your words in electronic discussions—belong to you and/or your institution, not to the students who use them. Advise your students that they must understand and abide by laws and guidelines protecting these resources. The same caveat holds true for discussion entries and other electronic artifacts that students produce while taking your course. Your statement should make clear that course materials are for class purposes only and cannot be distributed to others without violating the intellectual property rights and/or the privacy rights of the owners of these materials, whether the owners be the course instructor or students in the course.

In addition to officially notifying students about your intellectual property rights, there are several other ways to protect the elearning resources you create. These steps have the added advantage of protecting you from outside users of your resources as well as from students. The most formal step you can take is to submit a claim to the Copyright Office of the Library of Congress. In addition, there are several more informal approaches:

- Place a copyright notation on your materials.
- Place a dated copy of your materials in a sealed envelope and send the envelope by registered mail to yourself. Be sure to keep the envelope in a safe place and keep it sealed.
- Create course materials in formats that protect the materials from being changed or printed, as is possible, for example, using Adobe Acrobat to create PDF files.
- Restrict access to materials by password protecting your coursesite.
- Embed a registered ID number in every image or video so that when the image or video is downloaded, the ID number is included and serves as a copyright notation.
- Disable files from being downloaded. For example, stream media instead of allowing students to download files.
- Display an image as a background image instead of as a file.

A final obvious reason to make students aware of copyright issues has nothing to do with protecting your own rights. Rather, it concerns protecting the intellectual property rights of others. When students unfairly use materials created by others in elearning assignments, they are guilty of plagiarism. As every English teacher in the world knows, the Internet makes it very easy for students accidentally or intentionally to commit plagiarism. This subject is raised again in the section of this chapter on course policies.

Intellectual Property Rights for eLearning Resources Developed in a University Environment.   This subsection applies to elearning instructors working in a university environment. If you instruct in a for-profit or in a K–12 institution, it is probably clear that your employers and not you yourself own the elearning resources you use. By contrast, ownership rights of elearning resources created by a college or university faculty member are not nearly so well agreed upon. In what follows, we use the term *university* to subsume both undergraduate colleges and universities granting doctoral degrees.

Many universities view faculty members' ownership of elearning course materials differently from other publications they may author. When, for example, a faculty member writes and publishes a textbook, typically his or her university doesn't mind if a competing institution adopts the book for a course. In fact, a university usually views very positively the favorable publicity associated with a quality textbook written by one of its faculty members. However, the same university may be very much against the same faculty member's online course materials being disseminated publicly.

The reasons for this apparent anomaly seem various and far from obvious. Some universities seem to fear that competitor universities will obtain and use elearning resources developed by their faculty members. Others may see more potential profit from elearning course materials than from traditional publications and desire to share in those profits. Still others may fear perhaps that faculty will self-publish low-quality materials that—because they are not peer reviewed—fail to measure up to the university's perceived standards of excellence, thus affecting the university's reputation. Another major issue has to do with the significantly large expenses associated with creating elearning resources as compared to traditional learning materials. The support a university offers a professor who authors a textbook is pretty much limited to office space and perhaps a desktop computer and a supply of paper. In contrast, a professor who authors an elearning course uses institutional resources such as instructional technology personnel, instructional designers, web developers, graphic artists, student assistants, and proprietary LMS software hosted on third-party servers, among other resources. Such resources are very expensive. Under the circumstances, a university's desire to recoup some of its expenses in the form of profits from elearning materials may not be wholly unjustified.

Whatever the explanations for it, one thing is clear. The question of who owns intellectual property rights to elearning course materials developed in a university environment all too often remains unanswered. For this reason, it may be difficult for you as university faculty to determine whether you have intellectual property rights to your elearning resources. In fact, there is currently much controversy among instructors and institutions as to who rightfully owns elearning course materials, precisely because most universities have not yet formulated a coherent policy on the subject. At the same time, it is reasonable for you to want to know whether you will own what you create before you begin developing an elearning course. In addition, because you will spend a lot of time developing the course, you will probably want to know how your department chair and other academic leaders will value your efforts in the promotion and tenure processes.

The controversy in universities over elearning intellectual property rights has prompted the ▪American Association of University Professors (AAUP) to take a position on the issue. Because it is likely that only a few faculty will create marketable online courses—even as only a handful of faculty author textbooks—the AAUP recommends that the faculty in general should be conceded ownership of elearning course materials they develop. However, the

AAUP also sees three circumstances in which the faculty's intellectual property rights are in question:

- The creation of the course was required for employment, or the institution specifically directed the faculty member to create the course.
- The institution obtained contractual ownership of the course from the faculty member.
- The institution contributed significant resources to the development of the course.

The last circumstance seems most problematic, because what constitutes "significant resources" is surely open to debate.

To avoid an intellectual property rights controversy with your university, review its policies on intellectual property rights before starting a major elearning project that you desire to own. If there are issues in question, or if no policy exists, negotiate a formal agreement with administrators before you begin development. In the event that your university is among the many that do not have an intellectual property policy, you might desire to help it establish one. What follows is a list of questions that could form a basis of discussion with academic leaders at your institution on the subject of intellectual property rights of faculty.

- Under what circumstances do faculty own the elearning materials they create?
- Under what circumstances does the university have a claim to the elearning course materials faculty produce?
- What are faculty's rights in relation to marketing and selling elearning course materials they create?
- Does the institution have the right to market elearning course materials produced by a faculty member? If so, and profits will be generated as a result, what is the faculty's share of profits?
- Do other faculty at the same institution have the right to use course materials developed by a peer faculty member?
- When the faculty and the institution have a contractual agreement on the development of elearning course materials, what governs the revision of the course material? Will the original author be required to revise at the institution's request? Can the institution hire someone else to revise the course materials, or must the original author be given the right of first refusal? Can revision occur without the permission of the original author?
- When the author of elearning materials moves to another university, does he or she have rights to course materials developed at the previous university?
- When the author of elearning materials leaves the university, can the university continue to use the materials he or she developed?
- When a third party publishes elearning materials, what is the division of royalties between the faculty author of the materials and the university?
- What are the intellectual property rights of adjunct faculty?
- Should copyright be in the name of the elearning course developer or of the university?

When creating an intellectual property policy at a university, it is prudent to review similar policies of other universities. Figure 9.2 contains provisions of such a policy approved by the faculty at the ▪Stevens Institute of Technology (Ubell, 2001). At Wake Forest

FIGURE 9.2   Example Intellectual Property Policy

Stevens's Web-Course Ownership Policies Recommendations

1. Copyright: A course developer's copyright to an entirely online course should be assigned to the school when the faculty member agrees to enter a contract with the institution to develop it.
2. Compensation: The agreement should compensate developers for creating entirely online courses in "virtual space"—a provision that should not apply to online material presented in conventional classrooms in "physical space." Faculty should also be compensated separately for entirely online instruction.
3. Use: While copyright for an entirely online course is assigned to the university, the faculty member retains the right to use course material components (notes, slides, exercises, and so on) for other purposes, such as conventional classroom teaching, publication, and lectures.
4. Portability: In the event the developer delivers an entirely online course at other schools, a usage license fee should be paid to the originating institution.
5. Third-party licensing: If an entirely online course is licensed to a third party—publisher, corporation, distributor, or other school—the course developer should receive a percentage of the net licensing revenue.
6. Additional compensation and limitations: If an entirely online course is taught at the school by someone other than the developer, the faculty member who created it should receive a percentage of the net tuition revenue.

Stevens Institute of Technology, used with permission.

University, a special committee was organized to address the intellectual property rights of faculty. The committee recommended that ownership should reside with the author of the work except in a few well-defined cases such as "work for hire" scenarios (Wicker & Boyd, 2003). The committee's recommended policies can be viewed on the ▪Wake Forest University Copyright Policy website.

COURSE POLICIES

In any instructional environment, it is crucial that students have a clear understanding of what you expect from them, as well as what they can expect from you. Another very important purpose for establishing course policies is to aid you in controlling your workload. The best way to do this in an elearning course is to create clear course policies on applicable topics and to post them to your coursesite in a prominent folder, usually called *Policies*. Policies are even more important in an elearning environment than in a conventional learning environment, because many elearning activities are technology based and self-directed, and so the need for clarification cannot always be satisfied by a telephone call or a face-to-face meeting. Consequently, course policies are a critical component of an effective elearning environment.

A number of policies might become formulated at the university level, such as student privacy policies, discussion policies, software standards policies, and intellectual property rights policy. Such institution-wide standards will likely evolve in the future as implied by the efforts of the ▪Association for Colleges and University Policy Administrators to develop a policy development process applicable to information technology departments (Petersen, 2004).

In addition to creating policies, you must ensure that students understand the policies and agree to abide by them. Consider having students sign contracts at the outset of a course saying that they have read and understood your course policies and are aware that they must abide by them. Another way to reinforce student acceptance of course policies is to provide a getting-started activity such as an ungraded online test or a discussion question on the content of course policies. The following list identifies major policy categories and is followed by a discussion of each type of policy.

- Elearning policies in the course syllabus
- Student privacy policies
- Intellectual property rights policies
- Email policies
- Discussion policies
- Assignment policies
- Getting technical help policies
- Student code of conduct policies

eLearning Policies in the Course Syllabus

Virtually every academic course has a course syllabus that catalogs the course goals, sets a course schedule, identifies course texts and other required materials, and explains how to contact the instructor outside of scheduled class activities. Typically a course syllabus also sets forth general criteria used to administer the course, for example an attendance policy and a grading policy that explains how student performance will be evaluated.

In an elearning course, your course syllabus should of course be posted on your coursesite and should include several additional policy statements. First, because elearning involves electronic communication, you should require students to visit your coursesite once a day to view new announcements you may have posted, and require them to read email daily to peruse course information disseminated via this medium. Second, you should inform students that whenever they submit course assignments by email or on CD or disk, they are responsible for ensuring that computer files holding these assignments follow course file format standards and are virus-free, and that files that fail your virus checker software will not be opened or accepted. Finally, your course syllabus should contain a statement to the effect that ignorance of course policies set forth in the syllabus or posted elsewhere on your coursesite is not an excuse for failure to conform to these policies. Of course, the existence of your course policies and how to access them should be prominently publicized in whatever introduction you provide for students who enter your course.

Student Privacy Policies

You should establish a policy and related procedures to protect student privacy. Most educational institutions in the United States have a student privacy policy consonant with the ▪Family Educational Rights and Privacy Act (FERPA). If this is the case and your institution's policy is available online, post a link to it on your coursesite; otherwise, post a copy of the policy itself. If your own student privacy policy is distinct from that of your institution, you should, of course, post it also. If you plan to publicize students' work outside of the course—including, for example, their words in electronic discussions, email, or assignments—be sure to inform them of your intent and obtain their permission to do so. Figure 9.3 provides an example student permission-to-use form.

One way to protect student privacy is to restrict access to your coursesite, so that outsiders cannot see the resources that reside there, including, for example, students' discussion responses. Often students' privacy rights are violated when they are required to participate in activities to get to know each other and are asked to post photographs and personal information on a coursesite. These types of activities should be voluntary, not required. Also, references to personal traits such as race, ethnicity, disabilities, age, and gender should be made public only if a student initiates the actions to do so.

Intellectual Property Rights Policies

Include in your course policies guidelines requiring students to respect intellectual property rights. As mentioned earlier, provide a formal statement that your course materials are copyrighted and that students are not to use or distribute any portion of them without your expressed permission in writing, except as allowed under fair use guidelines. Also include a statement that students must respect the intellectual property rights of fellow students.

Plagiarism of course involves representing the work of others as your own. As such, it involves violation of copyright and fair use. Thus your intellectual property rights policy is essentially an implicit plagiarism policy as well. You should make this clear in the policy as posted to your website. You can provide more detail about plagiarism in your student code of conduct policy, as described later.

FIGURE 9.3 Example Student Permission-to-Use Form

Student's Name _____ Course _____

Instructor's Name _____

I grant the instructor identified above unlimited permission to make public or reference those items checked below. This permission applies to work I have completed in the course indicated. I understand that if my work is used, when possible an acknowledgement identifying the work as mine will be included.

□ My comments in chats
□ My comments in electronic forums
□ My comments in email
□ Examples of my written work
□ My name as part of a directory listing of students in the class
□ My photograph
□ My biography
□ Other _____

Signed _____ Date _____

Email Policies

Elearning instructors report that the number of emails they receive from students can be overwhelming, especially in totally online courses in which there is no face-to-face interaction between instructor and students. If you allow email to monopolize your time, it will be very difficult for you to manage your other course responsibilities. Posting an email policy is therefore highly recommended. Consider the following three approaches to minimizing the workload email imposes on you. Figure 9.4 provides an example email policy statement.

Define Appropriate Email Topics.   Provide clear policies stating the type of email you will respond to. For example, you may establish a policy whereby you will respond to email that deals with students' personal concerns, their difficulties comprehending course content, or their need for clarification about graded work.

Require students to refer to the coursesite for general course information instead of requesting it from you by email. Besides reducing your email load, this practice also encourages students to be self-sufficient in finding answers to their questions. Provide detailed information about your course in your syllabus, in assignment instructions, in announcements, in the course calendar, in your policies folder, and in other course material. Then establish as part of your email policy that you will not respond to email about test dates, how students' grades will be determined, or any other information that is clearly posted in general course information in the coursesite.

Set a Reasonable Response Time.   It is important to establish an email response time so that students will know when they can expect to hear from you. This will reduce the number of emails that are of the nature of "I haven't heard from you, so I'm resending this email." Also, if response time is clearly stated, it will help to reduce students' frustration when they don't hear back from you in what *they* consider to be a timely fashion. For example, you

FIGURE 9.4   Example Email Policy

This document sets forth guidelines for email communication with the course instructor. Excessive emails make unreasonable time demands on both sender and recipient. Please ensure you have a legitimate need before you write. Thanks.

- Your instructor will answer email about
  - Questions arising from difficulty in understanding course content.
  - Requests for feedback about graded assignments.
  - Private issues appropriate for discussion within the teacher-student relationship.
- Your instructor will *not* answer email that
  - Poses questions answered in the course information sections of the coursesite.
  - Lacks a subject line clearly stating the purpose of the email.
  - Raises an inappropriate subject.
- Your instructor will answer email received on a given day no later than close of work on the next workday.
- You are reminded that a policy in the course syllabus requires you to read email every day to ensure that you receive course information disseminated by email in a timely fashion.

might say you will respond to appropriate email from your students within 24 hours of the time they write the email, on a 7-day-a-week basis. Another approach would be to respond to email within 24 hours of the time the student writes, except on weekends and holidays.

Some instructors prefer to associate email response times with office hours. For example, email will be responded to on Mondays from 10:00 A.M. to 12:00 P.M. Eastern Standard Time (EST), Wednesdays from 2:00 to 4:00 P.M. EST, and Fridays from 12:00 to 1:00 P.M. EST. It is very important to include time zones when dealing with students who may be geographically disbursed.

Use Alternatives to Email.   As discussed in Chapter 5, the announcement component of the LMS provides an alternative to your responding to several emails on the same topic. For this approach to work, you must require students to visit the coursesite at least once a day to read new announcements.

As discussed in Chapter 6, an electronic discussion can be another alternative to email by providing opportunities for students to answer each other's questions. An ongoing forum for students allows them to post and respond to questions about tests, deadlines, or any other related course information. You, or your assistant, could visit the discussion to determine whether clarification is needed and post a response in the discussion or via a course announcement. This approach encourages students to work with each other and to be self-sufficient, yet allows you to provide them appropriate feedback as necessary.

As also discussed in Chapter 6, yet another alternative to email is to establish electronic office hours via the chat capabilities of your LMS. For example, you could arrange to be available to students via chat on Mondays, Wednesdays, and Fridays from 12:00 to 2:00 P.M. EST.

Discussion Policies

Your discussion policy should contain guidelines for participating in chats and forums, including the degree to which you yourself will enter into student discussions. For example, some instructors participate in a discussion only after all students have had a chance to respond. If you use this approach, state so explicitly, so that students will not be expecting more frequent participation from you.

If student participation in electronic discussions is required, this should also be clearly stated in the policy. Furthermore, if you are planning to grade students on their participation in discussions, you should clearly indicate what grading criteria will be applied. For example, will grades be based on the quality of responses as well as the number of responses? Will students be expected to respond to other students' postings? What are the deadline dates for postings? Figure 9.5 provides an example discussion policy.

Assignment Policies

Clear guidelines governing assignments are very important, in part because they reduce student frustration when they prepare their assignments and in part because they can reduce the amount of email students will send you asking for clarification. Three important considerations in devising an assignment policy and related procedures are discussed next. Figure 9.6 provides an example assignment policy.

FIGURE 9.5 Example Discussion Policy

- Forums will have an associated deadline by which time all students must have posted their responses to receive credit for participation.
- Chats will have a specified time period during which students must participate to receive credit.
- The instructor will not participate in a discussion prior to the discussion deadline.
- Within 24 hours of a discussion's end, the instructor will review all student responses and post a response as a course announcement.
- Students will be graded on discussion postings. Points are earned based on quality of responses and compliance with required number of postings as specified in individual assignment instructions.
- Individual discussion assignment instructions will indicate the number of points that can be earned on that particular discussion assignment.
- The points earned by each student on a given discussion will be posted to the online gradebook not later than one week after the discussion ends.
- Students are expected to focus on the specific topic of the discussion as assigned. The introduction of

irrelevant subjects is not permitted. Violators will be asked to leave the discussion, and a grade of 0 points will be recorded.
- All students have a right to express their own opinions in discussions, and every other student must respect this right. Any student posting a comment disrespectful of this right will be asked to leave the discussion, and a grade of 0 points will be recorded.
- *Flaming* is posting abusive or insulting messages. Any student who engages in flaming in a discussion will be required to leave the *class*. A grade of F for the course will be reported.
- Controlling behavior includes, but is not limited to, attempts to dominate a discussion by posting threads excessively, intentionally changing the discussion topic, or exhibiting an inappropriate or argumentative attitude. Controlling behavior is not permitted. Violators will be asked to leave the discussion, and a grade of 0 points will be recorded.
- Students required to leave a discussion will be notified of this consequence in a private email.

FIGURE 9.6 Example Assignment Policy

- Students will submit all assignments electronically via the coursesite.
- If there are technical problems with the coursesite, assignments can be sent to your instructor in an email. The subject line of the email must include your name, course alphanumeric designator, and the number of the assignment. No work received via email will be graded if the subject line is not properly completed.
- All assignment due dates refer to midnight EST on the listed due date. Late assignments will not be accepted.
- The course software standards are Microsoft Word, PowerPoint, and Excel. Assignments completed in other formats will not be accepted.
- When technical problems occur, and you cannot submit your assignment electronically, send an email to your instructor to explain the difficulty. If you cannot use email, call your instructor to explain the difficulty. If you reach your instructor's voicemail, leave a message explaining the difficulty and a phone contact where you can be reached.

- Your instructor will review assignments within 72 hours of the due date, and will send you feedback electronically, either by email or through comments posted on the assignment returned via the coursesite.
- Grades on assignments will be posted in the gradebook within 72 hours of the due date of the assignment. You must refer to the gradebook in the coursesite to determine the grade you earned on each assignment. Do NOT try to determine your grade by sending email or by calling your instructor.
- If you need to discuss your grade or the feedback you received from your instructor on an assignment, make an appointment with your instructor. This may be done in a visit during published office hours, or via email or telephone contact.
- Students are responsible for keeping a copy of all graded assignments. Absent a copy of graded work in question, no grade change or credit for a missing assignment is possible.

Establish Submission Guidelines.   Establish guidelines about how completed assignments should be submitted. For example, if an assignment is being sent via email, establish a procedure requiring that students place their full name, course identification, and an assignment identifier both in the subject line of the email and in a prominent heading on any attachments. Alternately—as mentioned in Chapter 4—you might ask students to place assignments in a common LMS storage area where you have read and write privileges, and students have only write privileges. Also, be sure to emphasize that you will accept files only if they are virus free and their file format conforms to your software standards policy.

In an elearning environment, it is inevitable that technical difficulties will occur from time to time. Such problems include difficulty with a home computer or its Internet connection, and downtime on the LMS server, among others. Your assignment policy must clearly state what students should do when they experience such difficulties while attempting to submit an assignment. One alternative is to have students fax their assignments to you, following the fax with an electronic submission when the existing computer problem is cleared up. Another approach would require that students call you by a designated time to explain their difficulties and negotiate with you a plan for submitting their assignment.

Inevitably, a few students will abuse your assignment policy by claiming technical difficulties when they do not exist. You probably need to include in your assignment policy a statement that students must have regular access to a reliable computer and Internet connection to enroll in your course. If a student repeatedly claims technical difficulties when submitting late assignments, you will then have justification to let this fact be reflected in the grade of late assignments.

Establish Feedback Guidelines.   To reduce the number of emails and calls you receive from students with questions about graded work, establish guidelines on the types of feedback students can expect. For example, you may want to respond to work submitted electronically by recording your feedback directly on the work and returning it electronically. Most word processor programs facilitate typing easily distinguishable feedback directly on files submitted by your students. If you are fortunate enough to have a tablet PC, you can handwrite on an electronic assignment, as discussed in Chapter 4. Also, establish parameters on when students can expect to receive graded work back, such as within five days after receiving the work, by the next or second-next class period, or within some other appropriate time frame.

You should also establish procedures for how students can discuss graded work with you personally. For example, if the course meets face-to-face, you can specify that you will discuss the work during your office hours, but only during a limited time period, for example, within five days of a student's receipt of the graded work. If your course is delivered totally online, you might make yourself available to discuss graded work—within the same time period—by phone, via email, or in a chat session.

Keep Permanent Records of Assignments.   It is a good idea to require that students keep a copy of all graded work, just in case there is a technology failure with an online gradebook and grades have to be re-created (Brown, 2002).

Getting Technical Help Policies

We have all experienced the frustrations of having technical difficulties with computers that we could not resolve. For elearning students, this kind of frustration is compounded when they are working under the pressure of assignment deadlines As a consequence, it is imperative that you have a policy explaining how a student may receive help for technical difficulties. If they are available, post institutional guidelines about how students can receive help on technical issues with the LMS, as well as with computers in laboratories. In addition, you should specify what kinds of problems students should *not* expect to get help with. For example, computers that students use off campus are their own responsibility, and this should be clearly established in your technical help policy. Some institutions are establishing technical help desks available 24 hours a day, 7 days a week. An example is Rio Salado College, which serves adult learners who often cite lack of timely support as a reason for abandoning their studies. The Rio Salado help desk, staffed by noninstructional personnel, assists students in resolving technical problems. In addition, the college has established an innovative *beep-a-tutor* program available 24 hours a day, 7 days a week. Students who leave a telephone request for help will receive a response within one hour. The tutors who supply responses are alerted by means of beepers, making it unnecessary for them to stay close by a telephone or a computer in case a request for help arrives (Oblinger, 2003).

If your institution has not established a technology help desk, consider setting up a help desk for your course that is managed by student assistants or teaching assistants who are available at designated times to talk with students by phone, by email, or in chat sessions. Another alternative for courses in which students meet face-to-face is to use student leaders with advanced technical skills. You would then specify how a student requiring help can make contact with a student leader. You, or your assistants, would stay in close touch with student leaders to coordinate technology issues and find solutions for difficulties that the student leaders could not resolve. Student leaders could be compensated with extra credit on their grades, as appropriate, or paid a modest salary if funds are available.

You should also specify how you will contact your students in case technical problems arise that cannot be solved expeditiously. You probably should know, in addition to your students' email addresses, their work and/or home telephone numbers and their fax numbers. Chapter 10 (Figure 10.3) provides a survey form useful for gathering these data and related information preferably at the outset of your course. Finally, your technical help policy should specify what you plan to do if technical difficulties arise when an online test is scheduled. Figure 9.7 provides an example of a policy on getting technical help.

Student Code of Conduct Policies

You should establish a student code of conduct policy explaining how you expect students to conduct themselves in your elearning environment. Consider making the code of conduct a signed contract between you and your students. An example of such a contract is presented in Figure 9.8. The following categories of student conduct guidelines are discussed next.

- Behavior in electronic communications
- Cheating and plagiarism
- Attendance
- Self-motivation and self-direction

Behavior in Electronic Communications.   Encourage students to be courteous and professional in email communications and electronic discussions. As discussed in Chapter 6,

FIGURE 9.7   Example Getting Technical Help Policy

- To obtain technical help with the LMS, call the Help Desk at 386-555-555 or send email to help@xyzcollege.edu.
- To obtain technical help while working in laboratories, report your problem to the lab assistant on duty.
- You are responsible for the operation of the computing system you use off campus. A malfunctioning computer system is not a valid excuse for submitting late work.
- To obtain answers to questions about the content in our coursesite for this course, call our course Help Desk at 386-555-555 between 9:00 A.M. and 1:00 P.M. EST Monday–Friday, 6:00 P.M. to 10:00 P.M. EST Sunday–Thursday;

or send email to our course Help Desk at elearning@xyzcollege.edu.

- If technical difficulties with university computers or network servers affect assignments, quizzes, exams, or scheduled class presentations, your instructor will use the following procedures to communicate with you to provide appropriate directions in the order listed below:
  - An announcement will be posted on the coursesite.
  - If the coursesite is unavailable, an email will be sent to all students.
  - If the coursesite and email are not in service, your instructor will place a message on his or her voicemail at 386-555-5555.

the code of conduct in electronic discussion should include guidelines governing unacceptable behaviors such as disrespectful responses to other students or the instructor, complaints about the course, or the use of inappropriate language. Provide students with examples of appropriate behavior and responses as well as inappropriate ones. If you are planning to allow students the freedom to initiate discussion forums, you must include a policy on the types of subjects that are appropriate and those that are inappropriate.

Cheating and Plagiarism.   The student code of conduct must in most cases treat cheating and plagiarism. We have seen that an intellectual property rights policy can to some extent address this subject as well. Provide students with institutional policies on cheating and plagiarism, as well as the penalties for violation. Plagiarism is a problem that is becoming more widespread through an increase in websites from which students can buy reports and papers. Students must be made aware that this practice is flagrantly dishonest and that engaging in it will result in dismissal from the course and perhaps from the institution.

Also, in an elearning environment, there are increased opportunities to cheat on tests when they are delivered online. Three popular ways in which students cheat on online tests are:

- Getting someone else to take a test
- Group test taking when students gather together in a lab or at home
- Printing out and distributing copies of online tests

Your code of conduct policy should indicate penalties associated with these kinds of behavior. Chapter 11 provides suggestions about how to reduce cheating and plagiarism in elearning courses.

Attendance.   A code of conduct policy should address attendance requirements. At the same time, taking attendance in an elearning environment, especially in a totally online

FIGURE 9.8   Example Student Code of Conduct Contract

Each student is an important member of our class community and has a responsibility to himself or herself, to the instructor, and to his or her classmates to support and contribute to the course's learning community. This code of conduct is established to ensure that all students have a clear understanding of the expectations your instructor has regarding your conduct in this class. Please review the following responsibilities and sign in the space below that you are in agreement.

It is the responsibility of each student to:

- Treat all other students, instructors, and guests with dignity and respect in face-to-face interactions and in electronic communications.
- Comply with the Information Technology policies of the institution.
- Comply with cheating and plagiarism policies of the institution and this course. Violations will result in dismissal from the course with a failing grade and may result in dismissal from the institution.
- Participate respectfully in team class collaborations and team projects.
- Participate respectfully and professionally in peer reviews.
- Be self-motivated and self-directed and exhibit the following behaviors.
  - Be a good time manager.
  - Approach the course with a desire to learn.
  - Assume a leadership role when necessary. Voluntarily help other students when you have knowledge they don't have.

- Develop needed technology skills.
- Submit constructive suggestions for course improvements.
- Become familiar with and abide by all course policies and procedures listed in the policies section of the coursesite, including the following:
  - File Formats and Virus-Free Files
  - Checking Announcements
  - Email
  - Assignments
  - Attendance
  - Electronic Discussions
  - Getting Technical Help
  - Cheating and Plagiarism
  - Intellectual Property Rights and Fair Use Guidelines

Printed Name: _____   Signature: _____   Date _____

---

course, is more problematic than in a traditional learning environment. A code of conduct policy should clearly state what constitutes an absence in an elearning course and the penalties, if any, associated with an absence. Participation in required elearning activities can be construed as attendance in an elearning course. Absence, then, is lack of participation. For example, when students fail to reply to an email, participate in a discussion, or attend a scheduled chat, this equates to being absent. One of the most effective techniques to promote participation in elearning activities is to ensure that participation counts toward students' grades. If you choose to use this form of motivation, your code of conduct policy should so indicate, and both your assignment policy and your course outline should specify how attendance will be figured into the final course grade.

Self-Motivation and Self-Direction.   A code of conduct policy should state your expectations of students with respect to self-motivation and self-direction in an elearning environment. Adult learners, who are typically more mature and more experienced than younger students, often have a better understanding of what is required in a self-directed environment. Young students and students new to elearning may need considerable help to achieve the same appreciation for self-reliance that adult learners have. Consider including the following recommendations in your student code of conduct policy.

- Be self-motivated and self-disciplined.
- Be a good time manager.
- Approach the course with a desire to learn.
- Assume a leadership role and be a teacher when necessary. Voluntarily help other students, bearing in mind, however, that doing other people's work for them is tantamount to cheating.
- Develop needed technology skills.
- Contribute to course discussions, listen to others, and respond respectfully to their comments.
- Contribute to team activities and respect the ideas of others.
- Comply with all course policies.
- Submit constructive suggestions for course improvements.

REFERENCES

Berg, G. (2000). How distance education affects faculty compensation. *EDUCAUSE Quarterly, 23*(3), 44–45.

Besek, J. (2003, November/December). Copyright: What makes a use "fair"? *EDUCAUSE Review, 38*(6), 12–13.

Brown, D. G. (2002, August). Please learn from my mistakes. *Syllabus, 16*(1), 26.

Carlson, S. (2000, July 21). When professors create software, do they own it, or do their colleges? *The Chronicle of Higher Education.* Retrieved September 23, 2002, from http://chronicle.com/free/v46/i46/46a02901.htm

Carnevale, D. (2003, March 28). Slow start for long-awaited easing of copyright restriction. *The Chronicle of Higher Education.* Retrieved March 24, 2003, from http://chronicle.com/free/v49/i29/29a02901.htm

Hagner, P. R. (2000, September/October). Faculty engagement and support in the new learning environment. *EDUCAUSE Review, 35*(5), 27–28, 30–32, 34–37.

Harper, G. K. (2000, November/December). Copyright endurance and change. *EDUCAUSE Review, 35*(6), 20–26.

Jafari, A. (2002). Conceptualizing intelligent agents for teaching and learning. *EDUCAUSE Quarterly, 25*(3), 28–34.

Ko, S., & Rossen, S. (2004*). Teaching online: A practical guide.* Boston: Houghton Mifflin.

Oblinger, D. (2003, July/August). Boomers, gen-Xers, and millennials: Understanding the new students. *EDUCAUSE Review, 38*(4), 36–40, 42, 44–45, 47.

Petersen, R. J. (2004, March/April). A framework for IT policy development. *EDUCAUSE Review, 39*(2), 54–55.

Read, B. (2003, May 21). Catholic U. web site aims to help colleges comply with federal regulations. *The Chronicle of Higher Education.* Retrieved July 17, 2003, from http://chronicle.com/daily/2003/05/200305210lt.htm

Seabrook, J. (2003, July 7). The money note. *The New Yorker,* pp. 42–55.

Stein, S. (2001, January/February). An alternative approach to intellectual property rights in distributed education. *EDUCAUSE Review, 36*(1), 26–30, 34–37.

Twigg, C. A. (2000). Who owns online courses and course materials? Intellectual property policies for a new learning environment. *Center for Academic Transformation.* Retrieved January 6, 2003, from www.center.rpi.edu/PewSym/mono2.html

Ubell, R. (2001). Who owns what? Unbundling web course property rights: A policy on web course ownership may settle conflicts on campus. *EDUCAUSE Quarterly, 24*(1), 45–47.

Ulius, S. (2003, July/August). Intellectual property ownership in distributed learning. *EDUCAUSE Review, 38*(4), 62–63.

Ward, D. (2000, January/February). Catching the waves of change in American higher education. *EDUCAUSE Review, 35*(1), 22–26, 28–30.

Wicker, S. & Boyd, B. (2003, November/December). Promoting faculty adoption of technology at Wake

Forest University. *The Technology Source.* Retrieved November 26, 2003, from ts.mivu.org/default.asp?show=article&id=1032.

Winograd, K. (2000, March/April). Practicing the good practice in faculty development. *The Technology*

Source. Retrieved September 23, 2002, from http://ts.mivu.org/default.asp?show=article&id=656

URL REFERENCES

American Association of University Professors Guidelines on Intellectual Property: www.aaup.org/Legal/info%20outlines/legdl.htm

American Library Association: http://ala.org

Association for College and University Policy Administrators: www.inform.umd.edu/ACUPA/Project/process

Center for Academic Transformation, Rensselaer Polytechnic Institute, Monograph on Intellectual Property: www.center.rpi.edu/PewSym/mono2.html

CETUS: Consortium of California State University, State University of New York, and City University of New York, Intellectual Property Guidelines: www.cetus.org/ownership.pdf

Copyright Management Center at Indiana University–Purdue University–Indianapolis: www.copyright.iupui.edu

Digital Millennium Copyright Act: www.copyright.gov/legislation/dcma.pdf

Family Educational Rights and Privacy Act: www.ed.gov/policy/gen/guid/fpco/ferpa/index.html

Harvard University Statement of Policy in Regard to Inventions, Patents, and Copyrights: www.techtransfer.harvard.edu/PatentPolicy.html

Library of Congress—United States Copyright Office: www.lcweb.loc.gov/copyright

Stanford Copyright & Fair Use Center: http://fairuse.stanford.edu

Stevens Institute of Technology Web-Based Course Intellectual Property Rights: www.educause.edu/ir/library/word/CSD1474.doc

The TEACH Toolkit: www.lib.ncsu.edu/scc/legislative/teachkit/

University of Arizona Intellectual Property Policy: www.abor.asu.edu/1_the_regents/policymanual/chap6/6-908.pdf

University of Texas System's Crash Course in Copyright: www.utsystem.edu/ogc/intellectualproperty/cprtindx.htm#top

Wake Forest University Copyright Policy: www.wfu.edu/organizations/CIT/docs/CopyrightPolicy.htm

World Intellectual Property Organization: www.wipo.org/

CHAPTER TEN

COURSE DELIVERY

This chapter explains how to apply elearning concepts discussed in earlier chapters. Specifically, it discusses some of the things you can do during course delivery to help your students have a rewarding learning experience. What follows is divided into three sections. The first identifies steps you can take to ensure that your course gets off to a good start. The second explains how to manage and motivate students. The third provides information for leading students who are working together on group projects.

GETTING A GOOD START

This section offers some suggestions to help you through the process of starting up your elearning course. A good start is critical in an elearning environment. You must make a concerted effort to help students become acclimated to your elearning environment. If your course creates a student-centered environment—and many elearning courses do—students used to traditional learning may express dissatisfaction, at least initially, and have trouble getting started. A related concern is that students new to elearning may need help learning to use the technology effectively. You must be well prepared when your course begins to head off these problems and others like them. To ensure a good start, you should perform a careful technology check before you meet your students for the first time. Next, when you initially meet students—whether it be face-to-face or online—you should give them a thorough orientation to your course and the technology it uses. Third, you may want to profile your students to obtain information you will use while the course is in progress. Fourth and finally, it is probably a good idea to conduct some kind of getting-acquainted activity to help you and your students get to know each other. The four subsections that follow discuss each of these subjects.

Technology Check

Before your course begins, you should carefully check out the technology you will use. The time you spend doing this will be time well spent. You should check your coursesite for accessibility and usability, and assure that the computer technology in classrooms and labs is completely ready for you and your students to use it. You should also be well prepared to deal with any technology failure that may occur in the classroom.

Coursesite Check.   The coursesite check should include a review of all course resources to ensure they are accessible. Check coursesite references to URL links to ensure they are still current. Resources that will be used very early in the course should be checked with special care. These include student profile surveys, getting-acquainted discussion and/or chats, and course information. In addition, be sure you are clear on student coursesite login procedures if passwords are required. You should also know how to proceed if a student cannot access your coursesite because of password or related LMS login problems.

Figure 10.1 provides an example checklist for ensuring the readiness of the coursesite.

Classroom and Laboratory Check.   If you will meet your class face-to-face, you should check the computers and related technology in your classroom and in the labs used by students enrolled in your course. Verify that lab computers have the required software installed, including appropriate web browser plug-ins, and that it works properly. In your classroom, check the instructor's workstation to ensure all elements are operational—computer, projector, screen retractor, multimedia hardware, and so on—and that software required to support presentations, class demonstrations, and web browsing is installed on the computer. You must also ensure that you can use this technology with comfort and ease. Few things diminish your credibility with students more than technology difficulties in the classroom that you cannot deal with gracefully. In addition, if your classroom has computers for students, check them out in the same way you did lab computers.

FIGURE 10.1   Coursesite Readiness Checklist

GETTING-STARTED RESOURCES POSTED

☐ Course syllabus
☐ Staff contact information
☐ Course orientation
☐ Course policies
☐ Statement on course prerequisites
☐ Statement on required technical skills
☐ Statement on computer technology that students must have access to
☐ Welcome message
☐ Overview of the LMS
☐ "How to" tutorials
☐ Self-test on how to use discussion forum
☐ Getting-acquainted discussion question
☐ Student profile survey
☐ Student code of conduct agreement

COURSE CONTENT RESOURCES POSTED

☐ Unit 1 resources
☐ Unit 2 resources
☐ Unit 3 resources
☐ Unit 4 resources

EXTERNAL LINKS

☐ Unit 1 links tested
☐ Unit 2 links tested
☐ Unit 3 links tested
☐ Unit 4 links tested
☐ External links tested

TECHNICAL RESOURCES POSTED

☐ Technical requirements for course
☐ How to get help with LMS
☐ How to get help with technology in labs
☐ Procedures that clearly state students' responsibility to maintain their personal computing systems

PROCEDURES INSTRUCTORS MUST KNOW

☐ Student LMS login procedures
☐ Instructor LMS login procedures
☐ How to get technical help for LMS login or other computer difficulties

In addition to ensuring that class and lab technology is working, you must fully understand how students are to gain access to the computing network that will allow them to access the Internet. Note that network login is not always the same as the coursesite login mentioned in the last subsection. Make sure you know what procedures to follow if some student does not know how to log in to the network or experiences password difficulties. Login difficulties can consume class time rapidly and invariably lead to intense frustration. If you can persuade a network expert to accompany you to your first class meetings to help students deal with login difficulties, you will substantially increase the probability that your students' initial experiences with your elearning coursesite will be pleasant ones.

Figure 10.2 provides an example technology checklist.

Technology Failure Backup Plans.   It is almost certain that you and your students will eventually experience a technology failure. These failures always constitute a significant disruption to course delivery, but they are especially devastating during the initial portion of a course, when students are still adjusting to your elearning environment. Consequently, it is wise to consider what kinds of things might go wrong and to formulate a plan to deal with failures when they happen. As explained in Chapter 9, your course policies should include procedures to follow when the technology fails, and you should publicize these procedures from the very beginning of your course. These procedures apply, for example, when students cannot submit an assignment on time due to a technology failure or when a technology failure occurs when an online test is scheduled.

FIGURE 10.2   Classroom and Laboratory Technology Checklist

COMPUTERS (CLASSROOM AND LABS)

☐ How to turn computer on/off
☐ Login procedures
☐ How to obtain help with login procedures
☐ Ensure computers are working properly, including all peripheral devices
☐ How to obtain technical help with computers

SOFTWARE (CLASSROOM AND LABS)

☐ LMS is accessible
☐ Microsoft Office and other class standard software available and working properly
☐ Internet browser(s) and required plug-ins available and working properly
☐ How to obtain technical help with software

PRINTERS (CLASSROOM AND LABS)

☐ How to turn printers on/off
☐ Location of paper and how to load
☐ How to restock paper
☐ How to obtain technical help with printers

OTHER INSTRUCTIONAL EQUIPMENT (CLASSROOM ONLY)

☐ Procedures for turning projector on/off
☐ Procedures for adjusting projected image
☐ Ensure that projector is working properly
☐ Procedures for using multimedia hardware—CD and DVD players, analog video player, and so on
☐ Procedures for operating projection screen in classroom
☐ Procedures for operating classroom lighting
☐ How to obtain technical help for classroom hardware

As for technology failures in the classroom, usually you must resort to conventional course delivery for the rest of a class when they occur. However, viable recovery procedures exist if your classroom computer still works but Internet access is disrupted. In this case, if you have loaded the resources you need on the hard drive of the computer ahead of time or if you have written them to a CD or other mass storage device, you will be able to continue. Another approach is to have hard copies of your course resources that can be displayed on the projection screen using an overhead projector. Either of these backup plans would suffice in an emergency. What is most important is that you devise some backup plan well ahead of the need to implement it.

Student Orientation

Orienting students to your course and its learning resources is an important part of getting off to a good start. We have broken down the required orientation activities as indicated in the following list, whose items are expanded in the rest of this subsection. However, it will be obvious to anyone reading our comments that there are many appropriate orderings of the information presented during student orientation activities. Whatever order you choose for the information, what is important is that your orientation be thorough and systematic.

- Welcome students before the course starts.
- Conduct a course orientation.
- Explain course technology requirements.
- Conduct a coursesite orientation.
- Introduce students to LMS functionality required for assignments.
- Emphasize course policies.

If your course meets totally online, the student orientation will have to be in writing using coursesite resources that provide the appropriate information and directions. Once students have reviewed the relevant resources, consider having them engage in an electronic discussion to ask questions or to comment on the course. If you do decide to have students engage in such a discussion, be sure you provide detailed instructions on how to use the discussion tool. As previously stressed, students become extremely frustrated when they experience difficulties using your coursesite, especially during their initial elearning experiences.

Welcome Students before the Course Starts.   No matter whether your course will meet face-to-face or totally online, consider posting a welcome announcement that will be the first thing students see when they initially enter your coursesite. You might also consider sending your students an email message before class begins to welcome them. In the welcoming email, you could provide information about yourself and ask students to reply by telling you a little about themselves. Of course, if you have a very large number of students, processing the replies may require more time than you can devote to a welcoming activity.

Even if students do not see your welcoming announcement or email prior to the time the course begins, they will eventually notice it, and when they do, they will appreciate the fact that you were thinking of them before they ever came to know who you are. Everyone likes to feel appreciated. The University of Dayton has taken the concept of welcoming students to an institutional level through a program called Personalized Virtual Room for incoming freshmen. Several weeks before freshmen are to arrive on campus, they are mailed a username and password to use to enter a personalized virtual dorm room. Once logged into the Virtual Room, students can find out who their roommates are as well as correspond with them online. A virtual dorm provides a means for students to learn about the layout of their rooms and share the information with family and friends (Young, 2000). In a related welcoming website maintained by Emory University, entering freshmen can log on and select their roommate according to the same principles used to match individuals on computer dating websites (Lewin, 2003). It is easy to see how such welcoming approaches could be adapted to welcoming students in an elearning course, if an instructor desired to spend the considerable time required to create the appropriate coursesite resources.

Conduct a Course Orientation.   In your course orientation, you will acquaint students with the contents and requirements of your course. If you meet students face-to-face, such an orientation involves displaying and commenting on relevant resources on your coursesite. In this case the orientation can serve as a lead-in to the coursesite orientation, which is the next step. Some instructors may in fact prefer to conduct the coursesite orientation before the course orientation or to combine the two topics into a single course/coursesite orientation. In your course orientation, start off by introducing yourself, your teaching assistants, and your student assistants. Then review the information provided in the course syllabus; explain course goals and requirements and how the course will be conducted. Mention course policies, including the student code of conduct policy, if you are using one. As explained below, policies are so important that we suggest you cover them separately as a wrap-up of your student orientation activities.

If your course is to be student centered, your course orientation should also include a discussion of how this approach to learning differs from a teacher-centered environment. Be very specific about how you expect students to behave in such an environment, stressing the fact that a student-centered environment requires students to be self-starters. Some students will be accustomed to the passive, teacher-centered environment where all they are required to do is attend class, listen to lectures, and take tests. At least initially, some of these students may exhibit frustration when you require them to be self-directed and to participate regularly in course group activities. Less mature students may actually be at a loss about what to do when they first begin to function in a student-centered elearning environment. The more information students have about the environment, the easier it is for them to accept it and become comfortable functioning in it. If your course is successful, probably most of your students will leave it actually preferring a student-centered learning environment.

Explain Course Technology Requirements.   You should of course advise students that basic computer literacy is prerequisite knowledge for your course. The focus here is to let students know what personal technology they will need to participate in course activities. If you teach in a face-to-face environment, your students will probably have access to institutional labs with technology adequate to complete your course requirements. Let students know they will have to visit these labs regularly if they do not have the requisite technology in their homes or offices. Totally online students, or students who prefer to work on course activities from their homes or offices, must clearly understand the technology requirements needed for participating in your course. Also, if your course uses multimedia resources that require Internet browser plug-ins, post instructions on your coursesite about how to obtain them *before* they are needed.

Conduct a Coursesite Orientation.   Your coursesite orientation should explain how to navigate the coursesite and what course resources the site contains. In addition, you should familiarize students with LMS functionality. In general, using an LMS is not much different from using any sophisticated website. However, some LMS functions will not be familiar to all your students. Students must learn how to participate in electronic discussions, take on-line tests, and submit assignments. It is a good idea to post "How To" tutorials on each of these LMS functions on your coursesite. In a totally online course, such tutorials may constitute the only information students will have about how to use your coursesite. The next subsection treats introducing LMS functionality in more detail.

Introduce Students to LMS Functionality Required for Assignments.   During student orientation, you should acquaint students with the existence of LMS tools they will use later in the course. Students likely will have little trouble navigating your coursesite after the coursesite orientation familiarizes them with its contents. Creating assignment files likewise presents little difficulty, because you are assuming computer literacy as prerequisite knowledge. For most students what remains is an explanation of how to use LMS functionality they may not previously have encountered on the Internet. You will have to show them how to create their LMS homepages and how to transfer files including assignment files to the LMS storage areas available to them.

Three other LMS tools deserving of your attention are those that accommodate forums, chats (including the whiteboard, if one is available), and online testing. However, now is not the best time to provide details about the online testing and discussion tools, both of which require hands-on experience to master. After orientation is complete, you can familiarize students with the testing tool by giving them an online quiz on coursesite functionality. Alternately—depending on the functionality of your LMS—you may be able to introduce the testing tool by using it to conduct student profiling.

At about the same time, you can introduce forum and/or chat functionality in a get-acquainted discussion. At this point, simply mention to students that you will be asking them in the near future to practice using the LMS online testing and discussion tools. Show them once again where on your coursesite they can find the instructions for using these tools, and assure them that learning to use the tools is easy. The goal during student orientation is to put at ease students who might be nervous about using LMS tools by letting them know they will have a chance to become familiar with these tools in a practice session before they are asked to use them in a graded assignment.

If your class meets face-to-face and you find that you have a student who is not computer literate, you can try pairing that student with a more knowledgeable peer to help him or her through a crash introduction to computers. Because it is not difficult to master the basics of using computers, this may work. However, the reality of elearning is that students must know how to use a computer to engage in it. Thus you may have to recommend that a student without the prerequisite computer skills enroll in a computer literacy course before taking your course. If your class is entirely online, you are not likely to encounter a student unfamiliar with computers, because computer literacy and access to a computer are usually required simply to register for the course.

Emphasize Course Policies.   By the time you reach this point in your getting-started activities, you most likely have previously mentioned some if not most of your course policies. Nevertheless, because policies are such an important part of an elearning course, we feel you should devote additional time explaining them. Show students once again where policy resources reside on your coursesite, and explain the purpose and broad content of each policy.

Your goal here is to alert students to the gravity and importance of your course rules and to the fact that you intend to enforce them. Make sure students understand that they will be judged in part by how thoroughly they abide by these rules. It is not necessary to describe each course policy in minute detail. Rather your intent is to let students know that it is their responsibility to know the course rules and that ignorance of policies published on your coursesite is no excuse for not performing in your course. This message is better delivered in a separate part of your getting-started activities, as opposed to being interspersed among other getting-started information.

If you conduct this recommended getting-started activity, you will feel much more comfortable later in the course about enforcing your policies strictly but fairly. Bear in mind that some students enjoy testing limits, and it is pointless to establish a policy unless you intend to enforce it.

Profile Students

Student profiling—if you decide to use it—should be one of your getting-started activities. Chapter 3 explained the advantages of profiling students to gather contact data and personal information. Contact information will prove useful if a technology failure or similar eventuality requires you to reach students by fax, conventional mail, or telephone. Personal information about any special needs students may have will help you address these needs. Try to remember as much information about your students as possible. The more you know about your students, the easier it will be to create a sense of community and personalize your course.

If your LMS makes it convenient for you to see answers from individual students for an online test, you can solicit profile information using the LMS testing feature. If it doesn't, you can ask students to post profile information to you by email or deposit it in a suitable LMS workspace. When it is convenient, we prefer the online testing approach to profiling, because it introduces students to online testing in a nonthreatening environment. Otherwise—as previously mentioned—you can introduce online testing by giving a quiz on your coursesite content and functionality after student orientation has been completed. In any event, regardless of how you solicit profile information from students, remember that you should never force them to reveal personal information to you in any form, because doing so would violate their privacy rights. In short, giving you profile information is entirely voluntary.

Figure 10.3 is an example student profiling form that could be translated into an online test or an electronic form that students complete and submit. Although the form is

FIGURE 10.3   Example Survey to Profile Students in an Introduction to Elearning Course

Personal Information

Name _____   Address _____

Home Phone _____   _____

Email Address _____   _____

Fax Number _____   Major _____

Status (Check All That Apply)

☐ Freshman   ☐ Sophomore   ☐ Junior   ☐ Senior

☐ Masters Candidate   ☐ Doctoral Candidate ☐ Non-Degree-Seeking ☐ Special Student

Employment (Check One)

☐ Full-Time   ☐ Part-Time   ☐ Not Employed

Technology Skills (Check All That Apply)

☐ Can Use MSWord   ☐ Can Use PowerPoint   ☐ Can Use Adobe Acrobat

☐ Have Experience with LMS (If checked, Which LMS? _____)

Typing Skills (Check One)

☐ None   ☐ Hunt and Peck   ☐ Poor   ☐ Modest   ☐ Good

Personal Technology Available (Check All That Apply)

☐ Have Access to a Computer Outside of Class   ☐ Have Access to Microsoft Office Software

☐ Have Low-Speed Internet Connection Only   ☐ Have High-Speed Internet Connection

Prerequisite Knowledge (Check All That Apply)

☐ Can Define the Term *Pedagogy* and Explain What It Means

☐ Can Define the Term *Androgogy* and Explain What It Means

☐ Can Describe Bloom's Taxonomy of Intellectual Behaviors

☐ Can Describe the ADDIE Instructional Planning Model

Learning Style (Can Be Determined by Taking an Online Survey—See Instructor for Details)

☐ Auditory   ☐ Visual   ☐ Tactile   ☐ Undetermined

Please introduce yourself to me in no more than three sentences. For example, you could tell me where you are from and supply some information about your family. Alternately, you could tell me why you are taking this course. Another approach would be to tell me an interesting fact or two about yourself.

_____

_____

_____

_____

Perceived Obstacles to Learning (Check All That Apply)

Are there circumstances that might hinder your success in this course? For example, for some of you English may not be your native language. Others of you may not know how to type. For both groups, you may feel that writing in chat sessions may be an obstacle. Some of you may have sight, hearing, or mobility difficulties. Others may face an obstacle not included in the list. After you check boxes, there is space for you to reply in writing. Please limit yourself to three sentences or fewer.

☐ Writing   ☐ Typing   ☐ Shy   ☐ Lack of Time   ☐ Language

☐ Vision   ☐ Hearing   ☐ Mobility   ☐ Other (Please Specify)

_____

_____

_____

_____

specific to the Introduction to Elearning course we have featured in other text figures, you should have little trouble modifying it to fit the needs of your course. If you decide to use a form similar to the one in Figure 10.3 to profile students, you should always accompany the form with a statement that protects student privacy. An example of such a statement is as follows:

> The information you supply in this survey will help me create the best learning environment possible for you. Your answers will be kept confidential. Nevertheless, completing the survey is entirely optional. If you do not want to answer a question, leave it blank. If you wish to discuss this survey with me personally, please send me email. I welcome your input and look forward to hearing from you.

Conduct Getting-Acquainted Activities

It is very important to establish a sense of community among your students, especially if your class is delivered totally online. Making an effort to get to know your students and providing ways for them to get to know you and each other sends the message that you care about them and their success in your course. There are at least two ways to help students get to know each other.

Biography Posting.   One way to help students get acquainted with each other is to request each student to post a brief biography and a picture in the coursesite. Your LMS will probably allocate each student a storage area where only the student can post files but anyone in the class can access them. The biographical information a student posts will in essence introduce him or her to the rest of the class. Make this activity optional so as not to violate student privacy rights. This practice has the additional benefits of giving students practice creating and uploading files to the coursesite and allowing you to assess their written communications skills by reading what they have written. This activity will be more successful if you provide specific guidelines on what to include in their biographies as well as examples. Figure 10.4 is an example of a student biography page. The following list is information you might suggest be included in student biographies.

- Place of work
- Place of residence
- Hometown
- Student status (full-time, part-time, class, adult learner, nondegree candidate, etc.)
- Motivation for enrolling in the course
- Career aspirations
- Hobbies and interests
- Favorite athlete, celebrity, sports team, and so on
- Information about families and pets
- Information about current significant events in a student's life
- Expectations and goals for the course

Getting-Acquainted Discussion.   A getting-acquainted discussion is another good way to help students get to know each other. Instruct students to keep their postings simple, and provide them with an example of the type of responses you are looking for by participating in the discussion yourself. In addition to getting to know you and each other, students will learn how to use coursesite technology when they participate in a getting-acquainted discussion. Naturally you will have to assist students in learning how to use the discussion tool. Instructions about how to do this should be posted on the coursesite.

As discussed in Chapter 6, chats with many participants are difficult to control. Thus, unless your class is quite small, a forum may be a better choice than a chat for a getting-

COURSES › EDTECH SANDBOX 1 › COMMUNICATIONS › ROSTER › STUDENT PAGES - MICHELLE REA

Student Homepage - Michelle Rea

Intro Message
Michelle Rea's Homepage

Personal Information
Originally from Naperville, IL, I came to Embry-Riddle Aeronautical University (ERAU) in the fall of 1997 in pursuit of a Bachelor of Science degree in Communication. After graduation in 2001, I completed internships with American Airlines, the Ladies Professional Golf Association and the United States Golf Association. Upon my return to ERAU in 2003, I began working with the Educational Technology department while I earn an MBA in Aviation. I am excited about taking this course due to how much I enjoyed marketing classes as an undergraduate. I look forward to doing group projects and presentations as I enhance my knowledge in this area of business. My career goals include communications or marketing management within the aviation/aerospace industry. I enjoy learning new things, going to the beach and being around good friends. I cheer for every sports team from Chicago and adore my Cavalier King Charles Spaniel named Charlee.

FIGURE 10.4   Michelle Rea, Embry-Riddle Aeronautical University Student Homepage in Blackboard
Used with permission.

acquainted discussion. However, you could decide to break your class into small groups containing no more than five or six students and have these students participate in a get-acquainted chat. Students in the small groups would get to know each other faster than would students participating in a forum involving the entire class. Of course, if you use this approach, students will not get to know anyone in the class outside of their individual group members.

MANAGING STUDENTS

Recall the discussions in Chapter 2 of Gagne's *Nine Events of Instruction* and Chickering and Gamson's *Seven Principles for Good Practice in Undergraduate Education.* Both emphasize the importance of interaction between student and instructor. Such interaction is perhaps even more important in an elearning environment than in a traditional learning environment, because elearning may limit or preclude face-to-face meetings with students. At the same time, the elearning environment provides better tools for communicating with students. In this section, we discuss instructor–student interaction in elearning. The section is divided into five subsections. The first offers suggestions for motivating elearners. The second and third, respectively, discuss methods for getting and giving feedback. The fourth explains how to manage student assignments. The fifth and last subsection addresses how to deal with difficult students.

Motivating Students

Keeping students motivated requires work in any learning environment and is especially challenging in elearning wherein students are often expected to be highly self-directed. The best motivator is a well-designed and interesting course in which students are challenged intellectually and they perceive that they are gaining valuable knowledge. As discussed earlier, another important motivator is the assurance that the elearning activities in which students participate count toward a grade. In addition, students are more motivated to complete assignments and activities enthusiastically when they understand the purpose of the learning activity. Finally, students are more motivated in an environment that is conducive to learning and one where they are respected and supported.

The signs and causes of low motivation are various. Unmotivated students are sometimes nonparticipants in electronic discussions. They may fail to submit individual assignments or be unwilling to collaborate with peers on group assignments. If there have been persistent problems with technology, the frustration that ensues may cause some students to cease making an effort to complete your course. Other students may allow personal problems or disabilities to affect their performance. Regardless of the causes of nonparticipation, however, one thing is clear. It can be harder to identify nonparticipants in an elearning environment than in a traditional learning environment to the extent that you do not have personal interaction with students. For example, taking roll is easy in a face-to-face class, but what constitutes "attendance" in a totally online course?

What can be done when a student seems to lack interest in your course or in a specific course activity? The first thing is to notice a student's inactivity. Some elearning instructors require students to send them a brief weekly email—three sentences or fewer—confirming that things are going well and that they are making suitable progress in the course. Reading this mail can be time-consuming, but it does let students know you are concerned about them. You can reply to the collective emails with a general announcement, and send individual email to only those students who do not contact you by the required time.

More generally, your ability to demonstrate to students that you are involved in your course and that you care about each of them is probably the most important motivator you can extend to students. If the course is totally online, you must devise methods to be visible and display a constant presence. This can be accomplished through frequent announcements, email to the class, participating in electronic discussions, and communications with individual students when needed. If—as is recommended—you profiled your students during your course getting-started activities, the information you gathered about skill levels and special needs may help you head off problems. When you do recognize a problem, take action as soon as you can. Contact a student personally by telephone or email. Use direct communication with the student to uncover and resolve difficulties so that the student can participate successfully in course activities.

Obtaining Student Feedback

Typically, instructor and course evaluation take place at the end of a course, when it is too late to make corrections for the current students. In an elearning environment, it is especially important to obtain student feedback on an ongoing basis, so that adjustments can be made as they are needed. We recommend that you frequently ask students to provide input on your course. Doing so will provide you with the information you need to make positive changes in your course. At the same time, seeking frequent feedback will build a sense of community and course ownership among students. Finally, it builds mutual respect by sending the message that you care about making the course better for your students and that you value their input.

One strategy for obtaining student feedback is to designate specific students to canvass your class informally and report critical issues directly to you. We previously have mentioned using student teams to provide assistance with technology difficulties. If you employ such teams, you could ask the team leaders to help you get this feedback. Additional approaches are to seek feedback through discussions and surveys, or to mine coursesite statistics for information, as discussed next.

Discussions and Surveys.   Discussions and surveys provide an easy way to obtain frequent feedback from students to determine what is and is not working in your course. Discussions obviously will be conducted online; a forum is by far more suitable than a chat. Some LMSs have evaluation functionality built into the system so that students can conveniently evaluate the course and the instructor as well as individual learning resources. You may also be able to collect survey information online using the LMS testing capability. Your LMS will almost surely allow you to set up the discussion or online test so that the student input will be anonymous. Students will not feel comfortable providing feedback—particularly negative feedback—unless they know their names will not be associated with their comments. The perfect anonymity of online discussions and surveys makes this the approach of choice for obtaining student feedback. Do bear in mind, however, that if you use a forum to get feedback, even though the threads are anonymous, every student with access to the forum can see what other students have recorded about you and your course.

Surveys of various types can also be conducted in class meetings if you meet your students face-to-face. Consider using a short survey to obtain feedback on subjects such as the day's lecture, confusion about assignment instructions, or any other topic on which you need information immediately. We will refer to such surveys as *one-minute surveys,* although the actual time to administer the survey and wait for students to complete it may be more than one minute. If students have computer access in your classroom, you can administer a one-minute survey very quickly using the LMS and see the automatically tabulated results just seconds after students complete the survey. This is far preferable to using a printed feedback form, but do remember that obtaining feedback is your primary goal and that how you obtain the feedback is secondary. A student response system such as the one discussed in Chapter 2, if available, is another method of obtaining almost instantaneous feedback. Figure 10.5 is an example of a one-minute survey designed to obtain feedback on a guest speaker. One-minute surveys can, of course, also be used in totally online courses.

In addition to one-minute surveys throughout the course, consider conducting a more detailed survey halfway through the course to help you determine necessary midcourse corrections. The following are the types of responses you might ask students to supply:

- Describe what you like best about this course.
- Describe what you like least about this course.
- Describe what needs to be done to make this course better.

FIGURE 10.5   One-Minute Survey—Guest Speaker

Instructions:
- Please answer the following questions to provide me with your feedback on Dr. Smith's presentation.
- Please be aware that your feedback will be anonymous.
- Please use the following scale:
  A. Strongly agree   B. Agree   C. Neutral   D. Agree   E. Strongly disagree

	A	B	C	D	E
1. The speaker was knowledgeable about the subject.	☐	☐	☐	☐	☐
2. The speaker was well prepared for the presentation.	☐	☐	☐	☐	☐
3. The presentation was valuable to me.	☐	☐	☐	☐	☐
4. I would recommend this presentation to my peers in this program.	☐	☐	☐	☐	☐
5. I would like to have other guest speakers visit our class.	☐	☐	☐	☐	☐

Please use this space to enter any additional comments about the topic or the guest speaker.

When you solicit online feedback, the construction of the survey instrument should always encourage students to think critically about the course issues that concern you. Open-ended questions will encourage students to provide specific input. Figure 10.6 provides examples of appropriately worded requests for feedback.

Coursesite Statistics.   Because they track a student's use of the coursesite and of specific course resources, coursesite statistics provide valuable feedback on student performance. Typically an LMS records information such as:

- The number of times a particular student entered the coursesite
- The amount of time a particular student spent in the coursesite
- The number of hits a specific course resource received
- The total time spent by all students on a specific course resource
- Item analysis for objective online tests

Figure 10.7 illustrates a pie chart indicating coursesite statistics reflecting the total time spent by all students accessing several different course resources.

FIGURE 10.6   Example Feedback Questions

- You recently worked on a project called *Why Portals Are Important.* Apparently there was some confusion about the project instructions. What are your recommendations for improving the instructions to make them clearer?
- Consider the activities you participated in at the beginning of our course, for example, the Introduce Yourself, What's in the Course Syllabus, and How to Use the Coursesite presentations. What other activities would have helped you get a better start in the course?
- The last unit exam our class took resulted in grades lower than I had anticipated. Please take a few minutes to analyze your performance on the test and report on it. Did your grade reflect the knowledge you had when you took the exam? If not, why do you think this is the case? Were there parts of the exam that seemed unfair or unclear to you? If so, which parts, and why? If you were the instructor, how would you change the exam to make it a better instrument for assessing student learning?
- Recently a student expressed rather strong dissatisfaction with the way forums and chats are graded. What is your opinion about the fairness of discussion grades in our course? If you were the instructor, how—if at all—would you change the

grading method? Based on your experiences in the course, what in your opinion are the benefits and drawbacks of online discussions?
- The response to a recent guest speaker's talk on airline safety was overwhelmingly favorable. What other subjects relevant to our course would you like to hear guest speakers talk about? Do you have a specific recommendation about whom we should invite? Perhaps you know someone in the aviation industry who is a likely candidate. Remember that we have very limited funds available; we can pay modest travel expenses but not a speaker stipend.
- Coursesite statistics reveal that the resource entitled the *invisible web* is underutilized. This surprises me, because it is relevant to recent course content, and I myself find the subject very interesting. Please help me understand what the coursesite statistics mean. If you have visited *The Invisible Web,* please give me your candid opinion of its usefulness. Comment in particular on whether the information it contains is important, interesting, and clearly expressed. Be specific about what you like and don't like. If you have not visited *The Invisible Web,* please explain why you have not yet used this resource.

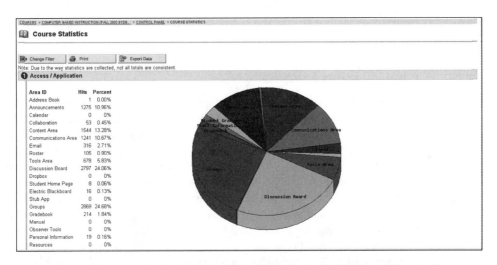

Area ID	Hits	Percent
Address Book	1	0.00%
Announcements	1275	10.96%
Calendar	0	0%
Collaboration	53	0.45%
Content Area	1544	13.28%
Communications Area	1241	10.67%
Email	316	2.71%
Roster	105	0.90%
Tools Area	678	5.83%
Discussion Board	2797	24.06%
Dropbox	0	0%
Student Home Page	8	0.06%
Electric Blackboard	16	0.13%
Stub App	0	0%
Groups	2869	24.68%
Gradebook	214	1.84%
Manual	0	0%
Observer Tools	0	0%
Personal Information	19	0.16%
Resources	0	0%

FIGURE 10.7   Pie Chart Indicating Coursesite Statistics in a Blackboard Coursesite

Course statistics have many uses. You can, for example, use them to see whether there is a correlation between questions students missed on an exam and how frequently they accessed related course resources. If such a correlation exists, the poor performance may well be due to lack of effort. More generally, if a student is performing poorly in your course and infrequently visits the coursesite, you might contact the student and encourage him or her to spend more time using course resources.

Another way to use course statistics is to ask why certain course resources receive high use while others go relatively unused. Is a frequently used resource unclear, requiring students to spend more time processing it? If so, the resource needs revising. Alternately, perhaps the frequently used resource is one that is particularly engaging for students. Are multimedia resources visited more frequently than other resources, indicating that students find such presentation of course content particularly appealing? If so, you may want to consider creating additional multimedia resources.

Reviewing coursesite statistics may lead you to discover unexpected student responses to course resources. For example, it may happen that a particular resource you thought would be popular is in reality not being used very much. There are a number of potential responses:

■ Revise the resource.
■ Publicize the resource.
■ Implement course activities that encourage students to use the resource.
■ Make the resource more visible on the coursesite.
■ Remove the resource entirely.

Notice how various these alternatives are. Which one might be the right course of action? In truth, coursesite statistics about resource usage tell only how often a resource is accessed, not why. To find out why a resource is underutilized, you will probably need to resort to student feedback. The last item in Figure 10.6 is an example of how such feedback can be solicited.

Giving Students Feedback

As stressed in the subsection on motivating students, it is very important for you to communicate frequently with your students, especially if your course is totally online. When events happen that would be of interest to the class such as news about classmates or relevant current events, post announcements or send email to the entire class. Another way to establish frequent communications is to routinely send out reminders about the next topic or assignment or summaries of the week's work. When you establish communications routines in your course, students will anticipate hearing from you on a regular basis and actually look forward to what you have to say. Besides communicating regularly with your entire class, you should keep in contact with members of class teams and with individual students when you perceive they need your attention. Be sure you keep routine announcements and email messages short. Like you, students are very busy.

In addition to announcements and email, virtual office hours and online tutoring are previously discussed elearning mechanisms that make it easy to communicate with students. We believe elearning instructors should use online communication liberally to recognize student achievement. Positive reinforcement properly used powerfully encourages students to dedicate themselves to your course. Do not hesitate to praise your class as a whole when you find good results on an assignment, project, or examination. Acknowledge as well the outstanding work of a class team or of individual students. If you are teaching a hybrid class, you can also bestow praise face-to-face. However, electronic praise perseveres longer than the spoken word, especially if the praise occurs in a coursesite announcement.

Electronic communication also makes it possible to counsel students online. Students using the Internet to communicate often feel more comfortable asking advice and discussing personal issues than they would in a face-to-face meeting. Electronic communication—typically email—is also more convenient than face-to-face meetings. You should strongly encourage students to write you when they are experiencing difficulties in your course. Eliminating frustration is an important factor in student success. Moreover, when students feel they have personal contact with you, their elearning experience is more likely to be a good one (Serwatka, 2002).

You might like to advise your students about institutional counseling facilities. Many institutions provide web counseling for students, including some with procedures to contact a counselor anonymously or in some other nonthreatening way. For example, ▪*Dear Uncle Ezra* at Cornell University allows anonymous questions to be sent to an equally anonymous trained counselor. Student feedback clearly documents the importance of anonymity in making them feel free to express themselves (Worona, 2003). The University of Wisconsin at Eau Claire provides a website with information about the university's ▪Counseling Services, homesickness, and drug addiction. Similar services are exemplified by the University of Chicago's ▪Student Counseling Virtual Pamphlet Collection and the Columbia University Health Education Program's ▪Go Ask Alice! website illustrated in Figure 10.8 (Carlson, 2002b).

For all its benefits, providing students with feedback and counseling them electronically has its drawbacks. One problem is that whatever you write electronically can be easily

FIGURE 10.8   Alice! Columbia University's Health Education Program
Used with permission.

distributed to others. Establish a firm policy that your students are not to send your personal communications to anyone unless you authorize them to do so. Also—as mentioned at several points in this book—encouraging email from students can increase your workload, especially if you are teaching a large class. As explained in Chapter 9, you should establish a clear policy about what you will and will not discuss in email communications. Do bear in mind, however, that the more attention you find time to pay to your students, the more likely it is that they will succeed.

Processing Assignments

You will of course carefully plan the assignments you require your students to complete. The first assignments are of particular significance, because one of your goals should be to help students experience early success in an elearning environment. Another important goal is to make assignments that foster learning without making unrealistic time demands of your students.

What follows contains suggestions about processing assignments, including strategies for managing assignment files when you receive them. Our comments are focused on treating students fairly when you make assignments. However, you must not forget to treat yourself fairly as well. Chapter 3 discusses the significant time demands elearning can make on instructors. It follows that when you make an assignment, you should take into account how much time will be needed to prepare and present the assignment requirements to the class, provide students with required feedback, and assess student performance. These factors are especially critical for instructors teaching large classes without the support of teaching assistants.

Realistic Due Dates.   Carefully planning the due dates for student assignments is one way to show respect for the workloads of students. Some assignments—for example, group projects—take much longer than others to complete. Rather than making time-consuming assignments sequential, alternate them with less demanding assignments. Remember that at the beginning of the course, students are adjusting to an elearning environment. Thus you should anticipate, for instance, that an early discussion assignment will consume more time than one made later in the course. Finally, define your workweek to consider student needs. For example, if your hybrid class meets once a week on Wednesday, you may want to consider Tuesday night as the end of the workweek. For totally online courses, you might consider Sunday night the end of the workweek. Either way, students can plan on having the weekend to complete an assignment before it is due.

Detailed Instructions.   Clarifying assignment instructions can be one of the most time-consuming activities you engage in with elearning students, especially in a totally online course. If you find different students asking the same questions about an assignment, it is likely the assignment instructions are less than completely clear. When you formalize an assignment and post it as a resource on your coursesite, consider using a checklist to ensure that the assignment file contains all the information students could reasonably expect you to provide. The checklist will help you assure that as a minimum the instructions contain:

- A thorough description of the assignment
- The assignment due date
- The assignment's relevance to the course content and course objectives
- What tasks must be performed and what must be submitted
- Special instructions if any for submitting the assignment (reference your assignment policy)
- How the assignment will be graded
- What kind of feedback on the assignment students can expect and when they can expect it
- Any other information pertinent to the assignment.

As explained in Chapter 9, students must know how to submit assignments electronically, including what file formats are acceptable. This information should be in a policy resource on your coursesite, and you should emphasize to students that you will follow your policy to the letter. In addition, if you use email for assignment submission, consider a getting-started activity whereby students write something about themselves and email it to you as an attachment to ensure that they understand the procedures for submitting an assignment. Alternately, if you use LMS workspace for assignment submission, have students post the information about themselves to this workspace.

Paced Assignments.   Ease into student assignments during the getting-started phase of your course. Too many assignments too early in a course can disillusion more than a few students. Avoid graded assignments entirely until you are sure that the technology is working properly and that students understand how to use coursesite tools. Make sure that your first assignments can be completed quickly and easily, so that students will feel good about their performance early in the course. We like to grade getting-started assignments on a pass–fail basis, with students receiving full credit if they demonstrate a mastery of the coursesite technology used to complete the assignment.

Assignment File Organization. In a traditional learning environment, assignments are typically submitted in hard copy, graded, and returned to students in person. By contrast, in an elearning environment, you will be receiving most if not all assignments in electronic form, either through email or by having students upload files to a designated storage area in the LMS, as discussed in Chapter 4. Once you have received a set of student assignment files, organizing them efficiently can be challenging. First of all, you must decide how you will discriminate between assignments as submitted and assignments after they are graded. Both submitted and graded assignment files should be saved, because the possibility exists that a dispute might arise as to exactly what a student actually submitted in an electronic assignment. Moreover, as explained in Chapter 8, you should ultimately store student assignments on your personal computer rather than exclusively on the LMS server, because otherwise you will not be able to retrieve assignment files if a technology failure erases them.

One method for saving submitted and graded assignments is to create a file folder for each assignment you give. You can create the folders yourself on your computer's hard drive or alternately use your email system to create the folders if assignments are submitted by email. For each assignment folder, create two subfolders, one for assignments as submitted, and the other for graded assignments. Immediately place assignments you receive from students in the submitted assignment subfolder. Then, when you grade the assignments and return them to your students, place a copy of each graded assignment in the graded assignment subfolder.

An alternative organization for assignment files is to create, for each student, an assignment folder with two subfolders, one for submitted and one for graded assignments. If your class has many students, this alternative for organizing assignment files may require more keystrokes and mouse gestures than organizing assignments by assignment number, but it has an advantage to offset this disadvantage. When you maintain a folder for each student's work, you are essentially establishing a portfolio of student work examples. To make a student portfolio more complete, consider pasting portions of each student's discussion comments in documents to be saved in the student's graded assignments subfolder. This provides additional examples of a student's critical thinking and communications skills, which may prove useful when you are determining a final course grade. Chapter 11 contains additional information about student portfolios.

Dealing with Difficult Students

Using common sense is perhaps the most effective method of dealing with difficult students. Most of the strategies you use in resolving problems with difficult students in a face-to-face environment also work in an online environment. The main problem is that when you do not have opportunities to be face-to-face with difficult students, creative remedial action may be necessary. What follows explains how to deal with three categories of difficult students: nonparticipants, disrespectful students, and domineering students.

Nonparticipants. Nonparticipants are students who fail to participate in course activities. While there are many reasons for nonparticipation, shyness is one of the most common, and it has become routine in the elearning literature to describe nonparticipants using the term *shy.*

There are a number of reasons why students shy away from online activities. Some are embarrassed to participate in discussions because of poor writing skills. People for whom English is a second language fall into this group. You might consider setting up guidelines that do not penalize such students for grammatical mistakes, assuming their written remarks are otherwise coherent. Other students do not participate out of an inertia stemming partially from shyness and partially from a lack of energy or motivation. Sometimes a friendly and encouraging "warning" about nonparticipation can help such students, though some of this kind of nonparticipator may be beyond the reach of most instructors. Still other students may not participate because they do not know how to use the LMS discussion tools. As previously indicated, such students can be instructed to review the online tutorials that explain how to participate in electronic forums.

As we saw earlier in this chapter, students' participation in course activities improves when it counts toward their overall course grade. A related method of encouraging participation is to send private email to students who are not participating. If you have gathered information about your students early in the course, you might use that information to draw out reluctant students by asking their opinions about an issue you know does not threaten them. Personalizing your contact with students makes it much more likely that they will be willing to discuss difficulties they are experiencing in course participation.

Another reason students may not be participating is that they have dropped out of your course altogether. If you do not come face-to-face with students on a regular basis, you may be able to determine whether a student has dropped out of the class by reviewing coursesite statistics to note what course resources the nonparticipant is currently accessing, if any.

Disrespectful Students.   Disrespectful students often manifest themselves in online discussions. It is best not to engage in an argument or in negative discussion with disrespectful students online. Instead, try to handle the problem by private email, in a phone call, or during a face-to-face meeting. As discussed earlier, you will be able to keep the number of disrespectful discussion responses to a minimum by establishing and firmly enforcing discussion policy. Include in the policy a statement that although students do not have to agree with an idea another student posts, every student must respect the right of others to express an opinion. Also, make it clear that students may be removed from a discussion or from the course for violations of netiquette. In addition to having clearly stated discussion policy, if you suspect problems may occur, you or your course assistants may need to monitor a forum carefully to minimize or eliminate disrespectful postings.

When rude comments are noted in a discussion or any other course activity, you can provide a general warning to all students by posting an announcement reminding students to follow the course discussion policy and to refrain from disrespectful behavior. If abusive behavior continues, copy and save the disrespectful comments so they can be verified, and notify your system administrator and appropriate institutional authorities. Many institutions have computer ethics policies that support punishing students who abuse the use of technology in any way. Such abuse includes exhibiting disrespectful behavior in online discussions through acts such as using obscenity or profanity or by directing abusive or derogatory comments to other students or to ethnic or racial groups. Ordinarily the penalties for violating use-of-technology policies are quite severe. Students should be made aware of this fact.

Domineering Students.   Some students may try to control or dominate class activities. Sometimes controlling students are also disrespectful, but it is possible to be domineering in less obvious ways. For example, posting an excessive number of comments in online activities is an act of domination. Students who exhibit such behavior frequently fail to realize that others find it objectionable, even as nonstop talkers often do not perceive that they are monopolizing a conversation.

More often, however, domineering students act consciously. As is the case with disrespectful students, domineering students often reveal themselves in electronic discussions. A domineering student may question the value of a discussion topic. Another common action of domineering students is initiating discussion responses that are intentionally off topic. Yet a third common act of control occurs when a student questions the instructor's course management or teaching style in an online activity. Surprisingly, some students who wouldn't consider arguing with you to your face may do so online, because being online conveys to some naïve individuals a sense of anonymity implying they don't have to answer to online colleagues in person. It is well known that domineering behavior is more common in email and in Internet forums and chats than in face-to-face interaction.

Course policies on electronic discussions and netiquette should clearly define and describe controlling behavior. When domineering students violate these rules, send them individual email reiterating the rules of online behavior and informing them specifically about how they have violated these rules. Ordinarily a warning suffices to cure the problem. However, you should be aware that a few domineering students thoroughly enjoy controversy. When you send email to such a student, your warning may simply provoke additional antisocial behavior. In that case, you may have to interdict the student's participation in online activities or drop the student from the class. Some LMSs enable you to disallow a student's ability to post discussion threads or to send email to students in the class. If your LMS has this capability, hopefully you will rarely if ever have to use it.

MANAGING ONLINE TEAM PROJECTS

This section is about team projects in an elearning environment. Most instructors and virtually all employers would agree that the ability to work as a member of a team is one of the most valuable skills an individual can develop. What follows consists of three subsections. The first catalogs the benefits and advantages of online team collaboration. The second subsection discusses how elearning tools can be used to promote teamwork. The third explains how you as instructor can promote successful team collaboration.

Advantages of Online Team Collaborations

There are several benefits and advantages of team collaboration in an online environment. First of all, the elearning environment makes it very easy, convenient, and inexpensive for team members to communicate with one another without having to meet face-to-face. One significant challenge to working on a team in physical space is finding a meeting time that is convenient for all team members. Virtual space allows teamwork among individuals who are widely separated geographically and/or temporally. Equally important—because we are discussing teamwork in an elearning environment—the same tools that promote team cooperation among students make it easy for you to monitor the progress of student teams and to guide them toward successful completion of their projects.

A second advantage of online team collaboration is that it builds a sense of community among team members. Team members collaborating online often establish a closer bond than those who rely on face-to-face meetings only. In face-to-face team meetings, often there is insufficient time for all team members to express their views fully. Some team members may be unable to formulate definitive ideas about a topic under discussion in such a limited meeting. Virtual space affords such individuals the additional time they need to contemplate an issue before reaching a conclusion. In addition, reserved team members may be more comfortable contributing ideas online as opposed to speaking out in a face-to-face meeting.

The third and probably most important advantage of team collaboration in elearning is that students participating in online team projects learn valuable real-world skills. For one thing, they develop proficiency with technology communication tools widely used in the workplace. More important, they learn—in an environment closely emulating the workplace world—how to cooperate with their peers in the pursuit of a common goal. For the latter reason alone, online team projects constitute perhaps one of the most important activities you can incorporate into your course.

Technology Tools to Facilitate Online Team Collaborations

By now you are no doubt familiar with elearning communication tools. If this is not the case, Chapter 4 provides an overview of the subject. The two most valuable of these tools for group collaboration are tools to create documents that can be shared among team members on the Internet and tools for engaging in electronic discussions.

Word processors are probably the tool of choice for creating documents that will be shared among team members. Because word processors enable tracking changes to a document, a team member's contribution to a document can easily be identified as to the author and the time the comments were placed in the document. Your word processor will probably allow you to assign a different type color to each person inserting comments in a document. When such a document is circulated among a team for each member's individual input, one convenient file containing the team's collective wisdom is generated (Klemm, 2002). Circulating documents, however, is usually not sufficient to allow team members to achieve all the goals of their project. At some point, a meeting will be required. Thus electronic discussion tools are fundamental to online group collaboration. Your LMS will most likely allow you to set up a private workspace for a student team. Use of this workspace is limited to students you designate as team members. Within this workspace, the team will have access to LMS tools allowing it to initiate forums and chats that can be visited only by team members.

Student teams will use forums in much the same way as they use circulating documents—to gather individual input on a topic of group concern. An individual team member contributes to a forum asynchronously in the same manner that he or she would modify a document attached to an email before forwarding to the next team member. In addition, because forums can be visited multiple times, team members who have already contributed to the team's collective thinking can return later and respond to other individuals who have seen their initial input and commented on it. Another advantage of forums is that individual contributions of team members are preserved electronically, making it easy to identify the major contributors to the team effort and to determine who—if anyone—is a nonparticipant. Discussion archives also allow an instructor to see where a team is having trouble with a concept or process and to intervene as necessary. We return to this idea in the next subsection.

For all these reasons, forums are probably the preferred communication medium for team deliberations. However, at some point team members will probably find it necessary to engage in a synchronous discussion to resolve differences of opinion before generating the team's final project report. Chats have a fairly high probability of succeeding when the size of the team is small. As we have already seen, chats need a facilitator, so student team members should be advised to elect a chat leader before a synchronous discussion starts.

Promoting Successful Team Collaborations

While students perform most of the work in team projects, you as instructor also have responsibilities. In essence, you are an almost-silent team member whose presence should nonetheless be apparent to every student on a team. What follows offers suggestions in six areas for discharging your responsibilities to student teams.

- Provide adequate instructions.
- Organize appropriate team membership.
- Require the use of collaboration technology.
- Build a sense of community among team members.
- Guide team progress.
- Determine a fair grading method.

Provide Adequate Instructions.   Before students begin work on a team project, they need instructions about how to set goals, plan group activities, conduct effective meetings, and resolve conflicts. Chapter 2 discusses learning styles and identifies various online inventories useful for determining an individual's learning style. Ideally, students working together in groups should have a basic understanding of this subject and be aware of each other's learning styles. When students are informed about these issues, team effectiveness improves dramatically (Poindexter, Basu, & Kurncz, 2001).

Team project instructions should detail exactly what is expected of each member. They should be very specific about what deliverables you expect and how the deliverable will be submitted. If a project entails multiple components, be sure to provide a due date for each deliverable. In hybrid classes—assuming time is available—you can ask teams to present their results in a talk to the class, backed up by a written summary. Such presentations are commonly required in workplace environments. For totally online classes, one method of presenting deliverables is in an online team portfolio posted on the LMS for other students to review and evaluate.

Besides being specific and complete about what you require from students in team projects, your instructions—or a coursesite policy on the subject—should state what each team member can expect of you and what your level of participation in the team's deliberations will be. For example, how often will you visit a team forum to provide feedback on what has been posted there? At what times—if at all—are you available to participate in a team chat so that team members can ask you questions about the project they are working on? To what extent will you respond to a team's questions about a project? Will you respond to email from any team member or only from a designated team leader?

In addition to all this, you might post a document to the coursesite containing general guidelines for students working in teams. The information in this document will undoubtedly grow as you gain experience in directing class projects through successive iterations of your course. Among other things, the document might suggest appropriate uses of discussions in a team project. For example, a Project Topics discussion allows team members to contribute ideas to the group at their convenience. An After Hours discussion provides team members an opportunity to socialize. An FAQ discussion—perhaps open to every member of the class—would allow students to answer each other's questions about a variety of generalized information pertinent to team projects.

Figure 10.9 illustrates the detailed instructions provided a team in an Introduction to Elearning course that is working on a course redesign project.

Organize Appropriate Team Membership. Graceful interaction between team members is essential to team success. For this reason, the selection of team participants is an important part of constituting student teams. Small teams are more effective than large ones. We recommend at most five or six participants, especially when team deliberations will be entirely online. There may be logical team groupings within your course, such as students who have the same major or students employed by the same company who want to work together on company-related issues. Also, if a variety of topics exists for a particular team project, team membership may form naturally based on the interests of individual students.

If students do not form teams on their own, there are several ways in which to organize them. Some LMSs have the ability to assign students to teams randomly. If you choose to determine team assignments, one way is to base membership on specific criteria such as by major, time zone, job, technical abilities, or declared personal interests. It is obviously advantageous to organize teams so that better prepared students, more motivated students, or more active students are evenly distributed in various teams. This makes it more likely that team leaders will emerge naturally. You should also do everything in your power to distribute evenly among teams any students you have identified as unmotivated or having limited capability. A student team composed primarily of such students may produce good results, but the odds are not high that it will.

Contradictory opinions exist about keeping the same team members together for the duration of a course when there will be several graded team projects. Many instructors believe that it is better to change team membership so that students will have greater opportunities to work in diverse groups. Also, if conflicts develop between team members on an initial project, team membership should most likely be changed for the next team project. If teams are to work together throughout a course on several projects, student leadership roles should be rotated to provide leadership experience for all team members. Also, consider rearranging teams by shifting members from collaborative teams that excel to teams that need student mentors or leaders to show them the way (Reinhart, Anderson, & Slowinski, 2000).

Require the Use of Collaboration Technology. To work together effectively in an elearning course, team members must make use of online collaboration tools. Hopefully, students will already have experience in using these tools by the time they reach the team

FIGURE 10.9   Team Project On Course Redesign Instructions

ASSIGNMENT DESCRIPTION

In this assignment, you will work as a member of a team to redesign a course that is currently taught in a traditional format. Your team redesign must include the use of elearning and it must focus on decreasing the cost of course delivery and the improvement of student learning. Your work will model the ▪Pew Program in Course Redesign in which 30 institutions received funding for course redesigns.

ASSIGNMENT OBJECTIVES

Students Will:

- Apply principles of the Program in Course Redesign to a course they may teach in the future.
- Apply elearning pedagogical principles to a course they may teach in the future.
- Experience the importance of team collaborations.
- Use team collaborations tools provided in most LMSs.

ASSIGNMENT INSTRUCTIONS

Part 1—Getting Started

- Your instructor will assign you to work on a team with five or six other students.
- You must nominate a team leader who will coordinate the efforts of the team.
- Sometime before the team presentation, you must determine who will be the team spokesperson. It does not have to be the team leader, although it can be the same person if the team chooses.
- Your team must review at least six of the institutions participating in the Pew Program in Course Redesign, and select three to model.
  - One way to work on this would be for each team member to review one or more institutions in the redesign program and report a summary of the findings to the team.
  - Your team will be responsible for modeling some of the methods used to assess the effectiveness of these redesigns.

Part 2—The Research and Collaboration

- The team must agree on a course to redesign with a goal of improving the delivery of the course and student learning through the use of technology. It can be modeled after a course one or more group

members have taken, or it may be a course one or more group members have taught. Please do not use the actual name of the course or any actual instructors. Let's keep this fictitious.

- The redesign must include all or some of the principles of the three institutions your team chooses to model from the Pew Program in Course Redesign.
- Through team deliberations including face-to-face meetings, electronic forums, chats, phone discussions, email, and any other appropriate methods of team communications, determine how the course will be taught when redesigned.

Note: A private team area has been designated in the LMS for your team. Take advantage of the electronic communications tools in this private area for your deliberations. For example, a private area has been designated for your team in forums, chats, and file exchanges. The How To Tutorials in the Coursesite Information section contain complete instructions on how to access and use these team functions.

Part 3—The Written Report (Due October 29)

The team must create a written report on the course redesign. The desired length is five double-spaced pages (10 point type). Do *not* produce a substantially longer or shorter report. The report must include/reflect the following elements:

- Adherence to the guidelines for creating documents viewable on the web. (Refer to the Creating Documents for Web Viewing checklist in the "Forms and Checklists" section of the coursesite.)
- A description of the way the course is taught in a traditional delivery mode.
- A description of the major problems with the way the course is taught in the traditional mode.
- A summary describing the major elements of the three institutions the redesign is modeled after. Please include the names of the institutions.
- A summary describing the major elements of your course redesign. Explain how the course will be delivered. Include details about the delivery method, the elearning technology that will be used, and any other information needed to fully describe your course redesign.
- A description of how you will assess the effectiveness of the redesigned course.

(continued)

FIGURE 10.9   Continued

Part 4—The Presentation (Due October 29)

The team must create a PowerPoint presentation to deliver within a 15- to 20-minute presentation in class on October 29. The number of slides in the presentation should be from 6 to 12. DO NOT exceed 12 slides. The PowerPoint presentation must include/reflect the following elements:

- Adherence to the guidelines for creating PowerPoint presentations viewable via the web. (Refer to the "Creating PowerPoint for Web Viewing" checklist in the Forms and Checklists section of the coursesite.)
- A description of the course in its traditional version with emphasis on the major problems encountered in the traditional delivery mode.
- A summary of the three institutions you choose from the Program in Course Redesign and a summary of the major principles you modeled in your redesign.
- A summary description of how your course will be delivered.

- A summary description of the major principles of your course redesign.
- A summary description of the anticipated savings in course delivery costs made possible by the redesign of your course.
- A summary of how you will assess the effectiveness of your course redesign.

Part 5—The Eportfolio (Due October 29)

The team must post the written report and the PowerPoint presentation on the coursesite in the designated team presentation space.

Part 6—Evaluation (Due October 30)

You must participate in a self-evaluation of your performance on the team as well as a peer review of the performance of your team members. Review forms are located in the Forms component of the coursesite. You must complete a separate form for each team member. Email your self-evaluation and the peer evaluation forms to your instructor by October 30.

DETERMINATION OF INDIVIDUAL ASSIGNMENT GRADE

Evaluation Category	*Criteria*	*Points*
Self-Evaluation	Thoughtfulness and Completeness	0–2
Your Completion of Each Peer Evaluation	Thoughtfulness and Completeness	0–4
Your Average Score from Peer Evaluations	Your Peers' Perception of Your Performance	0–4
Instructor's Review of Written and Oral Report	Same Score for All Team Members	0–4

■Program in Course Redesign: www.center.rpi.edu/PewGrant.html

project portion of your course. However, your coursesite should contain "how to" tutorials on using LMS tools for easy reference by your students. The following knowledge is required to participate fully in online team collaboration:

- How to set up and conduct forums and chats
- How to use a whiteboard
- How to exchange files by email
- How to send group email
- How to post files to the team workspace
- How to post a team calendar
- How to post a team portfolio

Build a Sense of Community among Team Members.   Teams will be more successful when provided opportunities to get acquainted and to build trust in each other before they begin their work. As a consequence, you should encourage teams to schedule activities that facilitate team building. A team's first activity could be an informal discussion—a chat or forum, as appropriate—in which team members provide general information and an interesting fact or two about themselves. At the same time the team can assemble logistical information, such as when members are available for chats and how comfortable they are with online collaboration technology. Such a discussion might also lead to electing a team leader or leaders.

Guide Team Progress.   Your goal as an elearning instructor is to guide team progress without intruding on the team's independent collaborations. To this end, you may want to enter the team discussion areas periodically and comment briefly on team progress. If you word your remarks carefully, you can assist and encourage the team without interfering in its deliberations. You will also be able to determine which team members, if any, are not participating, and identify any dominating students, students exhibiting inappropriate behavior, or students who are violating course policies. If you become aware that some students are not participating or participating inappropriately, contact them privately to give them constructive feedback and to determine whether a problem exists that requires you to provide assistance.

If your class is large, there may be too many teams for you to track personally without drastically increasing your workload. In that case, implement alternative monitoring procedures. One method is to have teams elect student leaders to monitor team activities and provide you status reports on a regular basis. Ask these leaders to play the same role you yourself would play if you visited the discussions personally. You might also ask the team to identify other team leaders, for example, a team recorder to summarize team deliberations and email them to other team members on a regular basis. If you are on the team mailing list, you can use these summaries to help you guide team progress.

Determine a Fair Grading Method.   When individual team members know they will be held accountable for their performances, they will work harder, and the likelihood of team success will increase. There are several ways to grade students on their participation in team projects. One method is to organize group projects into discrete portions and assign each team member overall responsibility for a portion. This method makes it easier to assign individual grades and provides a method of dividing work equally. A drawback of this approach, however, is that it can stifle organizational incentive and even encourage team members to work individually rather than as a group. If this happens, students may fail to develop the collaborative skills that are a primary goal of every team project. Be sure individual students know that although they are responsible for particular parts of a project, they must be sure to solicit input from every other team member in discharging this responsibility and that part of their grade will reflect their success in doing this. Knowing this, most students are apt to be quite persistent in asking team members for input, making it less likely that unmotivated students can avoid participating in team deliberations.

An alternative approach to grading projects is to assign the same grade to every member of the team. This approach has two merits. First, it stresses the idea that team collaboration is the best approach to problem solving and that the team as a whole is greater than the sum of its parts. (If students doubt this, just mention the Apollo program or the Space Shuttle program.) Second, it reflects the reality of the workplace world, where results are almost always considered more important than individual effort, and where there are always some individuals who work harder than others. However, assigning one grade to the entire team also has its drawbacks. We have all witnessed teams in which a few students did most of the work, while others did very little. Even though this situation again reflects workplace reality, some students will perceive it as unfair that unproductive students receive the same grade as those who actually accomplished the work. There are at least two ways to respond to this perception. Point out first of all that it is up to team leaders to motivate less productive team members and that there are rewards for individual effort—for example, personal growth—that far outweigh any grade for a team project. Of course, a procedure must be established so that team members have a way of notifying the instructor when the team leader is not fulfilling his or her responsibilities. Next, remind students that long-term rewards for persistent effort in the workplace are promotions, increased responsibility, and salary raises, and that the work habits they develop during the course of their formal education will carry over into their professional careers. Also remind them that unproductive workers fail at promotion, remain at low salary levels, and in the extreme lose their jobs.

Yet a third grading method is to assign an overall team grade, and an individual grade based on each student's participation, which you track in the coursesite by reviewing discussion dialogue. You can also use peer evaluation to determine a student's individual grade. In peer evaluation, each team member rates all of the other team members based on their participation and assigns a corresponding letter grade or awards a number of points out of a maximum possible numeric score.

Once you have chosen one of these grading methods, or synthesized a grading method from some combination of all of them, be sure to publish it as part of your grading policies. As with other grading criteria, criteria for evaluating team projects must be complete, concise, and crystal clear. Otherwise you open yourself up for reasonable criticisms of unfairness in grading. Be sure your team project instructions either contain your grading criteria or reference the course resource document that promulgates these criteria. If you plan to use peer evaluation, the form that students will use to evaluate their teammates should be disclosed to students at the outset of a team project.

REFERENCES

Bartindale, B. (2003, June 10). Online service pairs students, mentors. *The Mercury News*. Retrieved July 17, 2003, from www.siliconvalley.com/mld/silicon valley/news/local/6053553.htm

Brown, D. G. (2002, September). Accounting for team learning. *Syllabus, 16*(2), 27.

Brown, D. G. (2003a, February). How to customize big classes. *Syllabus*. Retrieved May 1, 2003, from www.syllabus.com/article.asp?id=7257

Brown, D. G. (2003b, May). Encouraging good student contact. *Syllabus, 16*(10), 32.

Carlson, S. (2002a, January 23). A community college offers a taste of online study. *The Chronicle of Higher Education*. Retrieved June 10, 2002, from http://chronicle.com/free/2002/01/2002012301u.htm

Carlson, S. (2002b, November 15). Virtual counseling: As campus psychologists go online, they reach more students, but may also risk lawsuits. *The Chronicle of Higher Education,* p. A35.

Carlson, S. (2003a, March 13). Ball State U. tests interactive system for answering students' health questions online. *The Chronicle of Higher Education.*

Retrieved March 18, 2003, from http:// chronicle.com/free/2003/03/2003031301t.htm

Carlson, S. (2003b, June 20). Help-desk diary: Tech-savvy students learn people skills and patience by solving campus computer problems. *The Chronicle of Higher Education.* Retrieved July 17, 2003, from http://chronicle.com/weekly/v49/i41/41a02701. htm

Danchak, M. M. (2002, September/October). Bringing affective behavior to e-learning. *The Technology Source.* Retrieved November 24, 2003, from http:// ts.mivu.org/default.asp?show=article&id=962

Hara, N., & Kling, R. (2001). Student distress in web-based distance education. *EDUCAUSE Quarterly, 24*(3), 68–69.

Hitch, L. P., & MacBrayne, P. (2003, March/April). A model for effectively supporting e-learning. *Technology Source.* Retrieved April 7, 2003, from http:// ts.mivu.org/default.asp?show=article&id=1016

Johnstone, S. M. (2001, December). Distance learning: Real-time faculty office hours. *Syllabus, 15*(5), 18.

Klemm, W. R. (2002, September/October). Extending the pedagogy of threaded-topic discussions. *The Technology Source.* Retrieved November 24, 2003, from http://ts.mivu.org/default.asp?show=article &id=1015

Knowles-Harrigan, C. (2003, May/June). Toward online success: The creation of a multimedia tutorial product. *The Technology Source.* Retrieved May 12, 2003, from http://ts.mivu.org/default.asp?show= article&id=936

Lewin, T. (2003, August 7). First test for freshmen: Picking roommates. *New York Times.* Retrieved December 3, 2003, from www.nytimes.com/2003/08/07/ technology/07ROOM.html

Lujan, H. D. (2002, March/April). Commonsense ideas from an online survivor. *EDUCAUSE Review, 37*(2), 28–33.

Murphy, C. (2002, September). ABCs of smart classrooms. *Syllabus, 16*(2). Retrieved December 3, 2003, from www.syllabus.com/article.asp?id=6704

Picard, M. M., Torcivia, E. M., & Younghouse, P. (2002, January). Collaborating to create narrative case studies. *Syllabus.* Retrieved December 3, 2003, from www.syllabus.com/article.asp?id=5915

Poindexter, S., Basu, C., & Kurncz, S. (2001). Technology, teamwork, and teaching meet in the classroom. *EDUCAUSE Quarterly, 24*(3), 32–41.

Quick, R., & Lieb, T. (2000, December). The Heartfield Project: Using computer technology to facilitate interdisciplinary collaborations in higher education. *T.H.E. Journal, 28*(5), 41–46.

Reinhart, J., Anderson, T., & Slowinski, J. (2000, October). Creating pre-service teachers' virtual space: Issues in design and development of cross-country collaboration. *T.H.E. Journal, 28*(3), 26–34.

Riffee, W. H. (2003, February). Putting a faculty face on distance education programs. *Syllabus.* Retrieved May 1, 2003, from www.syllabus.com/article.asp? id=7233

Serwatka, J. A. (2002, April). Improving student performance in distance learning courses. *T.H.E. Journal, 29*(9), 46–51.

Wald, M. L. (2002, December 25). An online course gets students thinking about drinking. *New York Times,* p. B8.

Worona, S. (2003, May/June). Privacy, security, and anonymity: An evolving balance. *EDUCAUSE Review, 38*(3), 62–63.

Young, B. A. (2000). Technology-enhanced learning and community with market appeal: Why the University of Dayton's personalized virtual room is attractive to students, parents, faculty, and staff. *EDUCAUSE Quarterly, 23*(4), 50–52.

Young, J. (2001, February 2). Time-management skills are one key to success for online students. *The Chronicle of Higher Education.* Retrieved October 22, 2001, from http://chronicle.com/free/2001/02/ 200102020lu.htm

Young, J. R. (2002a, May 31). The 24-hour professor: Online teaching redefines faculty members' schedules, duties, and relationships with students. *The Chronicle of Higher Education.* Retrieved May 31, 2002, from http://chronicle.com/free/v48/i38/38a0310. htm

Young, J. R. (2002b, June 11). Online education's drawbacks include misunderstood e-mail messages, panelists say. *The Chronicle of Higher Education.* Retrieved June 11, 2002, from http://chronicle. com/free/2002/06/2002061101u.htm

URL REFERENCES

Campus Blues: http://campusblues.com

The College of DuPage, Computer and Internet Experience Requirements: www.cod.edu/Online/exper. htm

Counseling Services—University of Wisconsin at Eau Clair: www.uwec.edu/counsel

Dear Uncle Ezra: http://ezra.cornell.edu

Go Ask Alice!—Columbia University's Health Center: www.goaskalice.columbia.edu

Harvard Business Online, Business Cases: http://harvard businessonline.hbsp.harvard.edu/b02/en/cases/cases_home.jhtml

SMARTTHINKING: www.smarthinking.com

Stevens Institute of Technology: http://k12science.ati.stevens-tech.edu/collabprojs.html

Student Counseling Virtual Pamphlet Collection at the University of Chicago: http://counseling.uchicago.edu/vpc

Tutoring Program at the University of Alabama, Program in Course Redesign: www.center.rpi.edu/PewGrant/RD2%20Award/UA.html

Tutoring Program at the University of Colorado, Program in Course Redesign: www.center.rpi.edu/PewGrant/rd1award/UCB.html

Tutoring Program at the University of Idaho, Program in Course Redesign: www.center.rpi.edu/PewGrant/RD2%20Award/UI.html

Tutoring Program at Virginia Tech, Program in Course Redesign Project: www.center.rpi.edu/PewGrant/RD1award/VA.html

University of Kentucky: Teaching with online case studies: www.uky.edu/~halesr/case.html

CHAPTER ELEVEN

ELEARNING ASSESSMENT

Elearning assessment involves finding out how well your students are learning. The process is ongoing, not something you do only at the end of a course. Ongoing assessment gives you the information you need to keep your course on track as you deliver it and also to make it better each time you teach it. The goal of this chapter is to give you some ideas about how to get the information you need to assess student learning, as well as to determine how effective your course and coursesite are in helping students learn. The chapter is organized into three sections. The first discusses measures for assessing student performance in elearning. The second discusses various approaches to assessing the effectiveness of your elearning course and the coursesite that supports it. The third treats comparing student outcomes in elearning and traditional learning environments. Although we have researched the chapter diligently, our goal is not to sum up the scholarship on elearning assessment. Rather, we present ideas we have used successfully in many years of college teaching and business consulting, with the hope that they will help you begin to think about the assessment procedures you will develop for your own course. We have used the assessment instruments presented in the chapter figures with good results.

ASSESSING STUDENT PERFORMANCE

Student learning in a traditional course is typically measured by testing, supplemented perhaps with a project such as a term paper. While both metrics are useful ways of assessing student performance, elearning—to the extent it results in a student-centered learning environment—supports a number of alternative approaches to evaluating student learning. In this section, we discuss four approaches to assessing student performance. While testing definitely has its place in elearning, the last three approaches have the distinct advantage that employers frequently use similar approaches to measuring an employee's value in the work world. The four approaches are:

- Testing
- Portfolio assessment
- Student participation
- Self- and peer evaluation

A separate subsection treats each of theses four approaches. In addition—because dishonesty is a subject of significant concern in the world of learning as in the business world—a fifth subsection discusses approaches to encouraging student integrity.

Testing

Testing is the favored measure of student learning in a traditional teacher-centered learning environment. It is also useful in a student-centered elearning environment. As discussed in Chapter 4, an LMS provides an online testing capability by which students can take online tests and quizzes with immediate computer grading and recording of grades. This testing format is very popular with students because it provides immediate results. Nevertheless, many elearning instructors are hesitant to use unproctored online tests because of the increased potential for cheating on such tests. Instead, they use online tests for self-assessment, because the instant feedback powerfully reinforces students' learning from their mistakes. The last part of this section advances suggestions for encouraging student integrity in taking online tests.

Portfolio Assessment

In a student-centered learning environment, students typically are required to complete a number of individual and team projects. In such an environment, portfolio assessment is an excellent method of determining what students have learned and whether they have met the objectives of your course. A portfolio typically consists of—in addition to examples of student work—self-evaluations, peer evaluations, and evaluations completed by the instructor. Also, portfolios can include excerpts from students' comments in electronic discussions.

The emerging concept of electronic portfolios, also called eportfolios, provides an electronic method of organizing and retrieving student work. These electronic processes make it possible to associate student work not only with student evaluations, but with those of instructors, academic departments, and institutions as well (Ahn, 2004). Some progressive institutions provide eportfolio services to graduates so that throughout their careers they will have a central eportfolio that can be updated on a regular basis, making it possible for potential employers to review samples of their work through various stages of their careers, as well as obtain reference information.

Most LMSs provide a private storage area where students can create portfolio websites. Web access to portfolios facilitates peer and instructor evaluation. In addition, if students choose to make their portfolios public, future students in the same course can view completed examples of the assignments they will work on, and potential employers can visit a portfolio website to help them assess a student's capabilities and job qualifications. Thus portfolios become a part not only of students' academic lives but of their professional lives as well. As such, they constitute a significant motivator for students to work diligently in an elearning course. If your LMS functionality does not support student websites, an alternative is to have students post their portfolios on a website they create on the file servers provided by their personal Internet providers.

Detailed instructions about portfolio design help ensure that students produce high-quality work. These instructions should be provided to students when your course begins, so they can plan their portfolios early in the course. Clearly state what kind of student work is to be included in the portfolio, as well as the minimum and maximum number of examples of each kind. The instructions should include a rationale for creating the portfolio, so that students fully understand its purpose.

Figure 11.1 provides an example portfolio grading rubric. Portfolio items are rated 0 to 10 inclusive, with fractional ratings—for example, 7.5, 8.1, 9.8—possible. You can use a similar form to grade student assignments such as individual or group projects.

Student Participation

We have seen that students are much more likely to participate in course activities when their efforts count toward their final grades. Thus strategies are needed to assess student participation in all course activities. Grading criteria reflecting these strategies should be explained to students when the course begins. They should also be posted on the coursesite for easy reference, either in the policies section or in the course outline.

Student participation may be measured in at least two ways. First, you can grade students' contributions to electronic discussions. Figure 11.2 illustrates an example form to use in evaluating students' participation in discussions. As indicated in the grading criteria explanation, the form reflects both the number and the quality of postings for each discussion.

FIGURE 11.1   Portfolio Assessment Form

Student's Name _____

Portfolio Component or Characteristic	Numeric Grade
Portfolio Item 1	_____
Portfolio Item 2	_____
Portfolio Item 3	_____
Portfolio Item 4	_____
Portfolio Item 5	_____
Portfolio Organization	_____
Overall Portfolio Quality	_____
Portfolio Average Score	_____

Comments

Explanation of Numeric Grading Scale

10 Excellent Quality Work
- Far exceeds course requirements
- Demonstrates superior effort
- Course content mastery

8–9 Good-Quality Work
- Exceeds course requirements
- Demonstrates commendable effort
- Good course content knowledge

6–7 Acceptable Quality Work
- Meets course requirements
- Demonstrates acceptable effort
- Acceptable course content knowledge

0–5 Unacceptable Quality Work
- Fails to meet course requirements
- Incomplete or unacceptable effort
- Poor course content knowledge

FIGURE 11.2 Discussion Assessment Form

Student's Name: _____

Discussion	Required Posts		Responses to Other Students		Total Points
	Posts	Points	Posts	Points	
Forum 1	_____	_____	_____	_____	_____
Forum 2	_____	_____	_____	_____	_____
Forum 3	_____	_____	_____	_____	_____
Total Points for All Discussions					_____

Comments

Grading Criteria

- Ten points is the maximum score on a forum.
- Two points are awarded if the minimum number of required posts is met.
- Two points are awarded if the minimum number of responses to other students is met.
- For both categories of posts—assuming the minimum number of posts is met—zero to three additional points will be awarded depending on the relevance of the posts and the extent to which they reflect critical thinking:
  - Inappropriate or otherwise unacceptable posts—zero points
  - Acceptable posts—one point
  - Good posts—two points
  - Outstanding posts—three points

A second way to assess student participation is to reward students for accessing and using materials in the coursesite. Many LMSs can track the number of times students enter the coursesite, measure the total time spent per session, and record the amount of time spent in specific coursesite areas. Such statistics allow you to determine a grade for student participation in the coursesite. You should view the LMS statistics with caution, however. Because students can manipulate the statistics, they are not always an accurate measure of participation. For example, a student can log in to the coursesite and then work on something else while the clock runs. Total time logged on a coursesite is less indicative of course participation than are which areas of the coursesite students visit and how much time they spend in the more sophisticated and demanding coursesite areas. A student who spends a few minutes in an area where the majority of students spend 30 minutes or an hour is probably not seriously engaged with coursesite materials.

Self- and Peer Evaluation

Self-evaluation and evaluation by peers is another approach to assessing student performance. A reflective essay is one suitable means of self-evaluation. Periodically ask your students to write a suitably short essay about what they have learned in your course and how they will apply the knowledge in future academic courses or in their careers. The reflective essay could also include a self-evaluation of their performance in the course. This process will help you determine whether the students met the objectives of the course. You might also consider asking your students to offer constructive suggestions for improving your course. Be very specific in your instructions about reflective essays, both as to the length of the essay and the specific subjects the essay should address. The following list provides subjects and questions you might ask students to discuss in reflective essays.

- Summarize what you have learned in this course.
- Summarize how you will use the knowledge you gained in this course.
- If you were going to co-teach this course with me, what would you change?
- What was the most valuable knowledge you gained in this course?
- What was the least important aspect of this course?
- What was the most important skill you developed in the course, and why?
- What advice do you have for future students?
- What additional comments would you like to make?

Consider using self-evaluation and peer evaluations as one of the assessment components for team projects and student portfolios. One of the major advantages of peer evaluations is that student evaluators often have more time than you to give detailed feedback. This is especially true if you are teaching a large class, so that it is difficult, if not impossible, for you to provide thoughtful feedback to all students.

Peer reviews of portfolios are perhaps best conducted by teams of student reviewers. This process models committee evaluations of employees sometimes used in the workplace. To maximize the value of the process, specify peer review guidelines and evaluation criteria in a document posted on your coursesite. The review teams can collaborate face-to-face or in a forum. One advantage of using a forum for input is that student reviewers may feel more comfortable commenting online, because they can take more time to provide thoughtful feedback. Because peer reviews of this nature are significant group projects, you should consider counting the results of the review toward the course grade of the reviewers as well as the grade of the individual whose portfolio is being reviewed. You can use a version of Figure 11.1 for team peer reviews of a student portfolio.

Performance in team projects can also be assessed both by self-evaluation and by peer evaluation. With the growing importance being placed on team projects in elearning, consider requiring students working together on a team to evaluate their own performance on the team as well as the performance of their team members. Figure 11.3 is an example team project assessment rubric suitable for use in self-evaluation or peer evaluation.

Blogs, derived from "web logs," might also be used as a form of self- or peer evaluation. Blogs are web pages created by an individual in the form of a log or journal where the author writes his or her thoughts on a specified subject and posts them on a website. Blogs could be a useful tool for students to use to reflect on a topic or to publish their thoughts and understandings (Ferdig & Trammell, 2004). In addition to instructor review, blogs could be reviewed by student peers. See the end-of-chapter URLs for information on how to find blogs of interest and places where you and your students can post blogs.

FIGURE 11.3   Form for Evaluating Performance on a Team Project

Project Name _____

Team Member's Name _____

Reviewer's Name (if different) _____

Performance Category	Numeric Score
1. Participated Actively in Team Collaborations	_____
2. Contributed Relevant Knowledge and Information	_____
3. Completed Team Assignments with High Quality and on Time	_____
4. Exhibited Good Interpersonal Skills	_____
Total Points	_____

Comment on individual's major contributions to the team:

Comment on how, if at all, individual's team performance and participation could have been improved:

Instructions
- Award 0 to 3 points in each performance category, as appropriate.
- Fractional points are permissible *only* in half-point increments, that is, 0.5, 1.5, 2.5.
- Use the following rating criteria:
  - 0 points: nonparticipant; unreliable, inappropriate behavior; failed to perform; difficult to work with.
  - 1 point: minimal participation; contributed little; submitted work with little value.
  - 2 points: participated when called on; contributed frequently; submitted good-quality work; pleasant to work with; exhibited modest leadership behavior.
  - 3 points: thoroughly reliable; displayed energetic team spirit; submitted high-quality work; actively participated in team collaborations; was considerate of team members; took significant leadership responsibilities.

Encouraging Student Integrity

Computers make it possible for students to obtain credit for work they didn't perform. Students can buy and download term papers, essays, and reports. In addition, they can copy and paste information verbatim from a website to the documents they submit to fulfill course requirements. It is also possible to obtain credit unfairly for an unproctored test administered online, because with current LMS technology there is no way to ensure that the person taking the exam is the same person who will receive credit for it.

There are a number of explanations for why students attempt to obtain credit for work they do not do. In the case of plagiarism, students not infrequently have the misconception that information found on the Internet is in the public domain. These students violate copyright because they lack a clear understanding of what constitutes plagiarism. Some students simply give in to the very human temptation to try to get something for nothing. Others, noting rampant, widely publicized dishonesty in the business and sports worlds, assume that cutting corners with respect to integrity is acceptable behavior in our society. Still others believe that in an instructional environment where dishonesty is not uncommon, they will in essence be penalized with respect to their course grades for being honest. In other words, these students cheat because they perceive that their peers will do so as well. The 2003 National Survey of Student Engagement (NSSE) found that 87 percent of students surveyed indicated that their peers at least "sometimes" copied and pasted information from the Internet for reports and papers without citing the source (NSSE, 2003).

Whatever the causes of integrity violations, it is clear that elearning instructors need to do whatever they can to encourage student integrity. Both positive and negative reinforcement to encourage integrity are desirable. It is not inappropriate to explain to your students the benefits of honesty to the individual and to society as a whole, particularly if your students are young and still evolving a personal ethic. However, you will probably need to use some negative reinforcement as well to promote student integrity. In what follows, we offer a few suggestions for minimizing plagiarism and discouraging dishonesty in the taking of online tests.

Dealing with Plagiarism.   Chapter 9 points out that your course policies should clearly define what you consider to be plagiarism in terms of individual writing assignments, collaboration, use of web resources, and any other activities in which your students will be involved. Because many students do not know how to properly cite sources they use in papers, your policies should include guidelines about citations or web links to information on the subject. In addition, the policies should clearly state the penalties associated with plagiarism when it is detected.

To detect plagiarism, some instructors are using *plagiarism websites* that will allow them to determine whether a piece of work submitted by a student was previously used in a course or downloaded from any one of a number of known websites that sell papers on the Internet. The end-of-chapter URL References identify a number of these plagiarism sites. Publicizing to your students that you intend to submit their papers to these sites for authentication is likely to encourage student honesty.

Another method to detect plagiarism is to obtain a sample of your students' writing skills to compare with work they submit later as their own. However, this approach must be applied very judiciously. In his autobiographical book *All the Strange Hours,* Loren Eiseley—the well-known paleontologist, nature writer, poet, and one-time provost of the University of Pennsylvania—relates a moving story about a paper he submitted to an undergraduate English instructor at the University of Nebraska. The instructor challenged Eiseley's authorship of the paper, claiming it was too well written to have been produced by an undergraduate. Nevertheless, Eiseley in fact wrote the paper. He reports that the experience discouraged him from taking further courses in literature, even though at that point he envisioned a career as a professional writer rather than as an academic. Ironically, Eiseley—who died in 1977—ultimately became much admired by college English instructors as a prose stylist. He is distinguished in part by his having been one of the few scientific writers ever elected to the National Institute of Arts and Letters.

Using Online Testing Appropriately.   Currently it is not possible to ensure that students do not cheat on unproctored online tests. As with plagiarism, your course policies should clearly delineate the penalties associated with dishonesty in taking tests. In addition, at least three ways exist to encourage student honesty in online testing. One good approach is to deemphasize testing and base students' grades on a number of other class activities. Students can be graded on team and individual projects, on their participating in electronic discussions and face-to-face class activities, and on time spent working with coursesite material, as measured by LMS statistics. In the extreme, you might consider using online tests solely for student self-assessment. In this scenario, students earn points for repeating a test exercise until they achieve a grade that reflects subject mastery. More than one test on the same subject is required here, to preclude students' learning the test instead of the material the test covers. Moreover, this approach obviously works better for some subjects than for others and may not be suitable for classes whose primary purpose is to provide professional knowledge or prerequisite knowledge for follow-up courses.

Another approach is to proctor online tests, ideally using testing centers. This essentially eliminates cheating, but it is quite costly. We suspect testing centers will become common in the future of elearning, perhaps with the identities of students determined by identity recognition software. If proctoring tests is not currently feasible, the appropriate use of the LMS testing tool will help minimize cheating. The following are suggestions for using the LMS to reduce cheating on online tests. Some of the suggestions may not be suitable for special needs students, for example, the suggestion about placing a time limit on a test.

- Use the timed-release function to control when students can begin a test.
- Set a reasonable time limit for taking a test. If students are unfamiliar with the test material, they will be unable to use notes and other reference sources quickly enough to complete the test within the specified time.
- Password-protect the test and disseminate passwords by email right before the test.
- Allow students to take a test only one time.
- Create pools of test questions and randomly generate tests. This makes it unlikely that two students sitting next to each other will be answering the same questions in the same order.

Finally tests themselves can be designed to discourage cheating. Some suggestions for designing tests to this end are as follows (some may not be suitable for K–12 instruction):

- Create open book tests and design questions that require extensive student preparation and subject knowledge.
- Create questions that require students to use critical thinking to answer them.
- Obtain samples of students' writing early in the course to use in comparisons to answers on tests to reveal inconsistencies. (Asking students to tell you about themselves with no grade assigned is a good way to ensure what you receive is actually written by the students.)
- Design tests that require essay answers.
- Relate test questions to subjects raised in online or class discussions or other class activities.
- Make tests lengthy, so that students will not have time to look up answers.

- Allow students to take tests only after specified tasks have been completed.
- Use the chat capabilities of the LMS, and ask students test questions they must respond to in chat. (This is time-consuming, so students or teaching assistants may be required to facilitate the process in a large class.)

ASSESSING COURSE AND COURSESITE EFFECTIVENESS

Chapter 10 recommends the use of frequent short student surveys throughout an elearning course to determine whether midcourse corrections are needed. After a course ends, a more thorough evaluation process is needed to determine how well the course accommodated student learning. Two categories of information are available. First, you can seek after-course feedback from students. Second, you can ask a peer to evaluate your course. This section provides evaluation forms you may use to solicit information in both categories.

Student Feedback

Feedback from students can be obtained either by soliciting the information directly from your students or by visiting various instructor/course evaluation websites that students sometime use to critique their instructors. We discuss these two sources of feedback in separate subsections.

Student Surveys.   End-of-course student surveys are useful for obtaining information to assess the success of your elearning instruction. We recommend using separate instruments to measure the overall effectiveness of your course and student response to your coursesite. Figures 11.4 and 11.5, respectively, are course and coursesite evaluation forms we have used in the past to obtain such information. The forms are designed so they can be administered online anonymously using your LMS testing capability. Of course, you will want to adapt the forms to your own special needs. Your LMS will probably be able to generate statistics telling you the average rating your course and coursesite receive in each category addressed by the forms in Figures 11.4 and 11.5. However, to read student comments—which they enter in text boxes generated by the LMS testing tool—you will have to read test results online or print hard copies of the individual survey form results.

Online Instructor/Course Evaluation Websites.   Currently there exist a number of websites on which students may anonymously rate instructors and courses in colleges and universities worldwide. There are obvious drawbacks to such sites—some are commercial and others reflect a lack of sophistication in content and design. More important, there is no way to verify that the online comments about instructors reflect the opinion of a cross section of their students, or even that individuals posting comments on the sites actually studied with the instructors they are rating. In addition, some instructors suspect that disgruntled students are more likely to enter comments on such sites than are students satisfied with the instruction they received, resulting in skewed online instructor evaluations. Nevertheless, for better or worse, First Amendment rights apparently protect online instructor evaluation sites. The ACLU

FIGURE 11.4   Form for Student Survey of Course Effectiveness

For each question, please select the number as defined below that best corresponds to your response.

5 Strongly Agree   4 Agree   3 Neutral   2 Disagree   1 Strongly Disagree

After each response, a text box will appear where you may type any comments you care to make.

1. Forums were a valuable part of the course.   5 4 3 2 1
2. The web research projects were a valuable part of the course.   5 4 3 2 1
3. The team projects were a valuable part of the course.   5 4 3 2 1
4. The reflective essay was a valuable part of the course.   5 4 3 2 1
5. The major individual project was a valuable part of the course.   5 4 3 2 1
6. The self-assessment tests were a valuable part of the course.   5 4 3 2 1
7. The chat sessions were a valuable part of the course.   5 4 3 2 1
8. The in-class lectures were a valuable part of the course.   5 4 3 2 1
9. My special needs were addressed.   5 4 3 2 1
10. Getting-started activities at the course beginning were adequate.   5 4 3 2 1
11. The peer review activities were a valuable part of the course.   5 4 3 2 1
12. I enjoyed the constructivist approach to learning.   5 4 3 2 1
13. I liked having my grade based on points earned.   5 4 3 2 1
14. I feel that this course was appropriately challenging.   5 4 3 2 1
15. I received sufficient feedback from the instructor.   5 4 3 2 1
16. I had sufficient interaction with other students.   5 4 3 2 1
17. I had sufficient interaction with the instructor.   5 4 3 2 1
18. I had adequate access to technology and any help I needed to use it.   5 4 3 2 1
19. My expectations for this course were met.   5 4 3 2 1
20. I received adequate introductory information on the syllabus, polices, and so on.   5 4 3 2 1
21. My complaints or suggestions about improving the course were heeded.   5 4 3 2 1
22. Course resources and materials were available when needed.   5 4 3 2 1
23. The course was worth what it cost me in time and money.   5 4 3 2 1
24. I received adequate orientation to succeed in the course.   5 4 3 2 1
25. I learn better in an elearning environment than in a traditional environment.   5 4 3 2 1
26. I learn better in a student-centered environment than in a teacher-centered environment. 5 4 3 2 1
27. Overall, the course was a valuable learning experience.   5 4 3 2 1

For each of the following four questions, please type your response into the text box that appears. Answer in as much detail as you care to express. Be assured that your replies will be taken seriously.

28. What course activities did you enjoy the most? Why?
29. What course content did you like best? Why?
30. What course content was not useful? Why?
31. How could the course be improved?

FIGURE 11.5   Form for Student Survey of Coursesite Effectiveness

For each question, please select the number as defined below that best corresponds to your response.

| 5 Strongly Agree | 4 Agree | 3 Neutral | 2 Disagree | 1 Strongly Disagree |

After each response, a text box will appear where you may type any comments you care to make.

1. Coursesite design made it easy to use the coursesite.   5   4   3   2   1
2. The LMS announcement component was useful.   5   4   3   2   1
3. Course resources were well designed and easy to read on a computer display.   5   4   3   2   1
4. It was easy to understand how to navigate in the coursesite.   5   4   3   2   1
5. It was easy to find resources and information in the coursesite.   5   4   3   2   1
6. The LMS forum component was easy to use.   5   4   3   2   1
7. The LMS chat component was easy to use.   5   4   3   2   1
8. The LMS online testing component was easy to use.   5   4   3   2   1
9. The online lectures were valuable and were easy to access and read.   5   4   3   2   1
10. The coursesite added value to the course.   5   4   3   2   1
11. The coursesite made it possible to *interact* with course content.   5   4   3   2   1
12. The LMS software and the coursesite were reliable.   5   4   3   2   1
13. The resources posted on the coursesite were relevant and useful.   5   4   3   2   1
14. The coursesite was kept up-to-date.   5   4   3   2   1
15. When I needed it, I could get adequate help about using coursesite features.   5   4   3   2   1

For each of the following seven questions, please type your response into the text box that appears. Answer in as much detail as you care to express. Be assured that your replies will be taken seriously.

16. What was the most valuable resource on the coursesite? Why?
17. What was the least valuable resource on the coursesite? Why?
18. What LMS functionality (chats, forums, calendar, online testing, etc.) was most valuable? Why?
19. What LMS functionality was least valuable? Why?
20. How did you use the coursesite?
21. How did the coursesite help you learn?
22. What recommendations do you have for improving the coursesite?

(American Civil Liberties Union) has defended at least one site—www.teacherevaluation. com—against a lawsuit brought by two faculty members at a college in San Francisco, and ultimately the instructors dropped the suit.

We suspect that in the not-too-distant future institutions will sponsor online evaluation of their instructors. Most instructors will welcome this move, because it will assure that the opinions posted are legitimate and reflect attitudes of all the students one teaches, instead of a self-selected few. In the meantime, you can use online teacher evaluation sites to determine what those students who visit them are saying about your course and the way you deliver it. The end-of-chapter URL References identify some of these sites; others would be easy to find using an Internet search.

Peer Evaluation

Student surveys are an excellent source of information about your course and coursesite, although some K–12 students may lack sufficient maturity to participate in such evaluations objectively. Another objection sometimes raised about such surveys is that they measure student attitudes about the course and instructor, which may or may not be related to how much students learn in a course. However, we personally feel that most students—and certainly mature or adult students—are objective enough to give honest feedback about a course, and that they generally are good judges of how much they learned. Nevertheless, corroborating information about the success of your course is desirable. One such source is peer input. Many institutions are formalizing evaluations of elearning through peer reviews. If there is no formal peer review process at your institution, you may want to initiate an informal process by asking an interested colleague to evaluate your elearning course, based on the contents of the coursesite after your course ends. If your institution has a Department of Educational Technology, you might also ask someone who works there to review your course. Figure 11.6 is an example rubric that could be used in a peer review of elearning. As with the forms of Figures 11.4 and 11.5, the form of Figure 11.6 can be administered using the LMS testing tool. It addresses a number of elements characteristic of effective elearning, including the following:

- Opportunities for students to apply critical thinking
- Appropriate use of technology
- Opportunities for students to interact with the instructor and with other students
- Opportunities for students to interact with course content
- Assessment methods
- Course resource effectiveness
- Overall coursesite design

ASSESSING ELEARNING VERSUS TRADITIONAL LEARNING

Student and peer feedback is one valuable source of information for evaluating course effectiveness. However, anecdotal feedback from individual elearning courses in itself cannot verify that the elearning environment is more conducive to student learning than a traditional instructional environment. Another approach is to compare student outcomes in your elearning course with student outcomes in the same or similar courses taught in a traditional learning environment. Areas of comparison include:

- Student course grades
- Student dropout and course completion rates
- Student performance in subsequent courses, based on grades and completion rates
- Quality of work produced by students

FIGURE 11.6   Form for Peer Review of Coursesite Effectiveness

Please give me your response to my coursesite in the categories indicated. For each category, select the number as defined below that best corresponds to your response to the coursesite.

5 Exemplary coursesite. A model of best practices.
4 Good coursesite. Well above the average.
3 Average coursesite. Adequate, but somewhat lacking in design and content.
2 Poor coursesite. Additional work clearly needed.
1 Unsatisfactory coursesite. Much more work needed.

After each response, a text box will appear where you may type any comments you care to make.

1. Course objectives (clarity and completeness)   5   4   3   2   1
2. Course requirements (clarity and completeness)   5   4   3   2   1
3. Technology requirements (prerequisite knowledge and   5   4   3   2   1
    equipment needed)
4. Coursesite design (ease of navigation; ease of finding   5   4   3   2   1
    specific resources)
5. Resource design (including ease of viewing on a computer monitor)   5   4   3   2   1
6. Opportunities for students to interact with each other   5   4   3   2   1
7. Opportunities for students and instructor to interact   5   4   3   2   1
8. Methods for student assessment (clarity, completeness, and fairness)   5   4   3   2   1
9. Use of external websites (frequency, relevance, up to date)   5   4   3   2   1
10. Use of LMS announcement feature (appropriateness)   5   4   3   2   1
11. Course policies (clarity and completeness)   5   4   3   2   1
12. Use of LMS forum and chat features (frequency, relevance,   5   4   3   2   1
    invoked critical thinking)
13. Overall coursesite excellence   5   4   3   2   1

For the following question, please type your observations into the text box that appears.

14. For items 1–13 above, enter any comments or observations you wish to make.
15. What in your opinion were the strengths of the course?
16. What recommendations do you have for improving the course and coursesite?

Gathering statistics in the first three categories is straightforward although time-consuming. Dropout rate is the percentage of students who formally or informally withdraw from the course before it ends, whereas completion rate is the percentage of students who complete the course successfully. These two figures do not necessarily sum to 100 percent, because there may be some students who finish a course but do not achieve a satisfactory grade. (Whether to count below average grades as "satisfactory" is open to debate.) In the fourth category, one would compare work such as term papers, individual examinations including essay exams, group projects, and the like produced by students in elearning courses and in traditional courses on the same subject. Work samples selected should include assignments that reveal critical thinking and communications skills. Comparisons in this category are based on a rating scale similar to the one used to grade the work in the courses where it was produced. Of course, the student work being compared must be blind-rated by the same individual or committee, rather than by simply using grades assigned by the teacher of the course in which the work was produced.

Unfortunately, once data are gathered in these four categories, drawing valid conclusions from them is not straightforward. So many variables contribute to effective learning that it is difficult to decide when an elearning course and a traditional course are similar enough to reveal meaningful information when they are compared with respect to student outcomes. Researchers have questioned the validity of grade comparisons in elearning and traditional deliveries of the same course because so many different variables contribute to a student's grade. The same objection to some extent applies to statistics about the other categories of student outcomes—dropout and completion rates, subsequent student performance, and quality of work produced.

Instructor variables that influence course outcomes include teaching style, familiarity with technology and elearning practices, attitude toward technology, and severity or leniency of grading criteria. Some instructors are so effective that their students will excel whether a subject is taught in an elearning or a traditional learning environment. Unfortunately, the relationship between teacher skills and student results also holds for poor teachers. The stability of the technology infrastructure, and student and instructor access to technology tools, are also important variables. The degree of appropriateness of course subject matter for delivery in an elearning environment is another significant consideration. There are also variables related to student demographics. For example, what prerequisite skills and knowledge do students have when they begin the course? What are the technology skills of students, and what is their collective attitude toward the use of technology in teaching?

Comparing outcomes in the similar courses conducted in an elearning and a traditional environment should be based on statistics gathered from many instances of the courses. When data from a large number of students taught by many different teachers are compared, one has more confidence that the results obtained are meaningful. Unfortunately, such experiments lie in the domain of research and offer little to individual instructors relevant to evaluating individual elearning courses. However, if you have taught a course in a traditional environment a number of times, after you have taught the same course in an elearning environment enough times to ensure a statistically valid sampling of students, you may be able to draw some tentative conclusions by comparing student outcomes over all instances of the course in both environments.

Most people familiar with elearning believe that computer technology can affect learning for the better. However, there do exist instructors who are skeptical about elearning's potential to improve teaching and learning. Such skepticism may seem supported by reports of high dropout rates among students engaged in distance learning programs. Many of these reports, however, have been attributed to low-quality elearning programs offered at higher tuition rates as compared to high-quality classroom-based programs in the same field (Christensen, Aaron, & Clark, 2003). It is difficult to defend elearning against skeptics because the field is so new that as yet significant research on elearning effectiveness has not had time to appear. With the exception of the Pew Program in Course Redesign data discussed in Chapter 1, there is very little documented research to support elearning's effectiveness. Distressingly, some studies have concluded that student performance does not change significantly when the elearning environment replaces the traditional instructor-centered environment. One explanation for this may be that most educators currently have an imperfect understanding of elearning, and that as a result current elearning courses fail to exploit its full potential. Time and experience will probably remedy this problem.

Time will also surely remedy the lack of research on elearning's effectiveness. Preliminary information on the subject may be found on two interesting but antithetical websites. One is the ■No Significant Difference Phenomenon site (and book) complied by Thomas L. Russell. This site provides a collection of more than 350 reports about distance education dating from the 1920s—a number are anecdotal—that reveal no significant difference in technologically enhanced courses compared to traditional instruction. Some of these reports focus on elearning. A related website, the ■Significant Difference Phenomenon, cites recent studies that show student learning improves in elearning courses. However, the fact remains that more high-quality research on elearning effectiveness is badly needed. Studies addressing the following questions might result in a more measured assessment of elearning's effectiveness. It is important to realize, however, that until the power of elearning is clearly and thoroughly reflected in existing elearning courses, comparing elearning courses with long-established traditional courses will be like comparing the achievements of adolescents with those of adults.

- Does the elearning environment improve student satisfaction?
- Does the elearning environment improve faculty satisfaction?
- Do the instructional strategies in elearning promote active learning?
- What are the benefits of elearning instructional strategies when compared to instructional strategies used in a traditional classroom environment?
- What are the benefits of a coursesite from students' perspectives?
- What are the benefits of a coursesite from faculty perspective?
- Does elearning contribute to preparing students for the workplace?
- Do electronic discussions contribute to improved writing skills?
- Do electronic discussions contribute to improved critical thinking skills?
- What effect does elearning have on a student's performance in future courses?
- Does elearning reduce the costs of course delivery?
- What is the return on the elearning investment?
- Does elearning improve student retention?
- Do students' grades improve when compared to the grades of students learning without the application of elearning?
- Do students feel they learn better in an elearning environment?
- Does elearning increase student enrollment?

REFERENCES

Adenekan, S. (2003, November 13). Students using the net to cheat. *BBC News.* Retrieved May 10, 2004, from http://news.bbc.co.uk/2/hi/uk_news/education/3265143.stm

Ahn, J. (2004, April). Electronic portfolios: Blending technology, accountability & assessment. *T.H.E. Journal, 31*(9), 12, 16, 18.

Baird, D. A. (2003, April). ePortfolios: A pocket full of ambition. *Syllabus*. Retrieved May 1, 2003, from www.syllabus.com/article.asp?id=7478

Brothen, T., & Wamback, C. (2003, May/June). Using WebCT quizzes in a high-demand environment. *The Technology Source*. Retrieved November 20, 2003, from http://ts.mivu.org/default.asp?show=article&id=1024

Brown, D. G. (2000, November). The venn of assessment: Transforming instructional design. *Syllabus, 14*(4), 36–40.

Brown, D. G. (2004, February). Demonstrating good teaching. *Syllabus, 17*(7), 19.

Bruce, L. (2003, September). The standards approach: Planning for excellence in distance education. *Syllabus, 17*(2), 29–32.

Butler, D. L. (2003, January/February). The impact of computer-based testing on student attitudes and behavior. *The Technology Source*. Retrieved November 20, 2003, from http://ts.mivu.org/default.asp?show=article&id=1013

Butler, D. L., & Sellbom, M. (2002). Barriers to adopting technology for teaching and learning. *EDUCAUSE Quarterly, 25*(2), 22–28.

Carnevale, D. (2002, February 25). Online students don't fare as well as classroom counterparts, study finds. *The Chronicle of Higher Education*. Retrieved February 25, 2002, from http://chronicle.com/free/2002/02/2002022501u.htm

Carnevale, D. (2003, February 26). Western Governors U. finally wins regional accreditation. *The Chronicle of Higher Education*. Retrieved March 5, 2003, from http://chronicle.com/free/2003/02/2003022601t.htm

Cennamo, K. S., Ross, J. D., & Rogers, C. S. (2002). Evolution of web-enhanced course incorporating strategies for self-regulation. *EDUCAUSE Quarterly, 25*(1), 28–33.

Christe, B. (2003). Designing online courses to discourage dishonesty. *EDUCAUSE Quarterly, 26*(4), 54–58.

Christensen, C., Aaron, S., & Clark, W. (2003, January/February). Disruption in education. *EDUCAUSE Review, 38*(1), 44–54.

Clayton, M., & Watkins, A. (2002, April). Assessment and integrity in the digital arts. *Syllabus, 15*(9), 31–34.

Cook, C. (2001, February). Regional accrediting commissions: The watchdogs of quality assurance in distance education. *Syllabus, 14*(7), 20, 56–58.

Diaz, D. P. (2002, May/June). Online drop rates revisited. *The Technology Source*. Retrieved November 20, 2003, from http://ts.mivu.org/default.asp?show=article&id=981

Eiseley, L. (1975). *All the strange hours*. New York: Charles Scribner's Sons.

Ehrmann, S. C. (2000, September). Evaluating instructional uses of the web. *Syllabus, 14*(2), 38–42.

Ehrmann, S. C., & Gilbert, S. W. (2003, July). Better off with or without your CMS? Kinds of assessment that can really help. *Syllabus, 16*(12), 37–40.

Ferdig, R. E., & Trammell, K. D. (2004, February). Content delivery in the 'blogosphere.' *T.H.E. Journal, 31*(7), 12, 16–17, 20.

Fleischman, J. (2001, February). Approaches and strategies for assessment: Project-based learning using technology. *Converge, 4*(1), 38–40.

Foster, A. L. (2002, May 17). Plagiarism-detection tool creates legal quandary: When professors send students' papers to a database, are copyrights violated? *The Chronicle of Higher Education*, p. A37.

Foster, A. L. (2003, March 7). Picking apart pick-a-prof. Does the popular online service help students find good professors, or just easy A's? *The Chronicle of Higher Education*, p. A33.

Gathercoal, P., Love, D., Bryde, B., & McKean, G. (2002). On implementing web-based electronic portfolios. *EDUCAUSE Quarterly, 25*(2), 29–37.

Groark, M., Oblinger, D., & Choa, M. (2001, September/October). Term paper mills, anti-plagiarism tools, and academic integrity. *EDUCAUSE Review, 36*(5), 40–48.

Heerema, D. L., & Rogers, R. L. (2001, December). Avoiding the quality/quantity trade-off in distance education. *T.H.E. Journal, 29*(5), 14–21.

Howell, S. (2003). E-learning and paper testing: Why the gap? *EDUCAUSE Quarterly, 26*(4), 8–10.

Krebs, A. (2000, November). Evaluation for success. *Converge, 3*(11), 26, 28.

Lambert, J. C., Lousteau, C. L., & Mochetta, P. T. (2001, August). New aspects of test security. *T.H.E. Journal, 29*(1), 55–59.

Lea, L., Clayton, M., Draude, B., & Barlow, S. (2001). The impact of technology on teaching and learning. *EDUCAUSE Quarterly, 24*(2), 69–70.

Lockee, B., Moore, M., & Burton, J. (2002). Measuring success: Evaluation strategies for distance education. *EDUCAUSE Quarterly, 25*(1), 20–26.

Long, P. D. (2002, January). Plagiarism: IT-enabled tools for deceit? *Syllabus, 15*(6), 8–11.

McHenry, B., Griffith, L., & McHenry, J. (2004, April). The potential, pitfalls and promise of computerized testing. *T.H.E. Journal, 31*(9), 28, 30–31.

McMurtry, K. (2001, November). E-cheating: Combating a 21st century challenge. *T.H.E. Journal, 29*(4), 36–41.

McNulty, K. T. (2002, February). Fostering the student-centered classroom online. *T.H.E. Journal, 29*(7), 16–22.

Moloney, J., & Tello, S. (2003, February). Principles for building success in online education. *Syllabus*. Retrieved May 1, 2003, from www.syllabus.com/article.asp?id=7252

Morrissey, C. A. (1998, June). The impact of the Internet on management education: What the research shows. *The Technology Source.* Retrieved September 23, 2002, from http://ts.mivu.org/default.asp?show=article&id=465

NSSE. (2003). The 2003 national survey of student engagement. Retrieved May 10, 2004, from www.iub.edu/~nsse/html/overview_2003.htm

Oblinger, D., & Kidwell, J. (2000, May/June). Distance learning: Are we being realistic? *EDUCAUSE Review, 35*(3), 31–39.

Olsen, F. (2000, March 24). Academic-technology group enters fray over what makes a "wired" campus. *The Chronicle of Higher Education,* p. A49.

Presby, L. (2001, February). Increasing productivity in course delivery. *T.H.E. Journal, 28*(7), 52–58.

Read, B. (2002, May 17). An online course teaches students to use libraries and the Internet—and avoid plagiarism. *The Chronicle of Higher Education.* Retrieved June 10, 2002, from http://chronicle.com/free/2002/05/20020517lu.htm

Read, B. (2003, September 4). Survey finds college administrators optimistic about the future of online education. *The Chronicle of Higher Education.* Retrieved December 1, 2003, from http://chronicle.com/prm/daily/2003/09/2003090401t.htm

Russell, T. L. (2000). *The no significant difference phenomenon.* Montgomery, AL: International Distance Education Certification Center.

Sistek-Chandler, C. (2000, November). Online assessment: Changing the way you test. *Converge, 3*(11), 38–40.

Sonwalkar, N. (2002, January). A new methodology for evaluation: The pedagogical rating of online courses. *Syllabus, 15*(6), 18–21.

Stith, B. (2000, March). Web-enhanced lecture course scores big with students and faculty. *T.H.E. Journal, 27*(8), 21–22.

Taggart, G. L., Phifer, S. J., Nixon, J. A., & Wood, M. (Eds.). (2001). *Rubrics: A handbook for construction and use.* Lancaster, PA: Scarecrow Press.

Terry, N. (2001, February). Assessing enrollment and attrition rates for the online MBA. *T.H.E. Journal, 28*(7), 64–68.

Thomason, A. (2004, March). Assessment with a new mindset: Portals in teacher education. *Syllabus, 17*(8), 31–32.

Townley, C. T. (2003). Will the academy learn to manage knowledge? *EDUCAUSE Quarterly, 26*(2), 8–11.

Woodfield, K. (2003, January). Getting on board with online testing. *T.H.E. Journal.* Retrieved May 1, 2003, from www.thejournal.com/magazine/vault/A4297.cfm

Young, J. R. (2000, January 14). Faculty report at University of Illinois casts skeptical eye on distance education. *The Chronicle of Higher Education,* p. A48.

Young, J. R. (2001, July 6). The cat-and-mouse game of plagiarism detection: Colleges provide professors with new online tools to give them the upper hand. *The Chronicle of Higher Education,* p. A26.

U R L   R E F E R E N C E S

American Association for Higher Education—Assessment Frequently Asked Questions: www.aahe.org/assessment/assess_faq.htm

American Federation of Teachers—Resolution on Ensuring High Quality in Distance Education for College Credit. www.aft.org/about/resolutions/2000/distanceed.html

Blogger: http://blogger.com/start

Center for Academic Integrity: www.academicintegrity.org

The Center for Academic Transformation—The Pew Grant Program Assessing the Impact of Course Redesign: www.center.rpi.edu/PewGrant/Assess.html

The Institute for Higher Education Policy—What's the Difference? A Review of Contemporary Research on the Effectiveness of Distance Learning in Higher Education: www.ihep.com/Pubs/PDF/Difference.pdf

My Drop Box: www.mydropbox.com/

North Carolina State University—Internet Resources for Higher Education Outcomes Assessment: www2.acs.ncsu.edu/UPA/assmt/resource.htm

No Significant Difference Phenomenon and Significant Difference Phenomenon: www.nosignificantdifference.org

North Central Regional Educational Laboratory—Technology Connections for School Improvement: Planners' Handbook: www.ncrel.org/tplan/tplanB.htm

Oregon University system—OUS Distance Education Policy Framework: www.ous.edu/dist-learn/dist-pol.htm

The Plagiarism Resource Site: http://plagiarism.phys.virginia.edu

Prince George's County Public Schools—Portfolio Assessment: www.pgcps.pg.k12.md.us/~elc/portfolio.html

Project-Based Learning: What Is It?: www.4teachers.org/projectbased

Project-Based Learning with Multimedia—Rubric—Scoring Guidelines: http://pblmm.k12.ca.us/PBLGuide/MMrubric.htm

The Quality Assurance Agency for Higher Education—Distance Learning Guidelines: www.qaa.ac.uk/public/dlg/contents.htm

RamRatings: www.ramratings.com

School Blogs: http://schoolblogs.com/

Schrock, Kathy—Guide for Educators: Assessment Rubrics: http://school.discovery.com/schrockguide/assess.html

Significant Difference Phenomenon: www.nosignificantdifference.org

Southern Illinois University at Edwardsville—Assessment Resources: www.siue.edu/~deder/assess/

Teacher Reviews: http://teacherreviews.com

Transformation of Learning—Rubric Development: www.k12.hi.us/~transfor/rubric.html

Triinfo: www.triinfo.com

Turnitin.com: http://turnitin.com

University of Illinois—Report of the University of Illinois Teaching at an Internet Distance Seminar: www.vpaa.uillinois.edu/reports_retreats/tid.asp?bhcp=1

Western Interstate Commission for Higher Education. Principles of good practice for electronically offered academic degree and certificate programs: www.wiche.edu/Telecom/projects/balancing/principles.htm

Western Michigan University—The Evaluation Center: www.wmich.edu/evalctr/ess.html

INDEX